What people are saying about *Managing a Small Business Made Easy*

Having worked with Martin Davis over 13 years, I fully understand the depth of his knowledge and ability to run a profitable, growing business. His wisdom, which he shared with me, is now available in this book.

The foundation he laid out for my company made it possible to foresee trends that would have a major impact on our bottom line. That capability, along with the business practices I learned from him, gave me the tools needed for my business to survive during the tough times experienced by all industries the past few years.

The ability to share such experience on an understandable level is a trademark of Martin's writing. If you want to implement the sound business practices that will help you build a strong company you'll find those here.

—*Charles David Larson*
President, Westland Corporation

Mr. Davis has served as a SCORE Management Counselor to my small business for the past year and a half. During that period, I carefully read and critiqued his book from the standpoint of a small businessman. It is difficult for me to separate the book from the counselor. Both have been critical to the success of my business. Mr. Davis's experience as an accountant, consultant, and small business owner have made him an extremely credible and well-rounded business resource. His insights regarding the things a small business owner really needs to know to be successful form the core of this book.

It's been my experience that a great book and a great SCORE counselor are an unbeatable combination. As an avid reader, I have no shortage of excellent books telling me how to run a successful company. These books cannot compare to the commitment and knowledge that a SCORE Management Counselor can offer, especially when using the right tool. Mr. Davis's book is the right tool!

—*Michael Uniacke*
President, Advanced Insulation, Inc.

Additional Titles in Entrepreneur's Made Easy Series

▶ *Accounting and Finance for Small Business Made Easy: Secrets You Wish Your CPA Had Told You* by Robert Low

▶ *Business Plans Made Easy: It's Not As Hard As You Think* by Mark Henricks

▶ *Meetings Made Easy: The Ultimate Fix-It Guide* by Frances Micale

▶ *Strategic Planning Made Easy* by Fred L. Fry, Charles R. Stoner, and Laurence G. Weinzimmer

▶ *Advertising Without an Agency Made Easy* by Kathy J. Kobliski

Entrepreneur® MADE EASY Series

MANAGING A SMALL BUSINESS MADE EASY

MARTIN E. DAVIS

John & Shirley
Best luck always
Martin

EP
Entrepreneur®
Press

Editorial Director: Jere Calmes
Cover Design: Beth Hansen-Winter
Editorial and Production Services: CWL Publishing Enterprises, Inc., Madison, Wisconsin, www.cwlpub.com

This publication is designed to provide accurate and authoritative information in regard to the subject matter covered. It is sold with the understanding that the publisher is not engaged in rendering legal, accounting, or other professional services. If legal advice or other expert assistance is required, the services of a competent professional person should be sought.
—From a Declaration of Principles jointly adopted by a Committee of the American Bar Association and a Committee of Publishers and Associations

ISBN 1-932531-54-8

Cataloging-in-Publication data is available.

Printed in Canada

10 09 08 07 06 05   10 9 8 7 6 5 4 3 2 1

Contents

Preface   ix

Introduction   xiii

1. Know Yourself   1
   Your Strengths and Weaknesses   1
   A Self Assessment   2
   A "Quiz for Small Business Success"   5

2. Understanding Leadership   8
   Definition   9
   What Leaders Know How to Do   9

3. Defining Your Business   13
   Where Are You Going?   13
   Do You Have Vision?   14
   Image and Attitude Are Part of It   16

4. People—Your Greatest Resource   18
   Finding the "Right Stuff"   19
   Be Aware of Employment Laws!   21
   The Employment Application   23
   Hiring the "Right Stuff"   23
   "Getting Acquainted"   25
   Training the New Employee   26
   Motivation and Involvement   27

 5. **People—Managing Your Greatest Resource** — 31
    Salary and Wage Administration — 31
    Compensation Policies — 33
    Personnel Handbook — 34
    Retirement Plans — 35
    Section 125 "Cafeteria Plan" — 36

 6. **Your Customer, the Essential Element** — 38
    Identify Your Customer — 38
    Developing a Marketing Strategy — 39
    Defining the Customer Base — 41
    Understanding the Competition — 44

 7. **Product Planning and Development** — 46
    Product Planning — 47
    Product Development — 47

 8. **Pricing Your Product or Service** — 53
    The Profit Maximization Approach — 55
    A Pricing-for-Profit Example — 58
    Gross Profit Percentage (Gross Margin) vs. Markup — 61

 9. **Selling and Distributing Your Product or Service** — 63
    Sales Management — 64
    Sales and Service Policies — 64
    Physical Distribution Systems — 66
    Technical Sales Literature — 67
    Sales Compensation Policies — 68
    Training and Monitoring Sales Personnel — 69

10. **Advertising and Promotion** — 71
    Advertising Opportunities — 72
    Promotional Opportunities — 74

11. **Developing a Business Plan** — 76
    Why You Need a Business Plan — 76
    What Is a Business Plan? — 77
    Not Just for Beginners! — 78
    Elements of a Business Plan — 78

12. **Gathering Financial Resources** — 83
    Are You Creditworthy? — 83
    Finding Financial Resources — 84

Contents

Selecting a Partner 87
The Partnership/Stockholder Agreement 88
How Good Is Your Banker? 91
Borrowing Money 93
The Role of Leasing 95
Suppliers as a Resource 96

13. **Understanding Accounting a Must!** **98**
Why Do You Need to Know? 98
Cash or Accrual Accounting 101
Understanding Debits and Credits (Double-Entry
  Bookkeeping) 102
How the Accounting System Works 106
Cost Accounting—a "Lost Art" 110

14. **Management and Control Systems** **113**
Internal Reporting Systems 113
Credit Management 116
Order Entry and Billing 119
Production Scheduling and Inventory Control 121
Quality Control 124

15. **Your CPA Firm** **128**
Selecting a CPA Firm 128
To Audit or Not to Audit: That Is the Question 130
Tax Matters ... You Don't Have Time to Learn! 131
Other Benefits of a CPA Relationship 132
Working with Your CPA Firm 133

16. **Why You Need an Attorney** **135**
Formation and Maintenance of the Business Entity 136
Contractual Matters 137
Employment Laws 137
Environmental and Safety Issues 137
Tax Laws 138
Consumer Laws 138
Licenses and Permits 139
Securities Laws 139
Protection of Intellectual Property 139
Litigation 141
Legal Self-Help 142

17. **Involve an Insurance Broker**   **143**

Types of Insurance   144

Selecting the Insurer   147

Handling a Loss Claim   147

Health Insurance   147

18. **Be a Good Communicator**   **149**

Communicating with Employees   150

Communicating with Customers   152

Communicating with Suppliers   155

19. **The Good Times ... and the Bad Times**   **157**

When All Is Well   157

When All Is *Not* Well   159

20. **"The Rest of the Story"**   **162**

The Intangible Factors   164

The Ultimate Reward!   166

Appendix A. Quiz for Small Business Success   **167**

Appendix B. Employment Application   **170**

Appendix C. Position Descriptions   **172**

Appendix D. Performance Appraisal System   **175**

Appendix E. Personal Financial Statement   **180**

Appendix F. Schedule of Start-Up Costs   **181**

Appendix G. Balance Sheet   **182**

Appendix H. Income Statement (P&L)   **183**

Appendix I. Cash Flow Statement   **184**

Appendix J. Funds Flow Statement   **185**

Appendix K. Chart of Accounts (Small Service Company or Manufacturer)   **186**

Appendix L. Chart of Accounts (Small Retailer)   **190**

Appendix M. Typical Accounting Entries   **193**

Appendix N. Trend Reports   **198**

Appendix O. Sample Business Plan   **203**

Index   **227**

Preface

SOME OF THE BEST-RUN AMERICAN COMPANIES HAVE STAYED ON TOP OF the heap by breaking the corporation into smaller companies and encouraging them to think independently and competitively. In a world of periodic cycles of centralization and decentralization of management control, "small" seems to have emerged as an effective philosophy, encouraging entrepreneurship and innovation. It would seem that even in large corporate endeavors "small is beautiful."

Thinking independently and competitively is a compelling element of small business. There is nothing as satisfying as knowing that a decision you made, which could significantly help your small business, was the right decision. There is also nothing more painful than knowing that you made a poor decision, which hurt your business. Small business owners are totally accountable for their successes and failures and face critical decisions daily without the benefit and guidance of a staff of experienced and well-paid technical personnel who are available in their large business counterparts.

There is a body of knowledge and skills that is *essential to the success* of the small businessman or businesswoman. The small business manager is confronted with problems relating to finance, sales, marketing, advertising, manufacturing, product engineering and design, pricing, inventory management, credit, human resources, and more. Yet, many small businesses are started by men and women who possess an unusual skill or have developed a unique product or service that satisfies a need or want that has value in the marketplace. How do these entrepreneurs gain this essential business knowledge that will permit them to successfully build upon their strengths? Sadly, such knowledge is often gained by trial and error and, unfortunately, many small businesses do not survive this educational process.

Many books have been written in an attempt to help small business owners and managers learn the business basics they need. Many of these books have presented a multitude of good management information but have failed to focus on the few *critical things that the small businessman or -woman* must *know to be successful.* Having helped numerous small businesses with this learning process, as a CPA, a management consultant, and a SCORE® Management Counselor, and having also learned from owning my own small business, I have written this book to help those entrepreneurs learn from my experiences (and mistakes) and not by their trial and error!

This book is dedicated to the men and women who have found the courage and resources necessary to start their own small businesses and the desire and perseverance needed to experience the ultimate reward of success.

Acknowledgments

The development of this book has taken nearly three years and has required the help of many people. My first attempt was much too technical in some areas, too detailed in other areas, and not focused on the major premise—that there are a few essentials that need to be understood to successfully manage a small business. I must thank my mentor, Merrill A. Joslin, retired KPMG Peat Marwick Consulting Partner, for enlightening me and helping me put the book on the right track. I worked for Merrill for nearly ten years and this is not the first time he has thankfully "set me straight."

Thanks must also go to four SCORE® counselors for editing the book and providing insights, corrections, and encouragement during the project: Russell A. Shedd III, Daniel Tokar, Jack Dunn, and Jim DiRienzo. Three of these men have served as Chairman of the Northern Arizona Chapter of SCORE®. Their knowledge of what the book should contain to be of maximum benefit to small businessmen and businesswomen was most beneficial.

My most critical editor was Michael Uniacke, President of Advanced Insulation, Inc., one of my SCORE® small business clients and a great student of business management. His perspective was from the eyes of the intended reader, the small business owner who is striving to be successful without the benefit of vast resources. Mike has seen the need for sound business advice to improve his own business and his insight and constructive criticism led to many changes that will make this book more useful to other small business owners. I owe Mike a great debt of gratitude for taking the time and effort to help me with this project.

Another business leader and my successor as the owner of a small business, Charles David Larson, President of Westland Corporation, supplied insight from the viewpoint of a manager who has lived with the principles presented in this book. He has seen many of them implemented that led to small business success. I am grateful for Dave's help in making this book a better tool for use by small business owners.

As I have become more involved in SCORE, I have also become aware of the positive and dynamic leadership offered that organization by W. Kenneth Yancey, CEO. His dedication to serving existing and emerging small businesses is the very backbone of the organization. His encouragement and help in developing this book was the key to its successful publication.

Finally, I must thank my wife, Vicki, who has spent many long and quiet hours "alone" while I have worked on the manuscript. Her support has kept me from aborting the project when things did not seem to come together. To all of these people goes a debt of gratitude and I hope that their belief in the project will not be in vain.

—Martin E. Davis

Introduction

WHAT ARE THE THINGS THAT *YOU REALLY NEED TO KNOW TO successfully manage a small business?* This book will define them for you and either help you learn those skills or guide you in securing outside help to fill any gaps. Learning by trial and error is very effective but it can also be very painful. Too many small business owners attempt to learn in this manner, only to find the penalty for their mistakes too severe, resulting in business failure.

Most businesses fail because the owner failed to understand the basic business management techniques. This lack of understanding can manifest itself in inadequate planning, financing, and marketing. Conversely, some small businesses fail because their growth was so rapid that the resources available were inadequate to keep pace. Key personnel are difficult to find and those who are available become spread too thin. Inadequate financial resources to support increasing working capital needs can cause the "successful" small business to be sold to a larger competitor or liquidated by a lending institution.

Managing a Small Business Made Easy is not an exhaustive treatise on all business knowledge that could be learned from a good college education and several years of business experience. This book sorts out those things that are *essential to success in managing a small business.* If you have a desire to know more than is presented here, there are other excellent books on the subject that are listed in our references.

This book will stress the importance of knowing your own strengths and

It is important for you, the small business owner, to better understand leadership as a key element in identifying your company's business objectives and in executing your plan.

weaknesses and taking action to deal with the deficiencies. It is important for you, the small business owner, to better understand leadership (a talent with which you may have been blessed) as a key element in identifying your company's business objectives and in executing your plan. You must know how to find, train, and retain the right people to help you in your business effort. Knowing your customers and all of the ways that they can help your business is also critical to your success. You must know how to plan, how to borrow money, and how to manage cash. A basic knowledge of accounting and an understanding of your financial statements are, in our opinion, also critical.

The good news is that outside help is available. It is expensive but necessary. You need to know how to select and utilize the talents of a CPA, an attorney, an insurance broker, and a banker. These resources can be highly instrumental in helping you build a successful, strong small business. Moreover, you must not overlook the resources available at your local SCORE® chapter. Many of these management counselors have successfully walked the same paths that you are following. And the best part is ... *their services are free!*

Finally, you must hone your communication skills. This is not as easy as it might seem. You must know how to develop a meaningful communication with your people, your customers, your suppliers, and the outside assistance previously described.

When things are going well in your business, none of what we present in this book may seem vital. However, when things go wrong, this how-to book of basic business elements will help you effectively and quickly resolve your business problems. After succeeding in these efforts, you will understand why we say, *"Small is beautiful."*

Chapter 1

Know Yourself

The small business owner who has the vision, initiative, skills, and persistence to start and manage his business is the single most important factor in its success.

THE QUALITIES OF A SUCCESSFUL ENTREPRENEUR ARE HARD TO ISOLATE and define. However, there are certain characteristics that are common among all successful small businesspeople. These qualities will become apparent to you as you progress through this book. This book will lead you to discover the ten key guidelines or traits that I believe are necessary to be successful in managing a small business or, for that matter, a business of any size.

Your Strengths and Weaknesses

Perhaps the most important quality that determines the success of an entrepreneur is the understanding of *his own strengths and weaknesses and the intelligence to deal with them effectively.* (Please note that, for the sake of simplicity, the terms *he, him,* and *his* in this text also mean *she* and *her.*) A manager's weaknesses might be referred to as "flat sides" in a perfect circle of understanding. The key is to understand your flat sides and complement

1

those with someone whose talents in those areas are rounded. I believe you will agree, after reading this book, that there are no businesspeople with perfect circles of understanding!

We can all recount the experiences of skilled people who started small businesses only to fail because they did not compensate for some absence of skills in their background. We have seen skilled tradespeople whose business failed because they did not understand how to price their service, talented salespeople whose business efforts died because they did not understand cash management, and brilliant inventors who ultimately had to sell their unique idea to a large company because they did not know how to market their product.

As we pursue a greater understanding of the things you really need to know to manage a small business, you will find that you have knowledge in many of those areas already.

As we pursue a greater understanding of the things you really need to know to manage a small business, you will find that you have knowledge in many of those areas already, have sufficient background and time to adequately gain the required knowledge, or have neither the background nor the time to pursue the required skills and must compensate for this shortfall in some manner. *Being honest with yourself is as vital to your success as being honest with your customer!* The failure to honestly assess your skills can result in the demise of your small business!

The book, *What's Luck Got to Do with It?*, puts it quite well, "Entrepreneurship … is a learning process, and part of that process is the ability to fail, to learn from failure, and then to seek the next opportunity."[1] *Remember that giving birth to anything does not occur without pain.* Despite this pain and the seemingly endless task of learning all that is required to be successful, all entrepreneurs should share one common emotion—*they must enjoy what they are doing!* If you don't share that emotion, despite the predictable difficulties, you should consider another line of work!

A Self-Assessment

As a guide for *assessing* your business knowledge, we have prepared a *list of 20 questions* for you to ask yourself. The answers should stimulate your interest in some areas and help guide you in the further use of this book. Read these questions and record your answers. Someday, you may look back at this exercise and better appreciate the results of your efforts at becoming a successful small business manager!

1. Do you fully understand the advantages and disadvantages of conducting your business as a corporation, an LLC, or an LLP?
   Yes _____ No _____

2. Do you understand the significance of and differences between a C corporation and an S corporation?
   Yes _____ No _____

3. Do you know the steps that should be taken before you choose a name for your business?
   Yes _____ No _____

4. Do you know how to write a business plan (complete with projected financial statements) that a banker would find suitable as the basis for long-term financing?
   Yes _____ No _____

5. Does your business have, or can you develop, well-defined, written personnel policies for:
   - Personnel procurement and dismissal? Yes _____   No _____
   - Salary and wage administration?   Yes_____   No _____
   - Employee benefits?   Yes _____   No _____
   - Disciplinary actions?   Yes _____   No _____
   - Use of company resources?   Yes _____   No _____
   - Emergency procedures   Yes _____   No _____

6. Do you fully understand the financial statements of your business, the balance sheet, and statements of income and cash flow and where all the numbers come from?
   Yes _____ No _____

7. Do you know your competitors, their strengths and weaknesses, to the maximum extent possible?
   Yes _____ No _____

8. Do you know how to price your business's products or services based on what the market will bear (rather than based on their cost to produce or procure)?
   Yes _____ No _____

9. Do you know how to involve your customers in new product or service development and testing?
   Yes _____ No _____

10. Are you familiar with the typical terms of a loan document, the positive and negative covenants, and how to structure the borrowing to your greatest advantage?
Yes _____ No _____

11. Are you well acquainted with your suppliers and have a system in place that ensures that you are being fairly treated as to price, terms, warranty, and service?
Yes _____ No _____

12. Are you familiar with the federal and state securities laws that govern how you can sell stock or securities in your company?
Yes _____ No _____

13. Are you acquainted with the federal and state laws and regulations regarding issues such as employment practices, environmental matters, and product packaging and labeling?
Yes _____ No _____

14. Are you aware of the regulatory requirements of the various taxing authorities that can affect your business, such as taxes on income, employment, property, and sales?
Yes _____ No _____

15. Do you understand the operation of a personal computer and use one in the normal course of your business?
Yes _____ No _____

16. Are there systems in place in your business, that you fully understand, to determine the accurate costs of each of your products or services?
Yes _____ No _____

17. Do you receive timely monthly financial statements that compare actual results of operations with planned results?
Yes _____ No _____

18. Do you have a strong business relationship with a banker? An insurance broker? An accountant? A tax expert?
Yes _____ No _____

19. Do you know the size of the market for your products or services and its growth pattern over the past three to five years?
Yes _____ No _____

20. Do you have a management succession plan in place to protect the equity of your business for your family if something happened to you?

Yes _____ No _____

If your answer to many of these questions was "No," it simply means that you need to either gain this knowledge yourself or acquire the services of professionals or employees who have such knowledge. The most intelligent leaders do not have "all the answers," but they do know how to acquire the answers.

You need to develop a list of the areas in which you are not completely comfortable with the extent of your knowledge. These are the areas where you need to acquire knowledge, hire knowledge, or contract for knowledge with outside professionals. It is OK to not know about many of these areas. It is not OK to fail to cover those bases.

Most of these questions are covered in the following chapters of this book. The answers to some of these questions are too complicated to fully address here and, accordingly, you will be referred to sources where the answers can be found.

A "Quiz for Small Business Success"

I cannot end this chapter without sharing a "Quiz for Small Business Success"[2] published by *Small Business Magazine* in 2002. The magazine conducted a survey of more than 100 successful small business owners in the state of California. Their comments about small business success guided the magazine in developing the quiz. The original quiz has 20 questions; I have selected ten of those questions that I believe are most appropriate for inclusion in this book. There are no "right" answers, but you will be able to compare your answers with those of the successful small business owners. I tried the quiz and found it to be most enlightening.

Each of the ten questions offers five answers, which you are asked to rank (from 5 points for "most important" to 1 point for "least important"). When you are finished, go to Appendix A to see how the small businesspeople answered the questions.

1. What is the key to business success?
   a. Business knowledge   _____
   b. Market awareness   _____
   c. Hands-on management   _____
   d. Sufficient capital   _____
   e. Hard work   _____

2. Which is the largest potential trouble spot?
   a. Too much growth   _____
   b. Too little growth   _____
   c. Too fast growth   _____
   d. Too slow growth   _____
   e. Sporadic growth   _____

3. My customers are:
   a. Always right   _____
   b. Too fussy   _____
   c. Demanding   _____
   d. Worth listening to   _____
   e. Dumb   _____

4. Rank these in order of importance for small business marketing success:
   a. Word-of-mouth   _____
   b. Advertising   _____
   c. Signs   _____
   d. Location   _____
   e. Community events   _____

5. Financially my firm:
   a. Has trouble with cash flow   _____
   b. Has a good line of credit   _____
   c. Is financed totally by receipt—no credit   _____
   d. Is making better profits this year than last   _____
   e. Knows exactly where it is all the time   _____

6. In hiring people:
   a. I take far too long   _____
   b. I look for the cheapest person   _____
   c. Personality is more important than experience   _____
   d. I look for the best person and am willing to pay   _____
   e. I only hire at the trainee level

7. The best competitive advantage is:
   a. Experience _____
   b. Understanding what the market wants _____
   c. Confidence _____
   d. Conducting a business ethically _____
   e. A detailed plan _____

8. I think business plans are:
   a. For the birds _____
   b. Nice but not necessary _____
   c. Something I can do with my accountant _____
   d. Useful and informative _____
   e. Essential—wouldn't do business without them _____

9. What makes a terrific entrepreneur?
   a. Creativity _____
   b. Discipline _____
   c. Consumer orientation _____
   d. Technical proficiency _____
   e. Flexibility _____

10. What is essential to marketing?
    a. "A sixth sense" _____
    b. Market research _____
    c. Customer awareness _____
    d. Experience _____
    e. Testing _____

Take a look at the answers in Appendix A. Your answers are not "right" nor are theirs. But any differences may be instructional to you as you pursue your business idea.

Notes

1. Ericksen, Gregory K., and Ernst & Young LLP. *What's Luck Got to Do with It? 12 Entrepreneurs Reveal the Secrets Behind Their Success.* John Wiley & Sons, Inc., 1997

2. "Quiz for Small Business Success." *Small Business Magazine*, 2002. www.sba.gov/BI/quiz.html.

Chapter 2

Understanding Leadership

Strength in leadership involves honesty, integrity, and a positive attitude!

L IKE IT OR NOT, IF YOU ARE THE OWNER-ENTREPRENEUR OF A SMALL business, *your values, honesty, integrity, and attitudes will be reflected in the image that your company portrays to the world.* Moreover, your people will tend to adopt those same characteristics and values in their business activities. It is not unlike the manner in which a football, basketball, or other sports team takes on the attitudes and character of its coach.

Jim Collins, in *Good to Great*,[1] stated, "Every good-to-great company had Level 5 leadership during the pivotal transition years." Level 5 refers to a "five-level hierarchy of executive capabilities, with Level 5 at the top. Level 5 leaders embody a paradoxical mix of personal humility and professional will. They are ambitious, to be sure, but ambitious first and foremost for the company, not themselves."

Let me repeat two important factors: every good company has a strong leader, but that leader must place the success of his company ahead of his own personal aspirations. Consider this carefully as you learn more about something that may have come naturally to you—leadership.

Definition

Leadership involves determining an objective, securing the necessary resources (especially the right people), and then guiding those resources to achieve the goal.

Leadership is the vision and character to guide resources to reach an objective.

It is important to note that these steps do not necessarily happen in the order listed. There is much merit in securing the right people *first* and then defining and pursuing the objective. Whatever the order, each of these steps is a prerequisite to small business success.

If you are not yet in business, but are considering starting a business (or simply want to reassess your personal traits as a leader), you may wish to complete this *personal assessment* by answering the following questions:

1. Are you self-motivated?
2. Do you enjoy competition?
3. Do you have will power and self-discipline?
4. Do you enjoy making decisions?
5. Are you a good planner?
6. Do you manage your personal finances well?
7. Are you willing to work long hours to succeed?
8. Are you physically and emotionally strong?
9. Is your family supportive of your endeavor?
10. Do you easily interact with people?

This self-assessment consists of ten questions. If you give yourself a 10 for each "yes" answer and a 7 for each "probably" answer (*no* points for any other answers), you need a score of *90 or better* to assure yourself that your endeavors as a small business owner are well-founded.

What Leaders Know How to Do

As a small business owner, you may have the traits that we have defined as leadership, but may not have given the subject of leadership much thought. Thinking about the following examples of this talent may even improve your leadership skills. These are things that a leader knows how to do!

1. Use vision to define a unique objective. Why is vision required? Because a unique objective is typically one that has infrequently or never before been achieved. In some instances, it may be difficult to visualize in advance whether the objective is even achievable. Keep in mind, however, that every successful endeavor is preceded by a vision of its fulfillment.

President Kennedy had a vision to define the objective of landing a spacecraft on the moon. At the time, many thought that this objective might not be achievable. Others did not see the merits of the trip. Despite these concerns, Kennedy delegated the responsibility to the "right people" to develop a plan to get to the moon, marshaled the resources necessary to make the trip (including vital human resources who were willing to put their lives at risk), and through skilled personnel directed the efforts to achieve the objective. The objective was achieved and beneficial to society, not because of Kennedy alone, but without his leadership, it may not have been attempted.

2. Develop a dynamic plan to achieve the objective. Determining the resources required, sequencing the timing of events, and developing a method of assessing the progress as the project moves toward its goal are all elements of the plan. *The ability to plan effectively is a critical element of business leadership.*

3. Gather the resources to achieve the objective. This is an even greater challenge to the small business entrepreneur. One of the most vital resource tasks is *finding the right people*, those unique individuals who will savor the trip, perhaps even more than reaching the destination. Without the right people, whose dedication to the objective is greater than their need for personal gratification, the trip may be a hopeless dream.

An equally critical resource is *money*. This requires the leader and his key associates to present convincing evidence to a financial institution (or other source) that his objective is achievable, has considerable merit, and, more importantly, will have a positive impact on the future success and profitability of the company. If Kennedy had had to convince a commercial lending institution of the merits of going to the moon, would he have been successful? No one will ever know. What we do know is that leadership includes gathering *all the vital resources* needed to achieve the stated objective.

4. Guide the resources to reach the objective. This is the last element of leadership. To plan, to organize, to procure resources, but not to lead the effort to accomplishment falls short of our definition of leadership. Much planning, organization and marshaling of resources was necessary to the effective conclusion of World War II. However, without Generals MacArthur and Eisenhower directing those resources, there may not have been a successful conclusion. The same is true in the field of business. Consider the efforts of Bill Gates in developing a product that has changed the world as we know it. Was he initially blessed with great financial resources? No, but he had the vision and character to marshal other resources to achieve a nearly miraculous objective … that of bringing the computer and its limitless capabilities to the personal use of individuals.

What elements of leadership did each of these men exhibit in their efforts? *Vision*, *strong character*, *a belief in their plan*, *confidence in their personnel*, *ability to gather resources*, and *a personal commitment* to achieving the objective. Their technical skills were important, but much of their success must be attributed to their character that was so strong and their attitude that was so positive, that their key personnel took on these attributes as if they were contagious. *Failure was never an option!*

One point that these and many other leaders in history have recognized: *leadership is not a popularity contest!* Many of the greatest leaders in history have had to make decisions that were not universally popular. It is agreed that being elected to the presidency of the United States involves the charisma and popularity of the candidates. However, once elected, they have had the courage and conviction to make decisions affecting the safety and well-being of millions of people and not all of these decisions have been popular.

Consider the following decisions: President Lincoln's determination to preserve the union with a Civil War, President Franklin D. Roosevelt's social programs to help recover from a depression (at the expense of big money interests), President Truman's decision to drop the atomic bomb, and President Kennedy's decision to become involved in the "Bay of Pigs."

None of these decisions was universally popular, but those who made the decisions remained strong leaders. Consider the following parable.

Leadership is not a popularity contest! *Many of the greatest leaders in history have had to make decisions that were not universally popular.*

Parable of the Donkey

The boy rode on the donkey and the old man walked. As they went along, some people remarked, "It is a shame the old man is walking and the boy is riding."

The man and the boy thought maybe the critics were right, so they changed positions. Later, they passed some other people who remarked, "What a shame he makes that little boy walk!"

So, the man and the boy decided they would both walk. Soon they passed some more people who thought they were stupid to walk when they had a good donkey to ride.

So they both got on the donkey! Later, they passed some more people who commented, "How awful to put such a load on the poor donkey."

The boy and the old man decided the people were probably right, so they decided to carry the donkey. As they crossed a bridge, they lost their grip on the donkey and he fell into the river and drowned.

11

Management Lesson: If you try to please everyone, you will eventually lose your … donkey!

Note

1. Collins, Jim. *Good to Great*. HarperCollins Publishers, Inc., 2001.

Chapter 3

Defining Your Business

What could be more simple than defining a business objective? It is, of course, to make a profit. Perhaps! But remember that profit is the desirable result of a well-conceived and properly executed business plan!

Where Are You Going?

I AM REMINDED OF AN EXPERIENCE WITH SOME BUSINESSMEN WHO HAD developed a unique process that, when applied to certain machine components, could extend their wear life. They met with me to learn more about the market that might find their process useful, a market with which I was familiar. Our conversations revealed that, although their process had merit, they had not defined their business, i.e., they had not answered the following questions: Were they to be a service organization or a manufacturer? Who would be their customers? How would their product or service be distributed to their customers? It was impossible to advise them when they had not identified their customer base or the nature of their business operation. In short, they had not determined the direction that their business should take. *It is difficult to develop a trip itinerary when you don't know where you are going!*

Let's contrast this approach with that of the Lanford Brothers Company, the 2002 Small Business Administration (SBA) Success Story Winner from the state of Virginia.[1] Stan and Jack Lanford struggled in the road construction industry for many years before finally focusing on a business objective that best fit their skills and experience: "They have overcome the uncertainty of their industry by finding a specialized niche in bridge construction and repair." Their philosophy, "We must grow or fail," led them to innovation (a word we will encounter again in this book) and, over a 15-year period, they slowly built their expertise and reputation in bridge construction and repair.

Lanford Brothers Company began in 1960 with eight employees. It now employs more than 200 people in Virginia and West Virginia, with annual sales of more than $15 million. Success did not fully materialize for this company until the owners redefined their business objective to a narrower niche in an industry where they could realistically become profitable.

Another 2002 SBA Winner in South Carolina[1] formed a very specific business objective based "on the vision that churches would one day own and use computer systems to perform many of their daily functions." This idea began for Computer Dimensions, Inc. (CDI) in 1978, long before personal computers became a major consumer industry.

Based on this vision, the company developed a primary product, an automated computer system for churches. The owners had the vision, focused on a well-defined objective, and developed a quality product designed for a very specific market segment, churches. Now ACS Technologies is the nation's leading provider of full-service church management software, with more than 300 employees. In 2003, Ernst & Young nominated the president and CEO, Hal Campbell, as a technology finalist in its Entrepreneur of the Year program. In addition to fostering a clear objective, the company has grown through excellent products and exceptional customer service.

Do You Have Vision?

What did President Kennedy and the leaders of these two small businesses have that the businessmen with the manufacturing process did not have? The answer is *vision*.

One of the dictionary definitions of vision is *"the perception of mental images, as of the fancy or imagination."* Another is *"something seen in a dream or trance."* I don't know if Kennedy saw the landing on the moon in a dream or trance, but I would bet that he had a mental image of the occur-

14

rence and its impact on the world. This vision was all that was needed to spur him to establish landing on the moon as a "business" objective for the United States.

Another businessman, Ely Callaway, the founder of Callaway Golf Company in 1982, combined vision with innovation in establishing a business objective. He believed he could revolutionize the golf club industry. "People had been making golf clubs for 300 years," Callaway told a group of entrepreneurs in 1994. "The major manufacturers of golf clubs weren't willing to take a risk on a radically new design."

Callaway had a successful background in the wine business but he also enjoyed playing golf. He found a small local company in California that was making a steel-core hickory wedge that was "meant to look old but perform like the best of modern clubs." The wedge, according to Callaway, worked beautifully. Although this company had only $40,000 in annual sales, Callaway decided to acquire it.

Not satisfied with the wedge alone, Callaway was determined to follow his vision and develop another product through *innovation*. The company created a driver that would do for the golfing world what the oversized racquet did for tennis players. The Big Bertha® driver was his answer. 13 years after he acquired the hickory-shafted wedge, the Callaway Golf Company had become publicly held and achieved annual sales of more than half a billion dollars.[2] As we know, Callaway Golf is still alive and very well with over 2,400 employees and sales now topping $2 billion! And Callaway now includes such names as Odyssey®, Ben Hogan®, and Top-Flite®.

Callaway, a golfer himself, knew that to make a successful golf shot requires a vision of the shot before it is executed. A painter must see a vision of the completed picture before beginning the painting process. The inventor must have a vision of his proposed device and how it works before dealing with the technical aspects of its development.

The inventor must have a vision of his proposed device and how it works before dealing with the technical aspects of its development.

Most certainly Bill Gates had a vision of people using a personal computer in their everyday lives and a vision of the methodology to accomplish this result. These visions were clear to him—despite some in the industry who commented, "Why would anyone want to have a computer in their home!"

Without vision, the ultimate objective is considerably more difficult to define. As I asked my wife before we began building our second home, "Can you visualize the completed construction before it begins?" From this visualization, plans can be drawn and timetables can be set. A contractor can be selected, based on his skills and character, to complete the project. But first, *there must be a vision.*

Let me assure you that all visions are not realistic! I can personally attest to this fact. They must be planned, researched, tested, and proven to be a practical objective. However, there is an important message here:

To define a business objective, you must first "see" it, whether in a dream or your imagination, as it will appear in its completion.

Image and Attitude Are Part of It

Large companies spend millions in advertising to develop an image in the marketplace. You are familiar with many of these efforts. Chevrolet trucks are built "like a rock," implying that the vehicles are well-constructed and virtually indestructible. Microsoft asks, "Where do you want to go today?" alluding to its boundless mastery of computer and internet software, allowing its customers to "boldly go where no one has gone before." Northwestern Mutual Life Insurance Company touts itself as "The Quiet Company," suggesting that you visualize it as a reserved, but competent entity with unlimited resources. The Lexus arm of Toyota has described its efforts as "The Relentless Pursuit of Perfection," a description that needs no explanation whatever. Obviously, these images must be supported by the actions of the companies or they will not be fully accepted in the marketplace.

Even the smallest business needs an image that reflects its focus and dedication to quality and service.

These concepts are true for small business as well as the large businesses mentioned above. Even the smallest business needs an image that reflects its focus and dedication to quality and service.

I was privileged to work for a leader whose business objective reflected his very strong personal commitment of service to the customer. All of his policies and actions, including his demands of those working for him, were focused on this principle. His highly successful career, in a business where service was the end product, attests to the validity of incorporating a positive image and attitude in the business.

Consider leaders from the past and how their image and attitude enhanced their ability to define and achieve their objectives. Regardless of your religious persuasion, you would probably agree that the attitude and image of Jesus Christ certainly enhanced his ability to achieve his objectives. George Washington, Abraham Lincoln, Franklin D. Roosevelt, Harry S. Truman, Dwight D. Eisenhower, Winston Churchill, and many, many others defined and achieved their objectives with the benefit of a positive attitude and strong image.

As a leader of a small business, you cannot avoid having your attitudes reflect in your business and its image in the marketplace. If you insist on integrity and honesty in dealing with your customers and business associates, your company will become known for those traits. To fracture an old adage:

"You will be known by the image you keep."

Notes

1. Small Business Administration. *Small Business Success Stories*, 2002. www.sba.gov.
2. Ericksen, Gregory K., and Ernst & Young LLP. *What's Luck Got to Do with It? 12 Entrepreneurs Reveal the Secrets Behind Their Success.* John Wiley & Sons, Inc., 1997.

Chapter 4

People–Your Greatest Resource

People are a company's greatest resource. We must not forget this!

I WAS WORKING LATE ONE NIGHT TO COMPLETE AN IMPORTANT PROJECT FOR our company, a medium-sized manufacturer of agricultural and industrial equipment. It happened to be a Saturday night and the second and third shifts were not working. The plant covered over 500,000 square feet and was equipped with all types of machinery, including huge 2,000- and 3,000-ton vertical presses that stood more than 20 feet high. During the day, when all of the workers were there, the noise and activity level in the plant was very high.

This particular night, I had to go across the plant to a supervisor's office to collect some reports that were vital to our project. The plant was completely dark, except for a few safety lights glowing at the end of some of the long bays. I turned on the lights to illuminate my way and was suddenly struck by the eerie silence. It was almost deathlike. Here was this huge facility and millions of dollars' worth of equipment, but without people it was a useless collection of idle assets, worth only their price at auction. People, working diligently, were the pulse, the heart of this plant. Without people, there was no activity, no life!

Finding the "Right Stuff"

How many times have we tried so hard to match the skills of a candidate to the demands of the open position that the most important characteristics of a person have been relegated to lesser importance or forgotten entirely?

The key to a person's worth (the "right stuff") is *integrity, honesty, intelligence, the ability to communicate, and the ability and willingness to learn.* Technical skills are important, but without the key ingredients, the technical skills of the applicant may be irrelevant.

Finding the candidate with the "right stuff" is not an easy task, but then my grandmother, after several years of urging, finally convinced me that anything that is worthwhile is difficult and requires considerable effort. There are *several roads to successful hiring.*

1. Personal knowledge of a candidate. The best candidates are usually not hunting for a job. They may be people employed by one of your customers, people in competing companies, people in the same industry but not in the same line of business, or people in other industries who have exhibited the talents necessary for the job. More important, do you or one of your key associates personally know the candidates? If so, you may begin to pursue them, but with a few admonitions.

If the selected candidate works for a customer, it is a good plan to contact the customer and let him know that his employee is a candidate for your position. I once hired one of my best customer's top men, believing that I would lose the customer. I decided it was worth the risk. I did lose the customer, but not forever. The man I hired is now successfully running the business from which I retired. It was well worth it!

People with the "right stuff" are absolutely essential to the future success of your business! A compromise in this area has come back to hurt many businesses: it typically involves terminating the "compromise" and repeating the hiring process. What's worse is that these "compromises" do poor work, cause internal problems, and end up costing the company in many ways.

Depending upon your relationship with a competitor who has a potential candidate, you may wish to treat that competitor much the same as recommended for your customer. The same may be said for candidates working for one of your suppliers.

2. A valued friend knows the candidate personally. This is the next best thing to knowing the candidate yourself. A referral from a friend, a business associate, or a present employee whose judgment you respect is a valid basis for

The key to a person's worth (the "right stuff") is integrity, honesty, intelligence, the ability to communicate, and the ability and willingness to learn.

19

pursuing a candidate. Note that your friend must be *more than a golfing buddy;* you must respect his judgment as you would a trusted associate.

3. "Pay the price." If the first two approaches don't provide a candidate, the next best avenue to the "right stuff" is a toll road. A search firm or a highly reputed employment agency is a good but expensive route (often in the area of 30 percent of the employee's starting annual compensation). Keep in mind, however, the value of an outstanding employee. It far surpasses the fee you may have to pay. Your agreement with the search firm or agency should include the right to reimbursement if the hired candidate does not work out within a reasonable time period, perhaps six months and sometimes longer. This may be negotiable with each individual firm. This avenue is most often appropriate for higher-level positions and not entry-level jobs.

The search firm or agency should do all preliminary screening, which often includes intelligence, personality, aptitude, and skills testing, the cost of which should be included in their fee.

The search firm or agency should do all preliminary screening, which often includes intelligence, personality, aptitude, and skills testing, the cost of which should be included in their fee. (Note: these efforts do not test judgment; you must do this yourself.) In addition, you should expect the firm to provide you with at least three good, qualified candidates who meet the requirements you specify when you contract with the firm.

4. Hire a temporary employee from an agency. It is quite common to contract for a temporary employee only to find that the temp is the right person for the job on a permanent basis and may be available. In this case, you should be prepared to pay a fee to the temp agency. This is a reasonably good way to hire clerical and lower-level technical personnel and it keeps your business moving while you are continuing your search.

5. Advertise in the right places. Although we have not found many "right places to advertise," they may include trade or industry magazines that you are reasonably sure are read by the type of person you are seeking. Sometimes the local newspaper can be a good source for candidates, but be prepared to "kiss a lot of toads to find the prince." Likewise, some have reported success with national publications such as *The Wall Street Journal* and the *National Employment Weekly*, and others report good results by advertising on the internet. Choose the ones best for you. Remember: if you hire an out-of-town candidate, you will be expected to pay for his moving expenses!

The hiring of a candidate assumes that you have carefully and thoroughly considered your own employees as a source. *You must not overlook current employee candidates!* Study the background and work history of those who might qualify. You may not be aware or have forgotten that one of them has all of the qualities that you are hunting for in the new position.

Many businesses post job openings on the employee bulletin boards. I believe this is a good practice.

Be Aware of Employment Laws!

The *interview process* and *application forms*, in today's arena, *are land mines waiting to be stepped on!* There are more employment laws today than ever before and questions you used to be able to ask are now grounds for discrimination lawsuits. *If you are not familiar with these laws, you must become so—and the sooner the better.*

Contact your legal counsel. Most law firms either have an expert on employee relations or can refer you to a source where appropriate literature can be found. By the time you read this book, the laws will have changed and more laws and regulations will have been added. For that reason, I have not attempted to provide specifics here. You can, however, obtain a very good document on the internet regarding employment laws, a document that will probably be updated regularly, *An Equal Opportunity Guide for Small Business Employers* at **www.sba.gov/library/pubs/equalemployguide.html**.

You may be astounded and frustrated to know that *the interview process* cannot *involve questions about the following:*

- ▶ age
- ▶ pregnancy
- ▶ religion
- ▶ race
- ▶ children

- ▶ disabilities
- ▶ marital status
- ▶ sexual preferences
- ▶ ancestry
- ▶ prior arrests

Everyone in your organization who may be in a position to conduct an interview *must* be aware of these and other limitations. We have recommended to companies that they develop a list of questions that *are acceptable* and provide the interviewers with some guidance that is meaningful.

A typical listing of questions that can be asked is presented on the next page. Obviously, if you have found a candidate because of your personal knowledge (or the knowledge of a business associate), you will already know the answers to many of the "illegal" questions. Even so, don't document such knowledge, even if the candidate is for the number-two position in the company.

Have as many key people as possible interview the prospect. More opinions will make for a better hiring decision and the other interviewers may uncover something vital that you overlooked.

Interview Questionnaire

1. What do you like most about your present job?
2. What do you like least about your present job?
3. Describe your responsibilities in detail.
4. Describe your relationship with your supervisor.
5. What do you like most about your supervisor?
6. Why are you considering a different job?
7. Why did you leave the job prior to this one?
8. Do you like most of your fellow employees?
9. Are you aware of the responsibilities of the job for which you are a candidate?
10. Do you have any physical limitations that would prevent you from fulfilling those responsibilities?
11. What do you consider your greatest strength as a candidate for this position?
12. What do you consider your greatest challenge as a candidate for this position?
13. What is your present compensation and benefits package?
14. What was your beginning compensation in your job?
15. What specific training have you had that might increase your ability to perform our job?
16. In which school subjects were you most successful?
17. Which subjects in school did you find the most difficult?
18. Can you provide some references for your technical abilities? What are their positions?
19. What do you know about our company that you find appealing?
20. Are working overtime and travel acceptable to you?
21. Are you willing to receive additional training to improve your ability to perform our job?
22. What is the most important factor to consider about becoming an employee of our company? For example: compensation, benefits, working hours, opportunity to progress.
23. What are the least important factors in your consideration?

Another aid in hiring is a *listing of employment preferences*. The answers can be quite enlightening when studied with the responses to interview questions and a review of an application form. The answers to these questions are important regardless of the level of the position that you are seeking to fill.

Employment Preferences

Rank the factors listed below, on a scale of 1 through 10, with 10 being the most important and 1 being the least important to you in considering a position with our company.

___ initial base compensation	___ retirement plan
___ health and dental insurance	___ 401(k) plan
___ opportunity for advancement	___ job security
___ working conditions	___ working hours
___ incentive bonus plan	___ vacation time

The Employment Application

Once you have identified legitimate candidates for the position, you *must* have them complete an *employment application*. Failure to do so may result in your inability to defend your decision to hire or not hire an individual. There are a number of sources available for securing a sample form that complies with all government regulations and laws. Or, you can develop one of your own and have your legal counsel review and revise it to ensure that it is acceptable in the eyes of the law. A *sample form* is provided as Appendix B, but you should have it approved by counsel for current compliance with the laws.

Do not use an employment application form that has not been approved by your legal counsel!

Hiring the "Right Stuff"

How you approach hiring the right person for a job depends upon the level and type of job. It goes without saying that hiring an entry-level person is substantially different than securing the services of a high-level technical person or a number two or three in the chain of command. In every case, however, *reference checking is mandatory*.

Despite your prior knowledge (assumed) of a key manager-level applicant, you may be surprised at what you find when checking references and credit. Remember: some of the biggest names in industry (and in our federal government) have been embezzlers, bankrupts, accused of sexual misconduct and harassment, felons, and convicted of lesser crimes. Check out their education, call prior supervisors, check for felony convictions, and verify prior employment. In short, *do your homework!*

Assuming that you have identified a good candidate and completed all of the homework with positive results, how do you convince him or her to become a part of your company? There are several *employment selling points* that you should emphasize.

1. Stress the positive factors that have influenced the candidate to favorably consider the position. They may include your company's reputation, a positive environment in which to work, an equity opportunity, the possibility of advancement, the prospect of securing improved monetary rewards for outstanding performance, or simply a "great challenge." *Remember that compensation is not the key incentive for people with the "right stuff."*

Any person who is primarily motivated by an immediate increase in base pay is not looking for the strong, long-term relationship that will contribute to the company's success.

2. Do not "buy" his services. Any person who is primarily motivated by an immediate increase in base pay is not looking for the strong, long-term relationship that will contribute to the company's success. Why wouldn't he leave your company six months from now for another immediate increase in base pay? This is quite different from a candidate's desire to be properly rewarded for an outstanding contribution to the company's objectives. Although you should not "buy" the candidate, you should be willing to "pay for what you get." Good people cost more! More about incentive compensation later.

3. Assure the candidate that his contribution to the company's objective is meaningful. What is more discouraging than being pursued by a company and, once employed, becoming an unnoticed number on the employee roster? The last section in this chapter, "Motivation and Involvement," will address this problem.

4. Consider involving more than one key manager in the hiring process to reinforce the positive factors. It is fine to discuss prospective employment with the key manager who is involved; however, if other managers are present, it will give the candidate a stronger feeling of being wanted. If you are hiring your number-two man or prospective successor, the group approach is not appropriate, unless that group involves other owners or directors of the company.

5. Consider an employment contract or offer letter. There may be occasions when a candidate for a high-level management position will be more comfortable seeing all of the conditions of employment in writing. The written document is a permanent record of the covenants between the candidate and the company and lessens the possibility for misunderstanding between the parties.

The written document may be as beneficial to the company as it is to the candidate. It would be desirable for you to have your legal counsel draft or at least review and approve either of these types of documents to prevent any potential future legal problems. Be especially careful with any noncompete language. Noncompete agreements are frequently not enforceable.

"Getting Acquainted"

One of the most common mistakes made by small businesses in the human resources area is believing that a new hire will perform exactly as expected. At the very least, there is an indoctrination phase that should be provided to every new employee. In addition to learning his way around the facility, the new employee must be provided information that will improve his chances of contributing immediately to the company's performance. This *indoctrination phase* should consist of the following, at a minimum.

Hiring the right candidate is just the beginning! He or she must be developed within the framework of your company and its objectives.

1. Presenting the company's personnel policies. Although the new employee will have learned a good bit about the company's personnel policies during the hiring process, he should now be provided a *personnel handbook* (assuming one is available) that explains the more important policies. These policies should include the hiring process just completed, a definition of salaried and hourly personnel (and their differences), salary administration, incentive bonus plan, profit sharing, retirement plan (if any), pay grade structure, time reporting, working hours, overtime pay, shift premium, pay for attending funerals and jury duty, and performance appraisals. Employee benefits should be explained, including vacation time, health and dental insurance, disability compensation, and other benefits, such as awards and company automobiles.

Note: The development of a good personnel handbook is not as difficult or time-consuming as it sounds. Check out Chapter 5 for help.

If the company has a 401(k) plan and a Section 125 "cafeteria plan," they should be covered carefully so the new employee understands how and when he can begin to participate. All of these matters, and others you may think of, are important to the employee and should be presented as soon as possible.

2. Teaching the company's safety programs. The Occupational Safety and Health Administration (OSHA) has issued standards and regulations designed to protect employees from *safety and health hazards*. These standards and regulations involve the communication of information about hazardous or toxic materials, infectious materials, respiratory hazards, and safety procedures for the operation of equipment. In addition, OSHA requires the development of a *fire safety program* that prescribes, among other things, fire exits, fire extinguishers, an emergency action plan, evacuation routes and procedures, an accounting for employees, assigned fire personnel, the alerting of fire emergencies, and training relative to all of the above. Check within your state for any other local regulations and related reporting that may be required.

Many companies also have plans that relate to local or regional weather problems, such as *tornados, hurricanes,* and *flooding.* All of these plans and programs must be communicated to the employee, who usually must also be trained in the execution of the plans.

3. Understanding the company's business. This may be the *most important part of the indoctrination program.* The new employee needs to learn about the company's operations, its objectives, and, in broad terms, the plan for achieving the objectives. The new employee should understand product information, competitive position, marketing strategy, manufacturing or service process, and personnel organization.

Obviously, the depth of this part of the indoctrination will depend upon the position. He must be involved and made to feel a part of the company's business; the best time to initiate that feeling is at the very beginning of his employment. If there is a plant, include a brief plant tour and introduction to other employees. If there are products, provide an explanation of what they are and why they are unique. If the company offers services, explain what those services are and how they are provided to the customer.

Training the New Employee

In some cases, you may have hired a person who has all of the character attributes that you desire but may not be well-versed in some technical area of his responsibility. He may be a good machine operator but not have adequate training in computer numerical controlled (CNC) equipment, or he may be a great salesperson but not understand the required data entry functions required of sales personnel, e.g., use of a point-of-sale device, cash register, and so forth. Many times a person with responsibilities in operations may have no background at all in accounting and financial controls. In all of these cases, a *training program* may be appropriate. There are several ways to provide the needed training.

1. Vocational technical school. Vo-tech schools are quite good in training people in industrial arts, such as machine tool operation, engineering design, computer-assisted design (CAD), computer-assisted manufacturing (CAM), and similar skills. You or the person who is responsible for human resources matters should be well acquainted with any vo-tech schools in your company's area and the types of skills for which they offer training.

2. Business schools, colleges, and universities. These institutions offer excellent training and education in traditional areas of marketing, sales, accounting, computer operation, clerical skills, and others. If the school is of sufficient size, it will offer these subjects at night, interfering less with the normal workday. If your company has a policy for doing so, you may offer to pay the tuition to attend such classes, provided the classes relate to the employee's primary job responsibility, the classes are approved in advance, and the employee completes the course satisfactorily. And, of course, I must mention the seminars and workshops offered by the local SCORE® chapters and by the Small Business Development Centers (SBDC). Most often, these educational opportunities are low cost and, in some cases, free to the participant.

3. Industry schools and seminars. Depending upon the background of the instructor and his or her teaching skill, industry-sponsored seminars or workshops can be an excellent way to provide "brush-up" training to new employees. The sessions are usually not lengthy and the value of meeting their peers from other companies may be even more valuable than the training itself.

4. In-house training. Many small companies do not have the facilities or time to offer formal in-house training. However, one-on-one or on-the-job training, focusing on the critical needs of the new employee, is an excellent way to make sure that the needed information is learned.

Keep in mind that such training may detract from the efficiency of the trainer but the new hire will learn "our preferred methods," enabling him to contribute more rapidly to the company's performance.

> *The most important thing to keep in mind relative to training and development is that it is necessary!*

Motivation and Involvement

Do you really know what motivates your people? Have you thought about what motivates you? We believe the answer can be expressed in this way:

Something or someone you respect has told you, in some way, "You have done well!"

The "some way" may be a silent nod, a communication from someone you respect, or your own knowledge (based on parameters you know and honor) that you have "done well." The more clearly this acknowledgment is perceived, the more effective the motivation.

The premise that "nothing succeeds like success" is illustrated by a research study involving ten adults who were given a puzzle to solve. The puzzle was the same for all ten participants. After they were completed, five of the adults were *told* that they did quite well, getting seven or more correct out of ten possibilities (which was *not true*). The other five (who may have done well) were *told* that they had done poorly, 7 out of 10 wrong (which was *not true*).

Then all ten were given another puzzle, the same for each person. The five who had been told they had done well on the first puzzle *really did do well* on the second puzzle. The five who had been told they had done poorly on the first puzzle *did poorly* on the second puzzle.[1]

The power of positive thought is immense.

Having coached little league baseball (ages 9 to 18) for 16 years, I can absolutely corroborate the results of the puzzle experiment. We created good teams out of players who were average in technical skills by reinforcing the good things that each player accomplished. We pointed out that poor performances were the result of some technical miscue of which the players simply were not aware and we were sure that they would do better now that they were aware. *This confidence that we expressed in the players was rewarded!*

In my own business, we often hired young men who had just graduated from high school and were known to some of our proven employees. Our on-the-job training program was essential to the success of these new recruits; however, positive recognition of their successful accomplishments played an immense role in their becoming valued and competent employees. We dealt with their mistakes as a learning process as long as their attitude remained good and they did not often repeat the same mistakes. *Positive reinforcement is a powerful motivator!*

Obviously, motivation is not as simple as a pat on the back or a person knowing that he has done well. You must *understand* the normal desires of people relative to their employment, regardless of the level of their responsibility. Most people desire the following:

▶ *Recognition* for their good work
▶ *Meaningful participation* in the company's efforts
▶ A *feeling of belonging* in a successful organization

▶ *Opportunities for growth and advancement* in their competence and responsibility

▶ *Security* in their job if they perform to expectation

▶ *Monetary reward* for an expected level of performance

▶ *Benefits that protect them* and their families from significant monetary loss

Even top-level management personnel, who are typically self-motivated, desire the same things as those in positions of lesser responsibility. A mutual recognition by their peers for a job well done or a project successfully completed may be sufficient. A brief recognition of their success by the top executive goes even further as a motivator!

In a recent survey, *employers* ranked what they believed was *most important* to new employees. The results are shown in the following table:

In the same survey, *employees* ranked the factors most important to *themselves*. The following table shows their rankings (with the employers' rankings in parentheses):

1. good wages	6. loyalty to others
2. job security	7. tactful discipline
3. opportunity	8. appreciation
4. working conditions	9. sympathy—personal matters
5. interesting work	10. feeling involved

There have been many such surveys published, but none that I have found have ever identified what I believe is the *most important factor in successful employment*:

1. appreciation (8)	6. interesting work (5)
2. feeling involved (10)	7. opportunity (3)
3. sympathy—personal matters (9)	8. loyalty to others (6)
4. job security (2)	9. working conditions (4)
5. good wages (1)	10. tactful discipline (7)

Enjoying the job ... enjoying going to work!

How many people do you know that sincerely like to go to work in the morning? How many people do you know who would say they honestly like their job? We all know people who have worked all their lives at jobs that they have *not* enjoyed. Considering that many men and women spend 35 percent to 50 percent of their waking moments at work, not enjoying that time would be very depressing.

So, how do you make an employee's work something that he or she enjoys? It is called *involvement!* Keep your people *involved.* Consider the following:

1. Communicate with them. Make them aware of company business that might affect them, either directly or indirectly. Make sure they know about new products or services, give them copies of new company brochures, and tell them about negotiations for new health insurance. They have a *need to know.*

2. Reinforce their contributions to the company's objective. Informal discussions are needed to bring the employees up to date on their role in the business. *Annual performance appraisals* offer an excellent chance to involve the employees in company affairs in addition to letting them know how effectively they have been working.

You can motivate your people by involving them in achieving your company's objectives!

3. Solicit suggestions for positive changes, whether in customer service, new products, manufacturing processes, or administration. Often, the employees who are closest to a problem will come up with the best solution. Involve them in problem solving and operational improvements. A lot of good ideas have come from a suggestion box and those ideas should be rewarded with recognition and monetary rewards.

4. Encourage a sense of belonging, a sense of being a part of a successful effort. This is much like being a part of a winning sports team, an experience that is never forgotten.

Note

1. Peters, Thomas J., and Robert H. Waterman, Jr. *In Search of Excellence: Lessons from America's Best-Run Companies.* Warner Books, 1982.

Chapter 5

People–Managing Your Greatest Resource

Helping your people succeed is the challenge of all managers. It's also the most rewarding activity you can undertake.

Salary and Wage Administration

A GOOD SALARY AND WAGE ADMINISTRATION PROGRAM IS A POSITIVE tool that provides an informed and objective method of fairly compensating your employees. Typically, a salary and wage administration program includes the following:

1. position descriptions
2. salary and wage pay grades
3. performance appraisal system
4. compensation policies

It also helps to establish salaries and wages that do not escalate beyond what the company should afford. We have watched more than one company provide liberal annual pay increases to employees until one day management discovers that the people are paid beyond what the company can or should afford for their positions. *The remedies are painful!*

Think about the math for a moment. If you hire a person at an annual salary of $30,000 and provide pay increases each year of only 6 percent, in ten years that employee will be making $53,725, not including other payroll costs. If the employee has been promoted to a position of greater responsibility, this may be appropriate compensation growth. But if that employee is doing the same job he had when he was hired, you have to ask, "Is the job worth that level of pay?" Viewed another way, over a ten-year period, *would you be able to increase the sales price for your products or services by approximately 80 percent?* A well-written salary and wage administration program can help prevent this situation. Unfortunately, this technique is used by very few small businesses and is foreign to most small businessmen. A good program includes the following.

If you hire a person at an annual salary of $30,000 and provide pay increases each year of only 6 percent, in ten years that employee will be making $53,725, not including other payroll costs.

Position descriptions. There should be a written position description that defines the *duties, responsibilities,* and *qualifications* of each position in the company. A position could be a secretary, a CNC lathe operator, a salesperson, a teller, and so forth. There may be several tellers employed, but for that *position*, there would be only *one* position description.

Position descriptions also serve as a factual basis for job evaluation decisions. They provide each employee with an understanding of what is expected of them in fulfilling the job assigned. Every employee should have a copy of the position description for his or her job.

Appendix C describes the format of a standardized position description and also presents a sample position description for an hourly position. Appendix D provides a sample position description for a salaried position.

Salary and wage pay grades. Pay grades are determined by the combination of a system of job evaluation and reference to salary and wage survey data for jobs common to companies in the immediate geographic region. These "benchmark" positions can be found in most of the current salary and wage surveys. Examples might include secretary, shipping clerk, accountant, machinist, sales clerk, and production foreman.

A *job evaluation system* is a procedure that enables the comparison of each position in your company with every other position based on selected factors. Quite often companies engage the services of a human resources consulting firm to design and implement a job evaluation system. An employee who has some training in human resources and time to devote to a special project can learn these procedures. The important result of job evaluation is the *pay grade structure* for both salaried and hourly positions that helps ensure equitable pay for all of your people and helps chart a career path for each of them. The pay grades also help prevent continued pay increases for employees when the positions they are filling do not warrant increases beyond specified levels.

Performance appraisal system. A system of evaluating and reporting the performance of each employee on a regular basis is an essential part of the salary and wage program. An appraisal system should provide the basis for promotions, pay increases, needed training, and sometimes termination. Appendix E describes a performance appraisal system and presents a sample form.

Compensation policies. There should be clear-cut policies that describe how base pay, overtime pay, holiday pay, and other compensation practices are determined. Oddly enough, writing compensation policies is not nearly as simple as it sounds. The next section deals with these policies and what they include.

Compensation Policies

All policies relating to compensation, including base pay, overtime pay, and pay day need to be communicated to the employee, preferably in writing. These policies should be part of the *personnel handbook*. The handbook should define a "normal work week," explain how overtime pay is calculated (not everyone does it the same), explain any shift premium, describe any piece rate plan, state when pay day occurs, and specify the pay period covered by each pay day. The handbook should also cover compensation for time spent on jury duty or attending funerals (including information on which funerals qualify), which holidays are paid, the treatment of time off for salaried and hourly personnel, payment for sick leave (if any), and when and how vacation pay is accrued and paid.

In addition to vacation time, you should explain to all employees other fringe benefits, such as health insurance, dental insurance, retirement plan, 401(k) plan, incentive compensation (bonus) plans, profit-sharing plan, and stock purchase plans. More complicated benefits, such as a Section 125 "cafeteria plan," disability (salary continuance) plan, life insurance coverage, and company-provided vehicles, all require more in-depth explanations. Some companies have awards for attendance, service, and other achievements that need to be defined.

If you are not familiar with the provisions of the programs and plans referred to above, you should engage the services of a human resource consultant and/or a tax consultant to provide an explanation. The personnel

All policies relating to compensation, including base pay, overtime pay, and pay day need to be communicated to the employee, preferably in writing.

handbook should cover much more than compensation policies. Some suggestions for items to include and how to develop a handbook are presented in the next section.

Personnel Handbook

In recognition of your pledge to communicate clearly, treat fairly, and provide a positive and enjoyable work environment for your employees, *a personnel handbook is essential!* Not only does this document support your effort to properly relate to your company's greatest resource, it may help insulate you from ugly legal problems that can arise in unfortunate occurrences involving employees. Earlier in this chapter, we discussed the myriad of laws and regulations that are designed to protect employees, but can also damage employers who do not understand those laws and regulations.

Although its contents will vary greatly from company to company, the *personnel handbook* should contain information regarding each of the subjects listed in the following pages:

Personnel Policies

- employment process
- disciplinary process
- e-mail and Internet use
- personal attire
- leaves of absence
- grievance process
- use of illegal drugs or alcohol
- sexual harassment
- discrimination
- smoking
- working hours
- termination process
- plant shutdowns

Salary Administration Program

- format and use of position descriptions
- performance appraisal
- job promotion policy
- bonus programs
- job evaluation process and pay grade structure
- compensation policies

Employee Benefits Program

- vacation policy
- life insurance
- disability compensation and insurance
- 401(k) program

- ▶ health insurance
- ▶ dental insurance
- ▶ section 125 "cafeteria plan"
- ▶ employee awards

Safety Programs

- ▶ hazard communication program
- ▶ fire safety program
- ▶ bad weather programs (tornado, hurricane, snow, flood, power outages, etc.)

All of these items and more should be included in the handbook, briefly but carefully worded. Every employee should be issued a handbook that is numbered and should return it when he or she terminates. The employee should acknowledge in writing that he or she has read the handbook and understands its contents. If your human resources person writes the handbook, *you should have a human resource consultant or attorney review its contents.* If you have no one able to write the handbook, write your policies in your own words and engage the services of a human resource consultant to formalize them suitably.

The employees should understand that the personnel handbook is for their benefit and they can rely on the commitments expressed in it. The handbook should be updated whenever required by a significant change. Many employers use a loose-leaf format to simplify that process.

In summary, the personnel handbook sets forth, in writing, the *commitments of the company* and the understood *commitments of the employee.* Although it does not need to be a fancy, bound document, it is most beneficial!

Every employee should be issued a handbook that is numbered and should return it when he or she terminates.

Retirement Plans

Although companies have long sought to provide for a source of retirement income and/or an accumulation of assets for employees, traditional retirement or pension plans have become increasingly rare in the corporate environment. In recent years, there has been a shift to employer-sponsored but largely employee-funded, income tax-deferred savings plans. One of the most popular is the *401(k) plan,* which, simply put, allows employees to take dollars from their *pretax* earnings and put them into an investment program.

The investment program, usually developed by the company with the help of an investment advisor, typically offers investment opportunities in various segments of the stock market, including stocks and bonds, usually in the form of mutual funds and many others. There is often a guaranteed, fixed interest rate option and sometimes contributions can be invested in the common stock of the employer.

The icing on the cake is the contribution that the company can make to employees' accounts, to match their contributions either fully or partially. The plan typically specifies a vesting schedule spanning five to seven years. But, for the employee, the employer contribution essentially represents "free money." *It simply doesn't get any better than this!*

There are severe restrictions on how and when employees may take the investment proceeds from their accounts, but the bottom line is that this is an excellent way for employees and employer to provide for the employees' retirement.

There are many other forms of retirement savings plans. If you would like to view retirement savings plans available to small businesses (including those listed above), go to **www.irs.gov** and download Publication 3998, *Choosing a Retirement Solution for Your Small Business*. This may be the best publication the IRS has ever offered!

Section 125 "Cafeteria Plan"

The Internal Revenue Code offers another benefit to employees and employers that is similar in concept. An employee can designate a specific sum to be deducted from his or her *gross pay* each pay period and set aside in an account to pay for various *health and child care expenses not covered by his or her health insurance policy*. The only admonition: the employee must estimate such costs for the year carefully, because any funds in the account that are *not used* are *lost* to the employee, forever!

Example: Suppose an employee believes that her unreimbursed medical costs, such as drugs or her share of the health insurance premium, will be $1,500 for the year. Accordingly, she contributes $125 per month to the plan. If those costs actually total $1,350, she loses the difference of $150. The company retains the $150 to help pay for the costs of administering the plan (which are not small).

But the bottom line is, the employee is paying for medical and child care costs with pretax earnings, rather than with net pay, after payroll taxes have been deducted. Check with your tax accountant about all the alternative plans and for assistance with your plan.

We have spent a significant number of pages in this book discussing people—how they are found, hired, trained, and otherwise "cared for." Why? How quickly we forget!

People (with the "right stuff") are a company's greatest resource.

Chapter 6

Your Customer, the Essential Element

WITHOUT THE CUSTOMER, THERE IS NO BUSINESS! IT IS THE customer who buys your service or product, pays the bill, and provides the cash flow that enables your company to survive and make a profit. The customer can also help in many other areas that benefit your company. A customer's input can be beneficial in new product or service development, competitor evaluation, pricing decisions, advertising and sales promotion, and product or service warranty considerations. Sound relationships with good customers must be a major focus of your efforts and good customers pay their bills on a timely basis.

Identify Your Customer

The first task in marketing is to identify that segment of the marketplace that constitutes your customers. If you manufacture airplanes, housewives are probably not your customers. On the other hand, if you manufacture clothes washers and dryers, housewives may be your customers. If you manufacture commercial grade washers and dryers, your customers may be self-service laundries and not housewives. It is not enough that you identify your market; you must find your niche (or market segment) that represents your customer base.

Too many companies try to be suppliers to markets that are greater than they can serve, in terms of either the scope of products they offer or the geographical area they try to cover. There may be nothing worse than developing a customer base that is too broad and then finding that you cannot serve those customers adequately to retain their business. These admonitions seem so elementary that they should go without saying. However, many bankruptcies have resulted when entrepreneurs failed to identify and focus on their *niches* in the marketplace. Develop an image of quality and service in a more narrow market segment that you *can* serve, then expand as your customer base dictates.

A *market* is defined as individuals or companies that have needs or wants and the willingness and ability to pay for them. If the broader market is defined as *individuals*, consider their wants or needs. For example, they *need* to eat, sleep, and dress and they may *want* to travel, own a luxury automobile, or take a cruise. *Companies* may *need* raw materials, equipment, or services and they may *want* to own their own buildings, provide special employee benefits, or have a corporate jet. The niche that is the *market segment* (or customer base) may be the satisfying of a *single need or want* for a specific group of individuals or companies.

Accordingly, your customer base may be identified as *men and women (and their children) who want to eat ice cream*, have the willingness and ability to pay for it, and reside in a particular locale. Hence, Ben & Jerry's, Baskin-Robbins, Häagen-Dazs®, and others have identified and strived to serve this narrow market segment. These companies have not attempted to serve a broader market but have worked to provide their product at the very highest quality possible to the market segment they identified. It is safe to say that they have been successful.

Developing a Marketing Strategy

Although a discussion of marketing strategy and all of its elements involve the customer in some way, we have opted not to cover all of those elements in this chapter. The importance of some of them requires that they be discussed fully and separately. As you read the following chapters, remember that without the customer a marketing strategy is academic.

Your ability to satisfy a specific need or want in a well-defined market is the key to identifying your customer!

A *marketing strategy* involves *all* of the following:

▶ Defining the customer base
▶ Understanding the competition

- ▶ Planning and developing products and services
- ▶ Pricing products or services
- ▶ Selling and distributing products or services
- ▶ Advertising and promoting products or services

Defining your customer base includes more precisely identifying your customers, how many there are, where they are located, and how they buy. In addition, you will need to determine the approximate annual dollar value of their purchases.

Another essential element of your marketing strategy is *understanding your competition*. Who are your competitors? Where are they? What competitive advantages, if any, do they have? How do they satisfy the needs or wants of their customers? Do they have any weak points that you might exploit? How well are they thought of in the marketplace? You need to know those with whom you are competing and their strengths and weaknesses.

You should establish a system of *planning and developing your products and services* so that they accurately address the needs and wants of the customer base. The system should also detect when you need to change products or services, add new products, or eliminate old products, in response to any changes in your customers' needs and wants. You may also need to make decisions with respect to the packaging and presentation of the products or services for delivery or at their point of sale.

You must develop a strategy for *pricing your products or services*. How many small companies do you know that determine the cost of what they sell and add a percentage to that cost to establish the selling price? Is this a strategy that you wish to follow? If not, you need to develop the *best* strategy for determining a selling price for each of your products and/or services that is viable in the marketplace and also permits your company maximum profitability. Note the following observation:

Inadequate pricing is one of the leading contributors to the failure of small businesses!

You must develop a plan for *selling and distributing your products or services*. You must determine how they will be sold, who will sell them, and how the sales personnel will be compensated. The plan should define how your products will be delivered to the customer and whether you will provide warranties for your products or services.

A final part of your marketing strategy is a plan for *advertising and promoting your products or services*. You must decide whether and how to

Defining your customer base includes more precisely identifying your customers, how many there are, where they are located, and how they buy.

advertise and how these ads will be developed and at what cost. Are there trade shows where you should exhibit or promote your products? What sales brochures, technical literature, or user manuals, if any, are required to adequately promote or explain your products? The answers to all of these questions become your *marketing plan* (see Chapter 10) and are discussed more fully in the following pages and chapters.

Defining the Customer Base

Most market research professionals talk about two approaches to gathering data about a market: *primary research*, where data is gathered directly from potential customers using a variety of techniques, and *secondary research*, where "ready-to-use" information is gathered from an array of third-party sources, such as the federal government, trade associations, and research organizations. Obviously, a combination of these two approaches will provide the best definition of your customer base. Assuming you already have developed a primary product or service that responds to a need or want of a specific group of companies or individuals, you need to determine the following:

Most market research professionals talk about two approaches to gathering data about a market: primary research and secondary research.

▶ How many potential customers are there? Where are they located?

▶ How do your potential customers buy the product or service—directly from a retail outlet, from a wholesaler, from a manufacturer or other source?

▶ From which of your competitors are these potential customers currently buying the largest quantities of the product or service?

▶ Is the product or service being supplied from an inventory (or service staff) rather than being manufactured or assembled to a customer order?

▶ If the product or service is not being supplied when sold, what is the lead time of delivery or installation?

▶ What is the annual dollar value of purchases of products similar to yours? What portion of that volume is purchased in each of the defined geographical areas that you intend to serve?

Let's consider an example of how these questions were answered for a small company; we'll call it ABC Company. By reading one of the most popular *industry trade magazines*, it was discovered that a research arm of that magazine had done primary research on a broadly defined market (which included ABC's market) for its own benefit, but subscribers to the magazine could have the results of this survey by simply requesting them. The data provided showed how many companies purchased the type of products that ABC offered, in what states the customers were located, and the number of customers in each of several size groups (in terms of the numbers of machines owned that used the products).

When requesting a copy of the survey, ABC asked the magazine research people if any additional information was available. The researchers indicated that the magazine owned part of an *affiliated research company* that would supply the names and key management personnel of each of the customer companies identified in the survey. The information was available for each of several geographical areas at a nominal price. ABC purchased the data for one of these areas, an area that it had defined as its primary marketing area.

To determine from which of ABC's competitors the customers were purchasing those products, ABC called several of *its customers* and asked the question directly. This inquiry disclosed that some were buying directly from the manufacturer of the products, responding to calls made by the manufacturer's own direct sales people; and others were buying from *manufacturers' representative organizations* that received a commission from the manufacturer. A careful review of another trade magazine revealed that the magazine offered a document listing *all* of the manufacturers' representative organizations, including the areas that they covered, the manufacturers that each represented, and the names of the principals in each organization, with their addresses and phone numbers and the number of salespeople.

ABC called several of the rep organizations and found out the terms of sale and the delivery lead times being experienced in the industry. The only thing missing was the total annual sales volume for the products, the size of the market that ABC desired to serve. It was unable to determine a completely accurate figure. However, a review of Dun & Bradstreet reports for ABC's largest competitors enabled ABC to make a reasonable estimate of their aggregate sales volume. Another survey done annually by yet another trade journal disclosed the names of all of the competitors offering these products for sale. Applying some rough estimates to these remaining competitors, ABC developed a compilation of the aggregate annual sales volume for products of the type that it manufactured and ... arrived at a pretty good idea which of the competitors were accounting for major portions of the volume!

It is not all as easy as the illustration given. It requires a *reasonable amount of effort*, a *generous amount of perseverance*, and some *common sense*. It should be clear that the techniques described in the example included both primary and secondary research. Large words for a commonsense solution!

There are many sources of data that are available to the small business owner (or prospective entrepreneur) to help determine an existing or potential customer base. We will not attempt to provide an exhaustive listing, but rather to illustrate the extent of such sources. Here are some places to begin.

Federal government. The single largest source of data available to business, it includes the *Statistical Abstract of the United States* (annual), the *U.S. Industry & Trade Outlook*® (annual) with industry reviews and forecasts, and a myriad of other data from the National Technical Information Service of the U.S. Department of Commerce. If you want to really be impressed, get on the internet and go to **www.fedworld.gov**, **www.fedstats.gov**, and **www.census.gov** and browse. Use the "search" capability there and then order (at a nominal price) the documents that fit your needs. You won't believe the information that has been gathered using *our* tax money!

Trade journals and magazines. These are a super source for information relating to your specific industry. Most journals offer "bingo cards" that you can check for free information from the various advertisers and contributors to the journal. If you don't know what journals and magazines are available, start with the Yellow Pages and find *trade and professional associations* that relate to your industry. Make a few phone calls or do a web search using Google or another reliable search engine.

Library. Go to the local library and ask the reference librarian to help you with your search. These people are usually well informed and quite willing to help persons with specific needs. Besides, your search may provide a break from what might otherwise be a rather routine day.

Universities and technical schools. These are another excellent source of information. Many universities have research organizations that publish considerable data regarding a wide array of industry information. You may have to ask a lot of questions to get to the right source, but it should be worth it.

Research foundations. These include The Conference Board (formerly the National Industrial Conference Board), the American Management Association, and the American Marketing Association. These foundations offer a huge assortment of information on various industries, much of which can be obtained or ordered on the internet. Try **www.conference-board.org**, or **www.amanet.org**, and **www.ama.org** and browse each of their sites.

Dun & Bradstreet reports. Although many businesses decline to provide D&B with information, most will give them some idea of their size, usually in numbers of employees and/or annual dollar volume of sales. This informa-

There are many sources of data that are available to the small business owner (or prospective entrepreneur) to help determine an existing or potential customer base.

tion may not be precise, but it does give you an idea of relative size of your competitors and may help you determine the size of the total market. D&B reports are available for a fee (unless you are a member), but you may enlist the aid of your banker or a business friend who is a member to help you get the reports you need.

All of the sources listed above are considered *secondary sources* because they come from third-party inquiries. The final effort in gathering data comes from *primary sources*. Talk with your *competitors, suppliers,* and *customers* and ask all of the questions for which you need answers. Surprisingly, some of your competitors are pretty nice folks and may give you some good information—so long as it is not detrimental to their business.

Intermediaries—including wholesalers, retailers, and others—are also a good source of information. Perhaps the best, however, is the *customer*. Ask several of your present or potential customers about their suppliers (your competitors) and gather their opinions. In the final analysis, their assessment may be the most important of all!

Having done all of your research regarding the customer base, you should be in a good position to determine the profile of your typical customer and the number of potential customers in your targeted geographical area. From this information, you may be able to estimate potential annual sales volume.

If all else fails, you may wish to contact or become a member of the American Marketing Association or other organization that can help you determine your customer base. Of course, there are plenty of marketing consultants who will give you a lot of help for a lot of money. But, sometimes it is worth it!

If all else fails, you may wish to contact or become a member of the American Marketing Association or other organization that can help you determine your customer base.

Understanding the Competition

Having gone through the exercise of determining the customer base, you will likely have a very good idea of who your competitors are, if you don't already know. The need to have a thorough understanding of your competitors and their strengths and weaknesses cannot be overemphasized.

You must know your competitors' reputations and where they are located. By careful inquiry of selected customers, suppliers, and others in the industry, you will be able to determine how well each of your competitors satisfies the needs and wants of the customer base. In other words, what are the *marketing strengths* of each and what *products or services* does each offer that gain an advantage in the marketplace?

Do any of your competitors hold *patents*? If so, you should obtain a copy of all such patents.

You should gather copies of all *literature and promotional material* distributed by each competitor. An understanding of their *sales and distribution system* is also essential. How do they sell? Retail, through distributors, with direct sales people, or with manufacturers' representatives? How do they deliver services or products to customers? With their own trucks, a common carrier, or other means?

Do any of the competitors fail, in any way, to satisfy the needs of customers? All of these *weaknesses* should be included in the documentation described below so that your partners and members of management can be made aware of such shortcomings.

You should prepare a *full documentation* of the information known about all major competitors. This documentation should include the following for each competitor:

▶ Ownership structure, members of management, and key employees

▶ Locations (offices, plants, stores, warehouses, etc.)

▶ Major products and/or services (including a detailed description of each, pointing out its strong and weak features)

▶ Any patents (or patents pending), trademarks, or trade names owned or applied for

▶ The strengths and weaknesses, especially as perceived by the customer, with a clear description of the strength or weakness

▶ A description of sales methods, sales personnel, and distribution system

▶ A description of advertising and promotional programs, media used, and estimated cost

▶ An estimate of annual sales volume and an indication, if possible, of the geographical areas of strong or weak volume

This information should be kept confidential to your key personnel, partners or co-owners, and others who have a need to know. Keep in mind that any weakness in a competitor's products, services, pricing strategy, or delivery capability represents an opportunity for your company to *gain an advantage*.

Chapter 7

Product Planning and Development

THERE IS A DIFFERENCE BETWEEN PRODUCT PLANNING AND PRODUCT *development*. Product *planning* is determining which products or services best satisfy the needs and wants of your customer base (that you should offer to them), consistent with your company's ability to provide such products or services.

Even if you are a professional, such as a physician, dentist, lawyer, or accountant, you must still concern yourself with product planning. Are you a specialist (internist, surgeon, pediatrician, and so on) or are you a general practitioner? Does your firm specialize in criminal cases or civil cases or something else, such as patent or water rights law? If you are a retailer or wholesaler, you must determine which products to stock in inventory. Determining the services or products to offer to your customer base is important: you should do research and define what you plan to offer.

The determination of your products and services relates to what you perceive your business to be. (See Chapter 3.) What is your unique skill, idea, product, or service and what is your vision of how that capability will perpetuate as a profitable business venture? Obviously, your training, education, and experience have a bearing on this decision, as do the present state of the business and the relative success of existing products/services.

Product Planning

The *product planning* procedure should include many, if not all, of the following activities.

Develop a listing of products and/or services that you believe are *absolutely necessary to the success of your business*. Then consider any products or services that might be added *to complement the primary products or services*.

Determine which of these products or services the company should *make* or provide from its own resources and which it should *buy* from a third party. Although the make-or-buy decision process is not within the scope of this chapter, it really boils down to which method would offer the greater return on the investment.

For those products or services that you will purchase, list potential suppliers and *solicit quotes* for various quantities of those products *to determine the most profitable source*. Delivery, service, credit terms, stocking plans, discount pricing, and other factors will enter into the decision. Also, in the case of retailing, brand name recognition, quality image, and diversity of styles are among the other considerations that influence the decision.

There are many manufacturing companies that have the *ability to manufacture* all of the products that they sell. But they must determine if that is the *most profitable approach* to take. The ability to make a product is *not* the primary determiner of the make-or-buy decision.

After considering all of the factors discussed, you and your associates should develop a *plan* that lists the products and services you intend to sell, whether you intend to make or buy the products and, if you plan to purchase, from whom and under what terms and conditions.

Product Development

Product *development* is different from product planning and includes the technical activities of product research, design and engineering. Product development is usually associated with manufacturing, engineering, or service companies rather than retail or wholesale operations. The introduction of new products, the enhancement or changing of existing products, and the elimination of ineffective or unprofitable products are all critical to the success of a small business.

Product development is different from product planning and includes the technical activities of product research, design and engineering.

A historically prominent economist, Joseph A. Schumpeter, concluded that:

"... dynamic innovative entrepreneurship is the engine that drives the entire economy."

With today's technological advances in electronics and computer science, there seems to be a bit of wisdom in that philosophy. Peter Drucker, in *The Practice of Management*[1], puts it boldly: "Because its purpose is to create a customer, any business enterprise has two—and only these two—basic functions: *marketing and innovation*." Another author put it even more bluntly, stating, *"Innovate or die."*

Although we believe the last assertion is a bit severe, we do believe that without *innovation* a company will never achieve the level of success associated with a creative, innovative competitor. Remember it this way:

Continuous innovation and product development is essential in maximizing the long-term success of a small business.

In Chapter 5, the subject of product planning and development was introduced. That is because *the customer is the very best source for ideas that can develop into new products or services.*

We can recite example after example that prove this belief and it will continue to be so in the future. How many patents have resulted from someone asking, "Why don't they develop this?" or "Why isn't there a way to do that?"

In my own business experience, my associates and I developed and patented a product that was the direct result of a comment from a large customer. The customer wanted a new product to enable them to accomplish something that previously could not be done. The new product became a significant success, both for our company (which developed it) and for our entire customer base, especially the customer who wanted it in the first place.

Product ideas come from the inability of existing products and services to satisfy a customer need or want!

Customers are often the starting point for new product development. Determine which of their needs and wants are not being satisfied and use that information as a basis for a new product or service. *New product ideas are* not *based on existing manufacturing or engineering capabilities*. Product ideas come from the *inability of existing products and services to satisfy a customer need or want!*

Microsoft created an operating system for personal computers that satisfied a need in the marketplace, the need to be able to operate a PC in a way that was so simple that all users (well, ... most!) could understand it. As a result, we have Windows®. The inventors of cell phones satisfied their customers' desire to be able to make phone calls easily and from any location. An anti-lock braking system satisfied a need among automobile owners to be able to use the brakes without locking them, thereby preventing disastrous skids and resulting accidents. With these illustrations as a background, *how then do you generate ideas for new products*?

Talk with your customers about the things that they would like to accomplish but cannot with existing products. Observe the customers' operations and consider potential improvements of existing products or services that customers would find desirable. Make the same inquiries of your *salespeople or manufacturing representative organizations*. They also see new product ideas and opportunities firsthand.

Examine the array of products offered by your best competitors. Do they have products that place your company at a disadvantage? Consider how Canon's Image Stabilization® camera lenses (for 35mm SLR cameras) stimulated Nikon to respond with its new Vibration Reduction® lenses. The move by Nikon was absolutely necessary to overcome a temporary advantage that Canon had gained. Make a list of the outstanding products and services offered by your competition and determine if your company should consider developing similar or better products to offer to your customer base.

Also, if high technology is involved in your product or service, make sure that you're familiar with all the *patents and registered copyrights* for your industry. Our company's selection filled two large, three-ring notebooks!

Continually stay abreast of the activities of research organizations in your industry. *Read their technical papers and journals* for new, pertinent information. Have they come up with data that could stimulate the development of a new product? Medical and nutritional research on the effects of fat and cholesterol on persons with heart disease gave rise to a huge number of highly profitable new products—egg substitutes, cholesterol-reducing drugs, low-fat margarine and many other low-fat foods, and ... look what it did for the poultry industry!

If you have *technical service personnel* who perform troubleshooting or maintenance functions in the field, solicit their ideas on how to make your products better or develop a new product that complements or replaces existing products.

These are some of the ways that new product ideas are discovered. Remember, however: product development only happens when management gives it a high priority among all company activities.

A word of caution: A new product idea is good, but doing something produc-

Make a list of the outstanding products and services offered by your competition and determine if your company should consider developing similar or better products to offer to your customer base.

Managing a Small Business Made Easy

tive with the idea requires a *careful assessment* of all the factors necessary to bring that product to the marketplace. *The cost of new product failure is extreme!*

I can personally attest to this fact, having had to recall and replace a large number of failing units of a new product that my company had introduced to the market. The new product had been field-tested, but not over a sufficiently long period. Over the longer period, but within the warranty period, the product failed. Regardless of the warranty period, the product had to be replaced to maintain the relationships that had been developed with the customers involved. P.S. No customers were lost!

There are some steps that your company should include in *evaluating and developing a new product or service:*

1. Screen the new product ideas and rank them based on your assessment of their relative marketability. Eliminate from further study those that may have good potential but lack market demand at the present time. Retain the product data! Also determine the suitability of the new product for inclusion in your company's product line. Does it fit your company's image?

2. Convert the product idea into a product definition, outlining its features, design, possible sizes (or stock-keeping units—SKUs), component materials, outward appearance, packaging, and mode of delivery. Develop blueprints and/or specifications for the new product so that others may assess its effectiveness or provide a quote for supplying it. Also, *sign and date all of these prints and specifications*. Doing so may allow you to use a "patent pending" designation for the product or service while it is being fully developed.

3. Develop a sales projection of the number of units of the product that can be sold over a given time period. State the sales numbers in categories, such as "Assured," "Quite Likely," and "Possible."

4. Determine the product source. Determine whether the product will be manufactured and/or assembled in-house or if it must be purchased from a third party. If made or assembled in-house, *determine the cost* of component materials, labor, and overhead required to make the product, considering the levels of production for the sales projected. If new equipment or facilities are required to manufacture or assemble the new product or provide the new service, those costs should also be determined.

If purchasing outside, select two or three sources and request quotations for the cost of the units at the same quantity levels. Add an estimate of packaging cost and calculate the total unit cost of the product, ready for delivery, in the quantities selected.

50

5. Study the market for similar items and **develop a proposed sales price per unit.** Identify what *the market will bear* based on the new product's likely appeal and benefit to the customer. *The price should* not *be based on the previously estimated unit cost.*

The price for the first Xerox copying machine bore no relationship to the cost of its manufacture. It was based on what the manufacturer believed they could be sold for in the market. Later, as other copiers appeared, Xerox reduced its prices. The same can be said of personal computers, scanners, and similar equipment. More later on pricing your products!

6. Determine the profitability of the product based on the estimated sales price and unit product cost previously calculated. Is the resulting gross margin comparable to the margins for other products in your line? Is the margin sufficient to generate a net profit after assessing the costs of selling, commissions, and administrative overhead? If the answers are *yes*, go on to the next step. If the answers are *no*, stop here and go to the *next product idea*. Experts point out that, even among well-managed companies, the *success rate of new products that actually reach the market is only two out of three!*

7. Test the new product in the marketplace. No doubt you work with some customers quite closely that would agree to use the new product and provide feedback. The buzzword for such a customer is a "beta site." Testing is important not only to determine if the product does what it is intended to do but also to gain an idea of the degree of benefit for the customer. The manufacture or purchase of a representative number of units also helps determine the accuracy of the estimated costs. Finally, depending upon the nature and complexity of the product, the testing period must be long enough to determine its durability and its continuing attractiveness to the customer. Testing is the final means to determine whether a new product will be viable and how profitable it will be. These determinations are essential. *Do not manufacture or buy a large number of units of a new product and attempt to sell them only to find that the product (1) doesn't work, (2) isn't profitable, or (3) is not perceived by the customer as satisfying a need or want.*

8. Determine if you can patent or copyright your product or service. Contact a good patent attorney and answer all of his or her questions about the product or service. The attorney will be able to make the proper determination for you and, if positive, help you achieve the product protection offered by law. By the way, if you are convinced that your idea is capable of being patented and your attorney is convinced otherwise, find another patent

51

attorney and secure a second opinion! *This is critical!*

A *patent* allows you to prevent others from making, using, or selling the patented item as set forth in the patent's claims. A patent can be a *utility* patent or a *design* patent. As briefly stated earlier, the *utility* patent covers (to quote the patent law) "Any new or useful process, machine, manufacture, or composition of matter, or any new and useful improvement thereof." The *design* patent covers "Any new, original, and ornamental design for an article of manufacture." If you think you can patent something you have developed, be sure to document the design early in its development and sign and date the design.

Also keep in mind that patents are awarded country by country. That is, a U.S. patent offers you no protection in Japan, Canada, or any country in Europe, except to prevent the import of competing goods to the U.S. Finally, remember that you can't use "patent pending" on your product until a patent application or a provisional patent has been filed and is, in fact, pending.

One additional word about patents. Sometimes it is better to *not* patent a process or idea rather than allow competitors to see, in print, how it works. (Note: The recipe for "Coke" has never been patented!) Their next step may be to copy your process but change it sufficiently to avoid infringing on your patent. Consider this possibility and discuss your options with the patent attorney.

Copyrights are used to cover books, articles, advertising copy, software, artwork, and similar things. *Trademarks* and *service marks* also provide protection for the words, names, symbols, logos, and similar items. Let your patent attorney explain their use as well. *Remember that the best solution to all patent questions is a good patent attorney.* (More about patents in Chapter 16.)

If you have taken all of the steps outlined above and the answers are positive, you then have a new product or service that you can add profitably to your product or service line. Now you can advertise and promote it!

Note

1. Drucker, Peter. *The Practice of Management.* Harper & Row, Publishers, Inc., 1954.

Chapter 8

Pricing Your Product or Service

PRICING PRODUCTS AND SERVICES IS ONE OF THE MOST CRITICAL aspects of running a small business. As we stated earlier, one of the biggest contributors to small business failures is improperly developed pricing for products or services. It is obvious that the price of a product or service is a major determinant in the attractiveness of the item in the eyes of a customer, affecting a company's competitive position and its ability to gain market share. The *most important consideration* is that pricing has a major bearing on the company's profitability. Although there are exceptions, I believe strongly that:

If you cannot price your product or service for an adequate profit, you should change the product or service so you can achieve that objective or drop it from your line!

Setting a price too high is usually not the problem with small businesses. Too many small businessmen base the price on the cost of the product, simply adding a percentage above that cost to determine the price. Cost is an important factor in determining whether to keep or reject a product from your line, but *cost is* not *a good basis for setting selling price!*

There are several pricing objectives that are used by successful companies and that studies have categorized into meaningful groupings, such as (1) achieving a target return on investment, (2) maintaining price stability, (3) maintaining or improving market share, (4) meeting or preventing competition, and (5) maximizing profitability.

Certainly achieving an adequate return on investment or on net sales is important, as is maintaining price stability. There are occasions when a company needs to improve its market share and meet or prevent competition but, in our opinion, these goals should not be long-term objectives guiding pricing. The main objective in business is to maximize profitability and to do so requires that your product be priced at what the market will bear!

Obviously, this approach requires that *you know what the market will bear,* which requires some research into the market to determine how your product compares with the competition. I should also admit that the *profit maximization* concept proposed here is sometimes considered "ugly" in the public mind. However, I believe that market forces will correct unduly high prices in the long run, avoiding the "ugliness" that is perceived by some. Isn't it interesting to note that studies have consistently shown that *consumers' perceptions of product quality vary directly with price? If it costs a lot, it must be good!*

A product typically has a price cycle. A new, patented product that will do what no competing product does can demand a price that is high in the range of expected prices. As time passes and competing products either match or approach the quality or effectiveness of the new product, prices may need to be reduced to maintain desired market share. Note that the word "may" is used. As long as quality and performance are maintained, pricing may be allowed to remain at a high level. Toyota's luxury automobile line, Lexus, has not reduced the price of its products, but has actually raised them since their introduction. The same can be said of high-quality photographic equipment (such as Hasselblad) and many other products with which you are familiar. The key is the *continuing quality, performance, and service.*

If competing products with lower introductory prices come onto the market (referred to as *penetration pricing*), some price reduction in your products may be required. Also, as a product nears the end of its cycle, it may be desirable to further reduce the price—but *never to a point that the profit is not satisfactory.* These reductions are illustrated in the computer and electronics industries, where the prices of PCs, scanners, and related equipment that started high have been reduced as lower-priced competing equipment comes into the market. There is little doubt, however, that the manufacturers consider the profit margin on their computer equipment adequate. Having said all of this, how do we determine prices using the *profit maximization approach?*

The main objective in business is to maximize profitability and to do so requires that your product be priced at what the market will bear!

54

The Profit Maximization Approach

1. You must determine the prices that are being charged for competitive products. In many industries, typically involving commodities, mass-produced products, and other products commonly purchased at retail you can simply observe the pricing. It is more difficult to determine the prices of specialty products, which are often highly technical, engineered, and proprietary. Many times, pricing is based on quotation and no price lists are available to the consumer. In these cases, research is the answer.

If you have good customers who are loyal, they may be willing to obtain competitive price data for you. Sometimes it is necessary to actually obtain a quote, through a friendly customer, for the specific product price that is needed. Occasionally, a friendly competitor may be willing to share information about another competitor's product pricing. (Beware of the Robinson-Patman Act. See Chapter 9.) In some cases, manufacturers' representatives may offer help in obtaining price information for competing products. You must use all of the tools at your command, and sometimes invent some, to secure the pricing information you need. Effort, imagination, and perseverance are the key words.

If you have good customers who are loyal, they may be willing to obtain competitive price data for you.

2. Compare your product or service with the competing product or service relative to quality, performance, and the ability to deliver the product or service in a timely fashion. Delivery can be a major determinant; as a wise economist has said, *"There will be two kinds of companies in the future, the quick and the dead!"* Sometimes service after the sale is also a sufficiently significant factor to warrant higher pricing.

Examine all of the comparison factors with competing products or services: quality, service before and after the sale, term and extent of warranty, and installation assistance.

3. Evaluate your ability to market the product or service as compared with your competition. If you are competing with the biggest in the industry and they have a superior marketing organization, you may need to set a price below theirs for comparable products or services to command the attention of the market.

4. Establish a selling price, based on the information you have gathered. You may wish to price above, below, or at the same level as the price quoted by your competition for a comparable product or service, but set your price as high as you believe the market will allow. Refer to the following table to assist you in this determination.

Pricing Consideration	Price Higher If	Price Lower If
Product type	Proprietary	Commodity
Manufactured	Custom-made	Mass produced
Production	Labor intensive	Capital intensive
Service before/after sale	Considerable	Little or none
Product obsolescence	Rapid	Slow
Product versatility	Multiple use	Single use
Product cycle state	New	Mature
Distribution channels	Long	Short
Market capability	Superior	Inferior
Promotion required	Considerable	Very little

5. Compare your selling price with cost and determine that the price selected will return an adequate profit and enable a desired return on invested capital. The definition of "adequate profit" varies by industry. It may be as low as two to three percent of sales in the food industry or as high as 15 to 20 percent in highly technical manufacturing industries. In all cases, however, the selling price must cover not only the costs of production, procurement, and/or installation but also administrative and selling costs and then yield a profit. If your first attempt at pricing does not yield a profit, change the product, service, method of delivery, or some other factor to allow a profit.

To illustrate the pricing strategy, assume the following data for a small business, based on average performance in recent months, in a little different profit-and-loss format:

If you can't make the desired profit from the products or services you market, you are in the wrong business!

Sales		100%
Cost of sales:		
Variable direct costs	35%	
Fixed direct costs	25%	
Total cost of sales		60%
Gross margin		40%
Operating expenses:		
Variable expenses	20%	
Fixed expenses	10%	
Total operating expenses		30%
Profit before taxes		10%

56

A sound pricing technique is facilitated by the recognition of all costs of doing business either as *fixed* or *variable*. This includes the costs of production, procurement, or installation and the costs of administration and selling.

Variable direct costs are costs that will increase or decrease as production or sales increase or decrease. Examples include product costs; direct labor and other payroll costs of production, installation, or warehousing personnel; raw materials; production supplies; power for machine operation; and similar costs. Wages for inventory stocking and handling personnel, and packaging and shipping supplies are also variable direct costs.

Fixed direct costs are costs that will remain the same regardless of the level of production or sales. Examples include:

▶ salaries and wages for supervisory, estimating, and installation,

▶ rent,

▶ maintenance and depreciation of manufacturing or inventory space (warehouse or retail floor space),

▶ long-term lease expense and the costs of production and material handling equipment,

▶ insurance on plant and/or equipment; and property taxes and depreciation based on facilities and equipment.

It's helpful if these fixed production costs are identified as such in your internal accounting system. You can accomplish this with some added coding in your chart of accounts (which is discussed in the chapter on accounting).

Variable operating expenses include the payroll costs of sales and billing personnel, sales commissions, warehouse shipping labor, travel expenses, warranty costs, bad debts expense, delivery costs and, in some cases, advertising and promotional costs. Also included are liability insurance premiums (based on sales volumes) and administrative supplies and expenses that relate to volume (packing slips, warranty registrations, costs of after-sale service, installation costs, and similar items).

Fixed operating expenses include the costs of administrative, sales management, and office personnel who are not sensitive to the level of production and sales; their associated payroll costs (taxes and benefits); facility rent; legal and accounting costs; and casualty insurance premiums. These costs will continue at the same approximate rate regardless of the level of production and sales.

As mentioned previously, the ability to identify all costs in your accounting system as variable or fixed is extremely helpful and not very difficult. If the accounts containing these costs are flagged in the system, they can be re-evaluated at later dates to ensure that their status is still appropriate. After distinguishing between fixed costs and variable costs, the abbreviated profit and loss (income) statement previously illustrated can be presented in a *different* manner:

Sales		100%
Variable Costs:		
Variable direct costs	35%	
Variable operating expenses	20%	
Total variable costs		55%
Marginal contribution		45%
Fixed Costs:		
Fixed direct costs	25%	
Fixed operating expenses	10%	
Total fixed costs		35%
Profit before taxes		10%

The reason for this segregation of costs is becoming more understandable. It is clear that any pricing strategy must be able to provide the marginal contribution needed to cover fixed costs and yield an adequate pretax profit, ensuring an adequate return on invested capital.

Consider the assumptions in the example that follows.

A Pricing-for-Profit Example

1. The product to be priced is *new and proprietary* with a patent pending. You have determined that it will compete with similar products offered by the competition that are priced in a range of $130 to $140 per unit.
2. You have compared the performance of your product with the competing products and have determined that your product is *superior* to competing products in several respects.
3. Further study indicates that your closest competitors are *somewhat larger* companies than yours and their ability to market their product is superior to yours. Their sales organizations are larger and the money that they are able to spend on advertising and promotion is much greater than your ad budget.
4. Your *product plan* is to sell approximately 1,600 units of the new product in the next year. Your cost studies, at that level of sales volume, indi-

cate a variable cost per unit of $50 (direct costs of production and sales associated only with this product) and a fixed cost of $40 (consisting mostly of allocated manufacturing overhead costs).

On this basis, the minimum price necessary should be at least $100 in order to cover total costs and provide a profit percentage of 10 percent (cost equaling 90 percent of selling price, i.e., $90 cost / .90 = $100). The total cost of 1,600 units is $144,000, consisting of total variable costs of $80,000 ($50 x 1,600) and total fixed costs of $64,000 ($40 x 1,600).

5. Research with your sales organization, customers, and competitors indicates that the *market will bear* a selling price of $130 per unit, which, after deducting total costs, will yield a profit of $40 per unit or 30.8 percent of selling price ($40 / $130 = .3077).

Accordingly, because of the superiority of the product, a price of $130 is chosen, giving consideration to the competitors' greater ability to market their products. The marginal contribution in this case is $80 ($130 selling price less variable costs of $50), which easily absorbs total fixed costs of $40, leaving $40 profit ($130 - $90) before any taxes on income.

An illustration of these figures, using an abbreviated profit and loss statement, will help you understand the approach.

Sales		$130
Variable costs:		
Variable direct costs	40	
Variable direct expenses	10	
Total variable costs		50
Marginal contribution		80
Fixed costs:		
Fixed direct costs	30	
Fixed operating costs	10	
Total fixed costs		40
Profit before taxes		$40

This approach to pricing is sound. However, there are other situations that may need to be addressed. *Your pricing approach may be different if you are in any of the following situations:*

1. You are trying to penetrate the market with a *new* product (which is one of several products in your line) and it is no better or worse than your competitor's.

59

2. You *must* have a particular product in the line because it is *complementary* to other profitable products.

3. You are trying to *secure a desirable customer* who has been buying this product from your biggest competitor.

4. You desperately need to sell this particular product to maintain a required *level of production* in your manufacturing facility or to provide this particular service to be able to keep a good *service installation team* during a down economic period.

These are all tough situations and require further analysis to determine how low you can set the price.

The answer to "how low you can go?" may be determined using the following approach, referred to as *marginal contribution pricing*. This technique requires that you know all of the costs to produce, purchase, or install and sell the product, in the same manner (variable and direct) as previously described.

The *marginal contribution pricing* makes the important assumption that the *company is profitable with product sales other than the sales contemplated on a "how low you can go?" basis*. Simply stated, pricing with this approach requires that the sales price per unit be in excess of the variable unit cost, so that there is a "marginal contribution" toward the absorption of fixed costs. Using our previous assumptions, a price above $50 (say $55) will allow the contribution of some of the selling price ($5) to the payment of fixed costs. It is obviously preferable to *recover all costs* (at a price of $90), but in some cases that may not be possible.

Marginal contribution pricing may be helpful if management wants to keep its labor force employed during a slack season. The judicious use of this type of pricing, selecting a price between variable unit cost ($50) and total unit cost ($90), can be beneficial for a *limited time*.

If you are trying to penetrate the market with a new product (situation 1), this approach helps you determine an appropriate price, but that price should be an *introductory price* or *special discount price* that, after some time period, will *rise to a normal price* yielding a desired profit.

Caution! If the company's entire product line were priced using the marginal contribution concept, it would be bankrupt in a very short time!

If you are trying to secure the business of a potentially large customer (situation 3), this approach gives you the guidelines needed to develop a price that is in a range from total variable unit cost to a figure that covers all costs (variable and fixed) *and yields some profit* to the company.

In this case, the price should also be an *introductory price,* to enable customers to evaluate your product in comparison with the competition. You should make it clear to your customers that this price is introductory and that the normal price would be much higher.

You can also use the *trial approach.* Sometimes it is better to allow your customers to *try your new product* without any reduction in pricing. Keep your desired "what the market will bear" price, but submit your product to the customers to "try" for a specified time. If they like it, it is theirs after paying the desired price. If they do not like the product, they can return it to the company without obligation. This approach may be quite successful if the product is clearly superior to the competing product and it is *not customized for a particular customer's application.* If the unit cost is quite low, you may wish to simply give a sample to the customer to try, with no obligation to return it. Do you remember the samples of soap you have received in the mail or the free hours of internet service offered by America Online and others?

Although the previous paragraphs may have seemed to relate to a manufacturing company, they also apply to a service or retail organization. The terminology is about the only thing that changes. "Production" becomes "installation" or "application" and the principal direct costs may be referred to as "installation labor," "application labor," or "sales clerks." It does not matter whether you manufacture a product, buy and sell a product, install a product, or supply a service, the pricing strategy is the same!

Gross Profit Percentage (Gross Margin) vs. Markup

One more matter regarding pricing needs to be addressed: understanding *gross profit* and the difference between *gross profit percentage* (or *gross margin*) and *markup.*

gross profit = selling price - cost of sale
gross profit percentage = gross profit / selling price
markup = gross profit / total cost

Below is an example assuming a selling price of $100 and total unit cost (cost of sale) of $75:

gross profit = $100 - $75 = $25
gross profit percentage (gross margin) = $25 / $100 = 25 percent
markup = $25 / $75 = 33.3 percent

If you want a *gross margin of 40 percent* and the total unit cost is $75, divide $75 by .60 (if gross profit is 40 percent of selling price, then total unit cost must be 60 percent) to yield a selling price of $125.

If you want a *markup of 40 percent* and the total unit cost is $75, then selling price must be cost plus 40 percent of cost, or $75 + (.40 x $75) = $105. Gross profit would then be $30 ($105 – $75).

Please, *carefully note the difference* in selling price when markup is used instead of gross profit margin. Both percentages are 40 percent, but they yield *substantially different pricing results!* Markup pricing is commonly used in the retailing industry to facilitate the later calculation of inventories using the *retail method of inventory valuation.* I have not described the retail method here, but there are numerous texts available that explain it clearly. If you are in retailing, you must read and understand the *retail method.*

The author believes that the use of *gross profit percentage* (rather than *markup percentage*) enables the businessperson to more easily relate pricing to his or her financial statements. Use markup concepts only if you are a retailer, and then in conjunction with a good understanding of the retail method.

Other factors having a bearing on the ultimate price to the customer include *trade discounts*, *quantity discounts*, and *promotional allowances*. Also the *terms of sale*, including FOB point determinations, freight allowances, unit pricing, cash discounts, and more. Although we will not dwell on these items, it is important for the businessperson to understand their application and formalize a policy regarding each.

Chapter 9

Selling and Distributing Your Product or Service

YOUR SALES ORGANIZATION WILL BE BASED ON THE SIZE AND FINAN-
cial resources of your business, the scope of distribution (local,
national, or international), and the nature of the product or
service (whether professional, consumer-oriented, or industrial). Your sales organization might include a sales manager,
technical sales personnel, customer service personnel, direct sales people, an
advertising manager, inside sales personnel (technical and/or order entry), or
... *no one except yourself!*

As you sense the need to expand the sales organization, the ideas in
Table 9-1 on the next page maybe useful.

Let me quickly point out that this is an oversimplification of some major
problems that you may encounter. However, this may give you an idea of the
difficulty in forming and maintaining a sound sales organization. Moreover,
when you start to add personnel, some costs increase, like: salaries, commissions, bonuses, travel expenses, per diems, cell phones, computers, awards,
office expenses, sales meetings, and more! Your *marketing plan* must deal
with both the organization required to generate the planned sales volume
and the costs of that organization.

When This Happens	You Add
You cannot process all the sales orders.	Inside sales personnel
There is too little time to answer all of your customers' technical questions.	Technical sales personnel
You need to add sales volume at a minimum cost.	Commission sales representatives
You need to add sales volume but with greater control over the organization.	Direct sales personnel
There is too little time to manage all the sales personnel.	Sales manager
There is too little time to manage a nationwide sales rep organization.	Regional sales manager
The development of new products and services becomes a full-time job.	Product manager
No one has time to manage the advertising effort.	Advertising manager

Table 9-1. Expanding your sales organization

Sales Management

Your sales organization, no matter how large or small (even if *you* are the sales organization), must establish and monitor the following:

▶ Sales and service policies

▶ Physical distribution systems

▶ Technical sales literature

▶ Sales compensation policies

▶ Training and monitoring sales personnel

Each of these elements is discussed in the following pages.

Sales and Service Policies

Sales and service policies include the discount and credit terms you are willing to grant to your customers. Policies regarding quantity discounts, trade discounts, discounts for paying cash, and seasonal discounts (to get rid of excess inventory of seasonal items) should be defined in writing and placed in a policy manual. If you have sales personnel, they should all have a copy of these policies. Your business may also be willing to use "floor planning" or consignment techniques, dating (delayed payment during certain time periods), and promotional allowances or discounts. These should also be described in your policy manual so that you and your sales personnel will not be confused about what you are and are not willing to do for your customers.

Although you may not be affected by these laws, you should at least be aware of the *Robinson-Patman Act* and the *Sherman Anti-Trust Act*. The Robinson-Patman Act prohibits discrimination in pricing and granting discounts. Special prices or discounts must be based on cost savings. You cannot grant special discounts or pricing to large customers or others unless those terms are based on verifiable cost savings resulting from longer production runs, less frequent setups, and lower costs of purchasing larger quantities of materials. The *Sherman Anti-Trust Act* prohibits any business activity that results in a restraint of trade or monopolizes trade or commerce in any fashion. Even though you may not be involved in acts that could be construed to fall within the parameters of these laws, keep in mind that the "long arm of federal law" is very strong and the penalties for violating these laws can be devastating.

If your business is not a retail or service organization, where title to the product or service transfers at the point of sale, you will need to establish an *FOB point policy*. The term FOB, meaning "free on board," is older than all of us and refers to the era when title to the product transferred when it was put on a rail car. Today, FOB still means the point where title to the product passes to your customer and establishes responsibility for freight and delivery charges. For example, if you use "FOB Destination," that means that title passes at your customer's door and you are responsible for the delivery charges and insurance costs to that point. The FOB point is discussed in greater depth in Chapter 14, "Management and Control Systems."

Even if you are a "one-person show," you will still need to establish *warranty and returns policies*. This should be carefully devised, approved by your attorney, and *shown somewhere on your sales invoice*. There are three types of warranties that may affect your business—express, implied, and limited.

An *express warranty* is a commitment by the seller to the buyer by which the seller makes a promise or declaration of fact on which the buyer bases his or her buying decision. For example, "This car has a six-cylinder engine that offers better gas mileage than a larger eight-cylinder engine" or "You will definitely see a longer life with this product versus product B."

An express warranty is a commitment by the seller to the buyer by which the seller makes a promise or declaration of fact on which the buyer bases his or her buying decision.

65

An *implied warranty* results when the seller knows the purpose for which the product is required and the buyer is relying on the seller's skill or judgment to select or furnish the product suitable for that purpose. For example, the local hardware salesperson states, "This product will, without a doubt, rid your house of mice and rats" or "The special tires on this snow blower will easily go up your steep driveway."

If you are going to grant a warranty for your product or service, label it a lim-ited warranty. Full warranties give the customer broad protection.

If you are going to grant a warranty for your product or service, label it a *limited warranty*. Full warranties give the customer broad protection. A limited warranty should specifically list what your warranty includes, such as the term of the warranty, what it covers, and situations in which the war-ranty no longer applies. Include the option to either refund the purchase price or repair or replace the product. Disclaim all other warranties, express or implied.

Important note: Have your attorney review and approve your warranty!

One more item regarding sales and service policies: you should develop and communicate to your customers the extent to which, if any, you will provide *service after the sale*, whether on-site or at your facility. You will want your customers to clearly understand what you will and will not do in connection with the sale of your product or service. Make sure to put your policy in writing and provide it to your customers.

Physical Distribution Systems

Depending upon the nature of your business, you may need to consider one or more of the following potential requirements of your operation:

- ▶ location and management of inventory
- ▶ warehousing (or materials handling) system
- ▶ order processing system
- ▶ transportation or delivery of your product
- ▶ delivery of your personal service

These systems can be somewhat complex and are discussed in Chapter 14, "Management and Control Systems." They are brought to your atten-tion in this chapter because they are a part of your marketing strategy.

Technical Sales Literature

The degree to which technical sales literature is important to you depends on the nature of your business. The subject includes the following:

Product packaging and labeling. This can be a very critical matter in some businesses. There are very specific laws governing the packaging and labeling of certain products. I am sure that you can recall many liability cases based on how a product was packaged or labeled, many of them involving claims on the package or label that the product would do certain things beneficial to health. Your best bet here is to discuss your product with your attorney and follow his or her advice.

Assembly or installation instructions. Have you tried to follow those assembly instructions that come with toys for your children and stayed up half the night trying to decipher them? Or, can you recall trying to assemble your new personal computer? If assembly or installation is required for your product, you will want to spend considerable time developing the related instructions. Nothing will kill your product image faster than poorly written instructions that frustrate your customers and delay or complicate their use of your product.

User guide or owner's manual. Even with a good user guide, some products are difficult to learn how to use. If you are into digital imaging, try the user guide to some of the imaging software. Many people are now taking pictures with digital cameras and at least some of the owners may never understand the imaging software, despite well-written guides for their use. If you want your customers to enjoy and maximize their use of your product and a user guide is required, it must be written well in language anyone can understand. Failure to provide a good user guide can undermine acceptance of your product and hinder sales. Spend the time to get it right and test those instructions with someone who has no initial understanding of the product.

Guarantees and warranty information. With the help of your attorney, these items need to be clearly written and legally correct. Warranties, discussed earlier, should be differentiated from *guarantees*; a guarantee is simply a pledge by the seller to replace the product or service if it is not as represented.

Troubleshooting and support information. Much like the user guide, these instructions must be clear, unambiguous, and stated simply. You have had experience with troubleshooting your computer, printer, or scanner. Nothing will destroy the image of a product faster than being unable to keep it running effectively.

The degree to which technical sales literature is important to you depends on the nature of your business.

67

Parts or service manuals. These serve a dual purpose. They provide instruction regarding the steps the user needs to take to ensure continued trouble free performance and they enable the user to easily buy replacement parts. Quite often, the parts carry a much higher margin than the product itself and you want to make it easy for your customer to identify and purchase them.

As you write your technical sales literature, remember that the success of many products depends upon the ability of the buyers to use them. Also keep in mind that much of the information users need can be provided in only one or two documents. Give them anything more complex or less informative than they need and it spells "death" to the product. In fact, there are technical writers who make lucrative profits writing simple, non-technical user guides where the manufacturer may not have done the best job. Look at the "Whatever for Dummies" books!

Sales Compensation Policies

If your business involves sales-people other than yourself, you should develop and document a policy for their compensation.

If your business involves salespeople other than yourself, you should develop and document a policy for their compensation. Your policy may be no more complicated than a straight salary plan, a straight commission plan, or a combination plan, but the people to whom it applies must be able to understand it.

A *straight salary plan* offers security and stability of earnings for the salespeople and ensures you a greater control of their activities and approach to customer needs. On the other hand, this plan may not offer an adequate incentive to the salespeople to close their sales and it represents a fixed cost, regardless of the sales revenue being achieved.

A *straight commission plan* offers tremendous incentive to the salespeople, whose compensation can vary directly with their effectiveness. This type of plan also represents a variable cost to the business that is incurred only if sales volume is generated. While beneficial to the salespeople, it can make them more difficult to control, especially in situations where no commission is involved (i.e., monitoring a house account or following up on past sales). In addition, there is always the possibility that salespeople will oversell products, putting the customer and the business relationship at risk.

Many companies use a *combination plan,* which offers the best of both worlds, helping the salespeople with travel expenses and a draw against the incentive-motivated commissions. The draw is a basic compensation amount that is guaranteed to the salespeople, regardless of their sales, and helps mitigate the ups and downs of sales cycles. This plan still allows the company control over the actions of the sales personnel. Of course, this plan does not achieve the level of control or the incentive offered by the straight plan and it still involves fixed costs (travel expenses and the draw). Under the straight commission plan, travel expenses are typically paid by the salespeople.

Compensating sales personnel is a topic that has been addressed by a great number of companies and consultants. If you wish to gain a greater depth of knowledge, the following highly rated books are recommended. *The Sales Compensation Handbook*[1] is based on the experience of internationally recognized consulting firm, Towers Perrin, and contains information and tools necessary to design and implement sales compensation programs. It includes designing base salary, bonus, and commission scales and cash and noncash incentives. *Compensating New Sales Roles: How to Design Rewards That Work in Today's Selling Environment*[2] is a guide to putting together compensation plans and rewards to ensure the motivation and organization of a sales staff.

Training and Monitoring Sales Personnel

Any discussion of marketing strategy must deal with the subject of training sales personnel and monitoring their effectiveness. A sales training program should emphasize a thorough knowledge of the product or service, a clear understanding of the sales policies (as presented earlier), and developing selling techniques. An unknown source has developed an approach to selling that is described as the Five P's of Selling. This approach is worth comment.

These are the Five P's of Selling:

1. **Preparation**—knowing your product or service, your competitors, and the market
2. **Prospecting**—identifying the potential or current customers you wish to call upon
3. **Pre-Approach**—learning as much as possible about the potential customers and their needs
4. **Presentation**—getting the customers' attention, stimulating their interest, overcoming any of their objections, ... and *closing*
5. **Post-Sale Activities**—reassuring the customers of their decision to buy your product and offering any post-sale services that are appropriate

A sales training program should emphasize a thorough knowledge of the product or service, a clear understanding of the sales policies (as presented earlier), and developing selling techniques.

69

I am sure that these concepts have been presented over and over in many different ways. However basic, they are vital to successful sales efforts. You may wish to adopt them, using your own terminology.

Monitoring sales effectiveness simply means evaluating sales volume in terms of units, dollars, and profitability. You need to measure sales by product/service/job or a product group and provide profitability information for each measured segment. Sales by salesperson, by sales location, and perhaps by customer is important information and is even more meaningful when related to the number of sales calls made.

This monitoring is best accomplished through normal internal financial reporting. Product or product line profitability, job profitability, and sales profitability by salesperson should be an inherent segment of your internal accounting system. This information can also be provided through special sales reports generated using spreadsheets or with more sophisticated sales-reporting software systems. However provided, such information is critical to the successful management of a small business—or a business of any size.

There are other ways to evaluate the effectiveness of your sales organization. Consider asking customers if they are being properly served, either through contact by sales managers or a personal letter or survey. There are independent survey firms that would be glad to assist you in this effort for a price. In my experience, it has been effective for the "boss" to periodically send a letter or make a phone call asking customers if they are being treated properly. It is best if the "boss" personally visits customers to make sure the relationship is as it should be. However you do it, just be sure to do it!

Notes

1. Colt, Stockton B. (Editor). *The Sales Compensation Handbook*, 2nd edition. AMACOM, 1998.
2. Colletti, Jerome A., and Fiss, Mary S. *Compensating New Sales Roles: How to Design Rewards That Work in Today's Selling Environment*, 2nd edition. AMACOM, 2001.

Monitoring sales effectiveness simply means evaluating sales volume in terms of units, dollars, and profitability.

Chapter 10

Advertising and Promotion

Your publicity, advertising, and promotional activities are limited only by your budget ... and your imagination!

SOME OF THE MOST EFFECTIVE METHODS OF GATHERING ATTENTION TO your business and its products or services are the least expensive. The very best of those avenues is *publicity*.

Publicity is the unpaid articles and TV and radio spots that illustrate a unique or new feature or capability of a product or service offered by your business that is of public interest or benefit (especially when supported by testimonials). If you are able to write technical articles for trade magazines or pieces for your local newspaper or to conduct free seminars that feature your expertise, your product, or your service, you can use the *most effective* and *least costly* method of advertising and promoting your business! Having written several articles for trade magazines (some of them with front cover illustration), I can personally attest to their effectiveness in drawing attention to expertise and products. If you are not a writer or a public speaker, there is another way. Read on.

There are many things that can occur in a community that may be viewed to be in the public interest. Consider the new restaurant, car wash, medical facility, state-of-the-art equipment, or a unique new customer serv-

71

ice, all of which the local media may perceive as being in the public interest. If your business is or has "one of those" and you believe there is a possibility of benefit to the public, contact your local TV and radio stations and newspaper. The worst result is that they don't agree. The best is that you get an article or spot in the news media that carries more weight than a paid advertisement and ... *it is free!*

Advertising Opportunities

There are many ways to advertise your product or service, starting with the media. You may use display advertising in *newspapers, magazines,* or *trade journals.* These ads are a bit pricey, but here are some things to make the ads look more impressive without much additional cost.

Bear with me while I digress, hopefully for your benefit. When you choose your letterhead, business cards, invoices, and other documentation to be seen by the public, you should select *one color* (one only!) that is *associated with your business.* For example, if you have a landscaping or gardening business, you might select green; if your business involves swimming pools, fountains, or water-related activities, you might select blue. Before you settle on the color, go to a good printer that specializes in color work and ask to see their color chart for the "standard" print colors used in the printing industry. These colors are universal and easy to duplicate. Try to select one of them to associate with your business.

Many of these relatively vivid colors will "screen" quite well, producing different tones or shades of the same color, giving the appearance of many colors. When you add those screened tones to black, which can also be screened to various shades of gray, you have the ability to design single-color (shades of black) or two-color (shades of black and your chosen color) display ads that can be very impressive.

Another suggestion is to develop a *well-designed logo* for your business. It must be simple, look professional, and use your new color. Do not go to your computer and pick out some clip art for your logo. If you do not have the talent to design your own logo, visit your local printer, the one that will print your letterhead, business cards, and brochures. Quite often small printers have people who are very talented and can develop several choices from which you can select. If you plan to do all your printing with that printer, the cost of developing a logo may be very reasonable. Find out the cost upfront and give it some consideration. Using your logo and your color in

When you choose your letterhead, business cards, invoices, and other documentation to be seen by the public, you should select one color (one only!) that is associated with your business.

all of your documentation that reaches the public helps your potential customers recognize your business more easily.

Important note: If your logo or letterhead is unique, you may be able to secure a trademark to protect both from unwanted infringement. Check with a patent attorney.

Visit your local newspaper and obtain their display rate card, which will provide you with some idea of the cost of any ad that you might wish to run. Also, contact trade journals and magazines and secure their rate cards. With these options, using black and your one color, you might be surprised how attractive and effective even a small ad can be.

By the way, you should always use your chosen color and logo, at least in some shade, with all of your documentation, such as letterhead, business cards, sales invoices, purchase orders, and so forth. Have you forgotten that IBM is also referred to as "Big Blue"? Another "blue" company is Dell. Kodak is known for its deep shade of yellow, Fuji for deep green, and so on. It doesn't cost very much and when people see your documentation, your delivery truck, or the sign at your premises, they will remember the color and logo!

Media advertising, including radio and TV spots, is fairly expensive and you may wish to avoid those alternatives until your company is more mature.

An ad in the *Yellow Pages of the phone book*, perhaps in more than one section, can be an excellent advertising opportunity. If your ad is well done, your potential customers may believe your business to be much bigger and better established than it really is, giving you an opportunity to compete with other advertisers.

Regardless of the nature of your business, you *must* have a *quality brochure* that presents the images of your business, emphasizes any unique capabilities, and discusses the products and services that you offer. A small business that has a well-designed brochure and business cards immediately gains in stature in the eyes of customers. If your promotional materials look professional, your business will also be considered professional!

The brochure must be printed by a printer on quality paper stock, using your color and logo. Do not attempt to use a "creative hands at home" brochure that is printed on your computer printer unless you are very talented in doing this. The same can be said of your *business cards*, which must also be done well and use your color and logo.

The brochure does not need to be more than one page, either letter size (with two folds) or legal size (with three folds). Be sure to put your address,

You must have a quality brochure that presents the images of your business, emphasizes any unique capabilities, and discusses the products and services that you offer.

phone number, fax number, cell phone number, e-mail address, and web site address in your brochure and on your business cards. Your printer can help.

Depending upon the nature of your business, you may wish to have a supply of your brochures in various public places where potential customers might visit. Stores, restaurants, the chamber of commerce, and banks are all places that, with the proper approach, may allow you to distribute your brochure.

Direct mail is a good and relatively inexpensive way to advertise, especially if your brochure is properly designed and sized to fit standard envelopes. Start with your customer base; after all, your current customers are your best potential source of future business. Be selective beyond the customer base, aiming at segments of the market that you wish to penetrate.

If you have a location that potential and current customers will see or visit, you will need to consider *signs*. Outdoor signs that show your name, color, and logo are important to your business. If your business is professional or indoors, you may wish to develop tastefully designed placards or banners to let people know of your business activities.

An inexpensive web site is a great addition to your advertising activities.

Last but certainly not least, is the internet. You should have an e-mail address through which people can contact your business, make inquiries, ask that you reply by phone, and so forth. An inexpensive web site is also a great addition to your advertising activities. If you or any of your people are adept at using word processing software, you don't need to hire a professional to establish your first web site. Many of the internet service providers offer inexpensive web sites that you can design yourself, either from scratch using their design software or with templates, requiring only the insertion of your business information. For an example, visit **geocities.yahoo.com**.

Promotional Opportunities

In your effort to expose your business to potential customers, do not overlook some effective promotional activities. Some of the promotions will *involve a cost*. These include:

- ▶ Chamber of commerce memberships
- ▶ Trade association memberships
- ▶ Sponsorships of educational, charitable, or fine arts events or activities
- ▶ Donations of products, services, or money for worthy causes
- ▶ Educational scholarships

- Free samples of products or services
- Newsletters sent to current and potential customers
- Support for children's activities (camps or schools)
- Giveaways, including printed caps, shirts, and cups

How many people have you seen wearing a ball cap that advertises the name of a company? Keeping the name of your business in the public eye is important.

There are some types of promotional activities that involve time and effort but very *limited cost*. They include:

- Volunteering your time at community or cultural events
- Mentoring or speaking at trade schools or colleges
- Participating in Boys & Girls Clubs and athletics
- Junior Achievement and 4-H mentoring
- Visiting senior citizens' homes
- Literary and fine arts counseling
- Conservation and environmental cleanup activities
- Providing on-the-job training or summer intern work

Start by designing your business card and brochure; that is a basic necessity. Then, before you select the advertising and promotional activities for your company, determine all of the costs of each alternative. *Develop a plan that will fit your budget while appealing to the greatest number of potential customers.* The resulting plan will become part of your *marketing plan*, your *business plan*, and your *financial budget*.

Chapter 11

Developing a Business Plan

H OW IMPORTANT IS A GOOD BUSINESS PLAN? A QUOTE FROM W. Edwards Deming, noted industrialist, author, and leader in the reconstruction of industry in Japan following World War II, expresses my sentiments exactly: "You don't have to do this—survival is not compulsory."

Why You Need a Business Plan

It is easy to understand why lending institutions require a sound business plan before they will consider loaning money to a small business, especially one with little track record. There must be a sound basis for the banker to go to his or her loan committee asking it to support the request. Without a plan, the business and the banker will have little prospect for establishing a commercial lending relationship that is necessary for the immediate and longer-term success of the business. Also keep in mind that the personal success of the banker is based on attracting and keeping successful business customers *that can repay their loans.*

You need a business plan for much more than financing. *It is your guide to developing an idea into a successful business operation.* Remember, too, that the lending institution will want you to update that plan every year so that your progress can be compared with the original plan.

Developing a business plan, either for a new, start-up business or for a business that is mature, requires some understanding of the techniques involved and *the initiative to get it done*. How many people have we known who had a great business idea that they never realized because they did not have the initiative to take it a step further? The "step further" is the *plan* that can help transform the idea into a reality. Lending institutions do not loan large sums of money based on ideas. Moreover, *they do not loan money if the loan request is not accompanied by a sound business plan* that embodies the essential elements required (including the great idea) to successfully achieve a defined business objective.

Developing a business plan, either for a new, start-up business or for a business that is mature, requires some understanding of the techniques involved and the initiative to get it done.

What Is a Business Plan?

If you were going to informally describe your plans for the future of your company to a lending officer in a bank, you would certainly discuss the *background* of your company, *your role* and the role of any key personnel in its development, and what makes your company (its products or services) *unique* and successful in the marketplace.

You would also define your company's current *products and services*, how you *sell and distribute* them, and what *ideas for new products or services* you have for the future. The overall *market* for your products and how your company's products or services compare with your *competition* would also be a subject of the conversation.

Because you may need additional funds to expand your business, you would likely indicate the amount of *funds required* and describe how the funds would be *spent*. You would include your *plan for repaying* the loan and over what period of time *repayment* would take place. Finally, you would point out how this added investment would substantially enhance your company's opportunities for *increased profitability*.

If you documented these comments and added detailed *financial projections*, your presentation could be described as a *business plan*. A true business plan simply presents all of these elements in a well-written and organized document.

Not Just for Beginners!

A plan is necessary whether to satisfy a lending institution or simply to document the company's current objectives and how well it is meeting those objectives.

We believe that *every year, every company should develop a detailed plan for that year and a more broadly structured plan for the following three to five years*. A plan is necessary whether to satisfy a lending institution or simply to document the company's current objectives and how well it is meeting those objectives. The annual plan does not have to be as exhaustive as the original business plan, but it should include all of the elements so that nothing is overlooked.

The plan for the current year will constitute a *budget* for that year's operation and permit a comparison of current results with planned performance for that period. This comparison will help determine what steps should be taken to get back on plan or to revise the plan. Simply put, *planning is an absolute essential for the success of any business, small or large, to secure financing, to interest additional investors, and to effectively manage the business.*

Elements of a Business Plan

Nearly every book that has been published on managing a business or business planning includes a description of a business plan. The *Small Business Kit for Dummies*[1] presents the subject in a separate chapter. The *Small Business Advisor*[2] dedicates two chapters to business plan development, including one chapter that illustrates a sample business plan. *The Harvard Entrepreneurs Club Guide to Starting Your Own Business*[3] also devotes an entire chapter (36 pages) to the subject.

These books, and several others, describe plan elements that are common to all. Let's examine those elements on which there is nearly universal agreement.

- ▶ Cover page
- ▶ Table of contents
- ▶ Mission statement
- ▶ Executive summary
- ▶ Marketing plan
- ▶ Operational plan
- ▶ Management control systems

▶ Financial statements and projections

▶ Long-range strategic plan

The purpose and description of each of these elements is presented in the following pages. As you write your business plan, you should observe some *guidelines* that will help others view it favorably. These points are not theoretical; they have been learned by experience (some of it painful!).

▶ **Write in your own style** (not academically), using the language of your business and industry, but don't be too technical.

▶ **Do not exaggerate or make unrealistic claims** for the future of your business. Be realistic and base your projections on hard evidence!

▶ **Say only what is necessary and important.** Do not embellish or elaborate to excess.

▶ **Include reference to other key personnel** in your organization and their role in the company's future success. Also acknowledge the importance of outside professional assistance.

▶ **Do not include confidential information.** If needed, that information can be communicated in person. You don't know who may read your plan.

▶ **Be grammatically correct** without *any* typographical errors. This is an absolute must, even if you have to hire a proofreader!

If you need help writing the plan or developing financial projections, a SCORE® management counselor or your accounting firm (CPA) is a good place to get advice and they can even help with the mechanics. Let's review the *elements*.

1. **Cover Page.** This page defines the document and should include the title or subject, the date of its preparation, and a statement indicating its confidential nature, thereby restricting its use. It should include contact information—company name, address, phone numbers, e-mail address, and the principal contact person (probably you).
2. **Table of Contents.** The purpose of this section is self-explanatory, but be sure to include both major and minor sections of the plan so that readers can quickly find the parts that interest them.
3. **Mission Statement.** This is a paragraph that describes for the reader exactly what business you are in. This may sound oversimplified; however, many small businesses have failed because the managers became confused about the nature of their business. This reaffirmation of the

business purpose, its target market, and the factors that separate its operation and value from its competitors is an essential part of your business strategy. It should be no more than one paragraph.

4. **Executive Summary.** The executive summary is designed to *briefly* tell the reader the structure and background of the business, the company's management and key personnel, its relative position in the industry, the future prospects for success, and what it needs to make those prospects a reality. If you are requesting funds, state the amount of funds needed and how those funds will be employed and repaid. *Write this section last!*

5. **Marketing Plan.** The marketing plan is a written documentation of the company's marketing strategy and how that strategy will be implemented. It includes:

   1. A description of the *product or service* to be offered and what need or want it is designed to satisfy
   2. A comparison of the product's *unique characteristics* with those of closely competing products
   3. A documentation of any *patents, copyrights, trademarks,* or other forms of intellectual property protection
   4. An identification of the *customer base*, location, and size of the market
   5. A listing of all *major competitors*, with their size, strengths and weaknesses, pricing strategies, and other pertinent information
   6. A description of any *environmental, legal, or governmental factors* that could influence the future of the market
   7. A documentation of the company's *pricing strategy* for its products or services
   8. An identification of *distribution channels* and methods and a definition of the sales organization
   9. A description of the *sales, service, and warranty policies* and the physical distribution systems
   10. A reference to all *product packaging, labeling, manuals, and technical literature*
   11. A definition of *sales compensation policies* and programs to monitor sales performance
   12. Documentation of *advertising and promotional plans* and how they compare with the competition.

   The marketing plan is an important and major segment of the business plan and its development is a considerable undertaking. A sample of a marketing plan is included in the business plan in Appendix O.

6. **Operational Plan.** This section presents in greater detail a description of who will direct the company's activities and how that will be accomplished. It includes information about the management team, how personnel are organized, and a description of how new personnel will be hired, trained, and indoctrinated, plus a discussion of the company's management and operational policies.

7. **Management Control Systems.** This section describes the systems that monitor the company's investment in inventory, equipment, and other productive assets; product or job profitability; sales management and effectiveness; sales and administrative costs; and cash flow management.

8. **Financial Statements and Projections.** This section should begin with a discussion of the present financial position of the company and what funds may be needed to further expand its operations. Specifically address how the needed funds will be spent and provide a plan for repaying those funds. You should point out how the proposed addition of funds will enhance the company's opportunities for increased profitability.

   These narrative comments should be supported with historical financial statements for the prior three years, if available. It is also helpful if those statements have been audited and certified without qualification by your CPA accounting firm. (More about the use of CPA firms later.) If this plan does not begin within a month or two of the past year-end, you should also provide the current financial statements for the most recent month-end. If the business is just beginning, you should present a balance sheet showing its present capitalization and other assets and liabilities as a starting place.

   Finally, this section should present your Personal Financial Statement and a Schedule of Start-Up Costs (if appropriate), and Projected Statements of Cash Flow, Income Statement (Profit and Loss), Projected Balance Sheets, and a Debt Repayment Plan. The projections should be in a monthly format for the first year and annually for the following two years. Samples of these statements are shown in Appendices F to J. A complete sample business plan is shown in Appendix O.

9. **Long-Range Strategic Plan.** This last section of the business plan presents a description of where you want your business to be in the next few years and how you intend to get there. Focusing on years two through five, include a description of the strengths and weaknesses in your business and the opportunities available to you. Then describe your strategy

The business plan is a dynamic, living document that should be updated annually. It is your guide to business success!

for exploiting your strengths, minimizing your weaknesses, and achieving your long-range goals.

Prepare an outline for the business plan before you begin. After you have a rough draft, let your accountant or SCORE® management counselor review and edit the document.

There are several software systems on the market that can also help you develop your business plan. Check the following web sites: *www.sba.gov/starting_business/planning/basic.html*, *www.bizplans.com*, and *www.bplans.com*. There are many others found with an internet search.

Notes

1. Harroch, Richard D. *Small Business Kit for Dummies*. IDG Books, 1998.

2. *The Entrepreneur Magazine Small Business Advisor*. John Wiley & Sons, Inc., 1995.

3. Sharma, Poonam. *The Harvard Entrepreneurs Club Guide to Starting Your Own Business*. John Wiley & Sons, Inc., 1999.

Chapter 12

Gathering Financial Resources

ATHERING THE FINANCIAL RESOURCES TO START OR EXPAND A SMALL business is probably the most difficult task encountered by the small business owner. Getting financing is always harder than you expect and always takes longer than you expect. In addition, some myths need to be exposed so that the small business owner does not waste time "chasing rainbows."

For example, the Small Business Administration does *not make loans*. (It may guarantee loans made by banks and other lending institutions.) Moreover, there are *no government grants* offered by the SBA, even to persons who are disabled or among business minorities, such as veterans, women, racial minorities, and others. The SBA web site addresses this issue quite clearly. However, your state may offer some grants for disabled persons or others. It is worth checking.

Are You Creditworthy?

An important factor to consider in pursuing resources of financing is your creditworthiness. It may surprise you to know that nearly every citizen in the United States is included in at least one (and usually all) of the major consumer reporting agencies (CRAs) that develop *credit reports* for use by lending agencies. Three of the major CRAs are Experian, Equifax, and TransUnion. These companies collect and organize information about you and your credit history from public records, your creditors, and other reliable sources. The information is extensive and is made available to your current and prospective creditors and employers, as allowed by law. Now you may be able to go to their web sites and download a copy of your report without charge. (There used to be a fee.)

Your personal credit report contains (1) your name, current and previous addresses, phone number, Social Security number, date of birth, and current and previous employers; (2) specific information about each credit account you have, such as the date opened, credit limit or loan amount, balance, monthly payment, and payment pattern during the past several years; (3) any federal district bankruptcy records and state and county court records of tax liens and monetary judgments; (4) the names of those who have obtained a copy of your credit report; and (5) statements of dispute over the particulars of a credit account and its status.

If all of this makes you feel uncomfortable, there is a law designed to promote the accuracy, fairness, and privacy of information in the files of every consumer reporting agency. The law is the federal Fair Credit Reporting Act (FCRA). As mentioned, you can find out what is in your report by going to a consumer reporting agency web site. In addition to individuals, businesses also have credit reports, which are available to you or your business for a fee. You need to get a copy of your report. The last time I did it, considerable information was not correct!

If you pay your bills on time, avoid bankruptcy, and have a successful record of incurring and discharging debt in accordance with its terms, your chances of further credit are enhanced.

Most of the CRAs develop a credit score for you, which is a numerical rating of your credit worthiness. For example, Experian credit scores range from 340 to 820; only 2 percent of people in the U.S. have the best possible score of 820.

The reason I bring this issue to your attention is that you may attempt to secure credit as a means of financing a start-up business. *If you have a poor credit rating (score), your chances of securing credit for this or any other purpose are minimized!* So, if you pay your bills on time, avoid bankruptcy, and have a successful record of incurring and discharging debt in accordance with its terms, your chances of further credit are enhanced.

Finding Financial Resources

Depending upon the status of your business (start-up vs. existing business with a track record), your principal sources of financing will include some or several of the following:

- ▶ Your personal resources
- ▶ Family and friends
- ▶ Direct bank loans
- ▶ SBA guaranteed loans
- ▶ Lease financing
- ▶ Vendor financing
- ▶ Strategic alliance or venture capital
- ▶ Business partner

Personal resources may include your bank and savings accounts, credit card, second mortgage on your home or equity line of credit, cashing in a retirement savings plan (401(k) or IRA), sale of investment assets (stocks, bonds, and real estate), sale of personal assets (e.g., antiques, furniture, and sporting goods), and the cash surrender value or loan value of life insurance. If you have chosen to use retirement savings to help develop your business, you need to remember clearly the risk you are taking relative to your long-term future.

Family and friends can help with a personal loan, an equity investment (i.e., a silent partner), co-signing on a bank loan, a convertible note (to equity when the business matures), a note with warrants or options attached, or a profit participation note (with repayment being based on the profitability of the business).

One of the most important things to remember when securing financial assistance from family or friends is to *keep it on a business basis*. This means that if it is a loan, you need a note agreement with a specified rate of interest and a repayment plan, and if it is an equity investment, there should be a document that defines how the relative or friend can recover that investment and on what basis, and so forth. The arrangement needs to be documented just as though your friend or family member were a disinterested third party.

Why the formality? You need to be protected if, for example, your brother who loaned you the money gets run over by a truck and his wife decides that *she* should help you run your business or if you get run over by a truck and ... on and on! Also, a well-documented loan protects you from IRS scrutiny. You do not want the loan to be considered a gift and taxed as such!

One of the most important things to remember when securing financial assistance from family or friends is to keep it on a business basis.

85

By the way, I should mention that, without a loan from my mother, I might still be among the employed! We did have an agreement and I repaid her as agreed. The best part: she was able to live to see a very good small business grow and thrive, due in large part to her loving assistance, ... and the repayment plan was part of her retirement income. Was there a risk? Of course, but she was willing to share that risk and I was willing to do whatever was necessary to repay her assistance.

Direct loans from banks usually require that your business have a *good track record* and *all of the following*: personal financial statement for you and any significant partners, prior year's financial statements and tax returns, a well-written business plan, a loan application document, a pledge of collateral, and a personal guarantee by the owners (you and your associates).

A bank loan to a business usually is accompanied by a long, wordy loan document that has a variety of covenants, both positive and negative.

A bank loan to a business usually is accompanied by a long, wordy *loan document* that has a variety of *covenants*, both positive and negative. These covenants include negotiable items such as due date, loan fees, interest rate, prepayment penalty, default conditions, payment grace period, late fees, collateral, co-signers, guarantors, attorney fees, and more!

To secure a bank loan, you need the services of a good professional (who has allegiance to you and your business), such as a CPA or corporate attorney or both. Your SCORE® management counselor can help you with a business plan and help get you to the critical point of the application, but professional help is suggested thereafter.

SBA guaranteed loan programs include a variety of choices, including the 7(a) Loan Guaranty Program, a LowDoc Loan Program, the SBA*Express* Loan Program, a Certified Development Company (CDC) 504 Loan Program, and a CAPLines Loan Program. (Nothing is simple!)

All of the SBA-sponsored programs are quite involved and can become very technical. You should contact your banker for assistance and also a SCORE® or Small Business Development Center staff member. If you wish to examine these programs on the internet, go to *www.sba.gov/financing*.

Equipment and facilities leasing is a good financing alternative for acquiring the use of a building, office facility, production, and automotive equipment. Financing leases (also referred to as *capital leases*) include the following benefits: the payments can be a tax-deductible expense, leases are usually quicker to gain approval than most debt financing, there is less paperwork and a more relaxed credit policy, and they can involve less risk of equipment obsolescence. Moreover, in some instances, they can allow you an option to ultimately buy whatever you are leasing at a nominal price. The downside to leasing is that your business does not develop any equity in the leased equipment and default on the lease can mean the abrupt end of your use of the equipment.

Vendor financing is frequently offered to successful, growing small businesses by (1) providing extended credit terms for purchases and accepting blanket orders for a one-year term, (2) consigning inventory (i.e., placing stock on your premises without obligation to pay until the stock is withdrawn), and (3) floor plan financing, similar to consigning inventory (common to the appliance and automobile industries). If possible, you should secure more than one quote for such assistance, especially if you have at least two good sources for your purchases.

Strategic alliance or venture capital is a form of financing that is used by small businesses that have developed a very unique product or service that may require further research and development. Usually the small business has a good track record of accomplishment and its future progress would be greatly enhanced by the new product or service. Large companies in the same industry are logical prospects for strategic alliances, but you must be very careful to protect the interests of your company in the new product or service. A corporate attorney is suggested!

Venture capital firms are also interested in companies that are involved in this type of new product development, especially if the company is already successful, albeit a small business. Their usual financing approach is to make a term loan with attached warrants or options to acquire a limited amount of equity. The agreement typically includes a redemption provision that would provide them interest during the term of the loan and an equity opportunity with the warrant or option. Simply put: they want interest on their loan and a capital gain on their equity instrument. It is not all that onerous if it is structured properly. Again, see your attorney.

Strategic alliance or venture capital is a form of financing that is used by small businesses that have developed a very unique product or service that may require further research and development.

Selecting a Partner

Having a partner is not a bad idea if you are both on the same page for the future. Consider Messrs. Hewlett and Packard. They were college friends and wanted to develop something of value with their combined talents. A source of financing? Maybe, but more often a good combination of talents to go forward with a business idea.

Keep in mind, as you seek financing (or partners), that many small business owners attempt to retain all (or most) of the ownership of the company for themselves, only to find that their personal resources are inadequate to sustain successful growth. These owners are plagued by a lack of money. You know the term for this condition—*undercapitalization*.

Selecting a *business partner* (whether for funds or knowledge or both) is as critical a process as selecting a wife or a husband, perhaps even more so! The selection of one or more business partners should be based on the following criteria, which, although obvious to most people, are worth listing:

Selecting a business partner (whether for funds or knowledge or both) is as critical a process as selecting a wife or a husband, perhaps even more so!

▶ **Honesty**—You must be able to trust your partner with your customers, your key employees, and your money. Your partner must be honest about business dealings and, when necessary, be willing to bring you bad news (in addition to good news). Honesty means being honorable in principles, intentions, and actions.

▶ **Integrity**—A bit different from honesty, integrity means an uncompromising adherence to moral and ethical principles in dealing with all people involved with the business—the employees, the customers, the suppliers, the bankers, and others. Above all, you must be assured that your business partner will adhere to those high standards whether you or anyone else is observing or monitoring his or her actions.

▶ **Technical competence**—A business partner must bring some form of skill to the organization, whether engineering, sales, manufacturing, or other. Without that talent and the willingness and effort to employ the talent, the business partnership will not be a balanced arrangement.

▶ **Financial investment**—Your business partner must also be willing and able to risk a reasonable financial investment in the business. Without investing "blood money," the partner may lack the commitment and motivation to share in the successes and failures that are sure to be present as the business grows to maturity.

Having been both frustrated with bad partners and pleased with good partners, I have thought about these criteria over and over again. I list them here in the hope that you might learn from my experiences.

Although the requirements for choosing stockholders are much the same, you rely less on your stockholders' technical skills. However, you would still want honesty, integrity, and financial commitment to the business.

The Partnership/Stockholder Agreement

Many partnerships are based on a verbal agreement and a handshake. (Again, the term "partner" may also include a major shareholder.) This approach may work quite well as long as conditions are "normal" and until one of the following happens:

▶ *Your partner gets a divorce* and his or her ex wants your business or, nearly as bad, wants to take his or her place in management.

▶ *A disabling disease strikes your partner,* preventing him or her from continuing participation in the business.

▶ *Your partner suddenly dies* and his or her heirs believe that they have a right to help you run the business or be paid a large sum of money for your deceased partner's interest.

▶ *Your partner decides he or she has had enough* of the business and wants to get out, demanding payment for what he or she perceives to be his or her "fair share," which is usually well in excess of its true value.

If you have partners or stockholders, you must have a partnership or stockholder agreement, in writing!

I could present more of these scenarios, but you probably already understand the point I am stressing. I can assure you that I have seen enough of these dramas in real life (and lived through one myself) to convince me that there are *critical issues* that can arise in any partnership or stockholder relationship.

Therefore, if you have partners or stockholders, you *must have a partnership or stockholder agreement, in writing!* Moreover, your attorney must confirm that the agreement is legally binding to all parties. For a good source of preliminary information, go to *www.nolo.com.*

In addition to being legally valid, the partnership/stockholder agreement (referred to as Agreement, for short) must contain the following *business elements*:

1. **A way out.** If any partner or shareholder decides that he or she wants or needs to dispose of his or her interest and withdraw from the business, the Agreement should allow for this possibility and prescribe how to accomplish the withdrawal. However, the Agreement should also place appropriate restrictions on the transfer of ownership interests to protect the remaining owners and the business.

2. **Procedures to be followed in case of the death of a partner/stockholder.** If a partner or stockholder dies, the Agreement must specify the disposition of his or her financial interest in the business and at what value. (See #8 below.)

3. **Procedures to be followed in case of the disability of a partner/stockholder.** The Agreement should set forth the procedures to be taken in the event that a partner/stockholder becomes permanently disabled, restricting his or her involvement in the business. It should also define the term "disability."

89

4. **Procedures if a partner/stockholder becomes a party to a divorce.** It is not uncommon for the ex-wife or ex-husband of a partner or stockholder to want to include the partner/stockholder's financial interest in the business among the assets to be distributed in the divorce proceeding. The remaining partners/stockholders may not wish to have a new partner/stockholder. The Agreement must address this concern, perhaps requiring the stockholder to sell his or her stock back to the business if he or she becomes involved in a divorce. It is always possible to allow him or her to reinvest later.

5. **Procedures allowing a partner/stockholder to be terminated for just cause.** Over long periods, people change in ways that may affect their ability to properly contribute to the well-being of the business. Sometimes it is necessary to terminate an employee, even one who is a partner or stockholder. The Agreement must allow for termination and also provide for returning the terminated partner/stockholder's equity value to him or her.

6. **Procedures for allocating profits among partners.** Although this may be applicable for the members of an LLC, it is especially needed for any type of partnership. The provision may also define how the partnership interest or percentage ownership is determined and how it may be modified.

7. **A definition of the authority of the owners in managing the business.** Management responsibilities of each owner, if not spelled out in the articles of organization or incorporation (or bylaws), should be defined, including the "pecking order."

8. **The method of valuing a partner/stockholders' interest.** A valuation method should be agreed upon and established *in the beginning* of the business entity, not after someone dies, withdraws, or becomes a party to divorce. There are several ways to value a partnership or stockholder interest; the one selected should be unambiguous, easily determined at any time, and fair to all parties. Your CPA and your attorney can help you with this.

The valuation of a small business is extremely difficult and appraisals to determine value should be avoided, if possible.

If a well-defined valuation method is not provided in the Agreement, an appraisal of the business may be required if a stockholder leaves. Appraisals can be costly and may not result in a fair or reasonable valuation. The valuation of a small business is extremely difficult and appraisals to determine value should be avoided, if possible.

Another method used by some to solve the valuation problem is the "I will buy or sell at a specified price" approach. This approach, referred to as a "buy/sell agreement," has merit—assuming that there is a willing buyer and a willing seller and both are alive. However, this frequently is not the case. In no case should the Agreement permit a "locked in" partner or stockholder, that is, a partner who desires to withdraw but cannot recover his or her rightful share of the business equity.

How Good Is Your Banker?

After your partners and stockholders, a banker may be the next most important selection as a financial resource for your business. Bankers are interesting persons with whom you will do business. Too often, they will not loan you money unless you don't need it. Too often, they will offer you extensive business advice, but have never been in business. Too often, they will counsel you on risk taking, but have never taken a risk themselves.

If it sounds like I am critical of bankers, I do not mean to be. I mean only to enlighten you about bankers in general and the *importance of selecting* the *right banker* for your business in particular.

You should know that my business life has been doubly blessed in having two absolutely outstanding bankers, each from a different part of the country, dealing with two totally different types of businesses in which I was involved. As a result of this experience, I feel qualified to provide you with some guidelines for selecting a banker. The guidelines set forth below are illustrations of the collective characteristics of the two bankers just mentioned.

A good banker will come to your business, tour your facility, and spend a considerable amount of time listening to you describe your business operations.

1. **Understanding your business.** A good banker will come to your business, tour your facility, and spend a considerable amount of time *listening* to you describe your business operations. He (or she) will ask questions about your marketing methods, your manufacturing processes (if any), how you develop new products, the competition, and what makes your business special.

2. **Understanding your systems.** A good banker should be vitally interested in your systems for accounting, cash management, credit and collection, inventory management, product quality control, and the timeliness and accuracy of your internal financial statements. He will spend time reviewing these systems and learn how they help you control your operations.

3. **Understanding your external resources.** A good banker will want to know the name of your attorney, your insurance broker, and your accounting firm and may even wish to contact these references, with your blessing. He will ask about any pending litigation and the extent of your company's

insurance coverage. If your financials are audited, he will want to have copies of the accountant's report and a copy of the accounting firm's recommendations for improving internal control systems.

4. **Understanding your financial statements.** A good banker will be most interested in your financial statements, how and when they are prepared, and what they reveal about your business. He will want to know who prepares your income tax returns. He will also want to know how well *you* understand your company's financial statements.

5. **Understanding your people.** A good banker will want to know the key personnel in your company, their role in the business, and the extent of their experience. He will especially want to know your partners and stockholders, their backgrounds, and the levels of their financial commitment to the business. If you have a labor union, he will want to understand your union agreement and the status of your relationship with the key union officials. He will likely want to know how you procure key personnel, whether in sales, manufacturing, engineering, or marketing, and their skill levels.

6. **Understanding your banking needs.** A good banker will want to understand why you need to borrow money, how much, and for how long. He will want to know how you intend to repay the loan, what you intend to provide as collateral, and, quite often, your willingness to personally guarantee the loan. Equally important, he will want to understand the risk and the downside to the loan arrangement. He will advise you of the *loan covenants* that the bank will require and determine how willing you are to live with those covenants.

Of course, all of the understandings set forth above are facilitated with a properly prepared *business plan*. However, a good banker will want to come to your business and clearly understand the factors that are important to your success. These criteria may help you to answer the important question, *"How good is your banker?"*

The two bankers referred to earlier embodied all of these understandings and became very involved in the business. They shared in the good accomplishments and understood the hard times because they had these understandings up front. When times became tenuous, they did not back away from the issues and hide behind their loan agreement. They stepped up and helped the businesses weather the storms. They were good bankers. *You will need one of these!*

A good banker will want to know the key personnel in your company, their role in the business, and the extent of their experience.

Borrowing Money

One of the reasons that a good banker is so important is because borrowed money is an excellent financial resource. The following statement is vitally important for you to remember:

If your company cannot borrow money, pay the interest, and effectively use the money to make a profit (after the interest cost), you are in the wrong business!

We are not suggesting that your business overextend by creating more debt than it can service, but we do want you to understand the value of being able to leverage equity capital to maximize your business opportunities. Many years ago, small business owners thought borrowing was shameful and a sign of weakness. Those were the days when the business paid cash for its assets (and the owners rode in buggies!). Those days are gone forever.

If your company can generate a return on assets (net income divided by total assets) of 20 percent, which is not unreasonable, isn't it good business to supplement the equity capital to enable additional assets (paying interest at a rate as high as 10 percent) and return an additional 10 percent (or more, depending upon income tax considerations) on assets to the shareholders?

As long as you have a legitimate need for the extra money to add *productive assets* and the debt does not exceed the company's ability to repay the loan, including the interest, I believe the added borrowing is good business. By contrast, if you decide to sell additional stock in your company to enable the purchase of productive assets, that capital will reduce the relative equity percentage ownership for you and your business partners.

So, what are the steps you need to take in borrowing money?

1. **Prepare a business plan.** It should, in addition to its other contents, describe the legitimate need for the money, identify the amount you intend to borrow, and demonstrate how it can be repaid and over what time period.
2. **Discuss the borrowing with your banker.** He should not only endorse your plan but provide helpful insights that you may not have considered. The data provided should include everything necessary to enable him to present your proposal to the loan committee successfully. He will also be able to review a sample loan agreement that will help you understand the extent of your commitment to the bank. The commitment includes the terms of the agreement and the *positive and negative covenants* that are typical of most loan agreements.

3. **Review the loan agreement terms** and determine those that you are or are not willing to live with. In most cases, the terms are somewhat negotiable. A sampling of the *terms* found in most loan agreements includes:

   ▶ *Repayment provisions*, including the duration of the repayment period, interest rate, late fees, and grace period for determining a late payment.

   ▶ The ability to *prepay the loan*, in whole or in part, and any penalties for doing so. This is an important provision.

   ▶ The amount of *loan fees* charged by the bank.

   ▶ *Events of default* that could enable the bank to call for the immediate repayment of the entire loan amount.

   ▶ *Collateral required*, including the need for a personal guarantee. If the terms of the loan agreement require the pledge of machinery and equipment as collateral, you will want to know the current loan value of those assets.

In some cases, you may be able to establish the value by referring to equipment manufacturers and dealers. The use of an appraiser may also be appropriate. There are several appraisal organizations listed on the internet, including Machinery Dealers National Association (*www.mdna.org*), Association of Machinery and Equipment Appraisers (*www.amea.org*), and American Society of Appraisers (*www.appraisers.org*). Before you select an appraiser, make sure that it is acceptable to your banker.

4. **Review the loan agreement covenants.** These are agreements on your part to cause the company *to do* (positive covenants) or *not to do* (negative covenants) certain things. The levels or degrees defined in these covenants are usually negotiable, but the inclusion of the covenants is usually not negotiable.

   Sample *positive covenants* would include:

   ▶ Maintaining a certain current ratio, that is, the ratio of current assets to current liabilities.

   ▶ The guarantee of positive net earnings, meaning that the company will not lose money for any fiscal year.

   ▶ Maintaining a positive cash flow (and the term "cash flow" is usually defined in the Agreement).

   ▶ Giving assurance that the company will continually meet a certain level of net worth, at least equal to and often a bit higher than the net worth at the time the Agreement is signed.

   ▶ Agreeing not to exceed a certain ratio of total liabilities to net worth. Sometimes this is referred to as a *debt-to-equity ratio* and is usually defined in the Agreement.

Typical *negative covenants* might include:

▶ Agreeing not to purchase property and equipment in excess of a certain amount annually, without the consent of the bank.

▶ Agreeing not to exceed a certain annual dollar amount for lease payments.

▶ Guaranteeing not to enter into any new loan agreements of any nature, except with the lending bank.

There are many other types of positive and negative covenants, but those listed above are examples of what you might expect to encounter.

One of the issues that typically confronts small business owners is that a bank insists that the owners *personally guarantee the loan.* Usually an owner's entire worth is in the business and he or she may not be able to repay the loan out of resources other than those in the business. What the bank really wants is evidence of your *personal commitment* to the business and its obligations. Do not be offended by the request for this guarantee. It is more often the rule than the exception.

There is one more important concern in borrowing money—*paying it back!* You *must not miss a payment* to the bank. If you anticipate that you may not be able to make a payment, discuss the reasons with your banker, *in advance!* He will likely understand and make some arrangements to accommodate you. What he will *not* understand is that you were unable to anticipate the shortfall of funds necessary to make the payment. You don't like surprises in your business and the banker's reaction to surprises (especially bad ones) is no different!

One of the issues that typically confront small business owners is that a bank insists that the owners personally guarantee the loan.

The Role of Leasing

There are pros and cons relative to leasing assets that are used in your business. The *advantages* may include less initial cash outlay, fewer restrictive financial covenants, and the ability to avoid asset obsolescence by using a short-term lease and updating the asset when desired. The *disadvantages* may be a higher long-term cost, lack of equity in the asset, and a possible lease clause preventing cancellation or early termination. You can compare the interest costs of leasing versus buying, which may give an advantage to one of the two forms of financing.

If you are not comfortable analyzing the costs of one form versus the other, you should seek the assistance of your CPA. He will also tell you that, with certain types of leases (capital leases), financing assets using a lease will be accounted for the same as if you had borrowed the money to finance them. Your banker may also provide insight in the cost comparison.

We believe one of the most important financing considerations for the small business owner is the *judicious use of borrowing power*. If you have borrowed extensively to construct a building to house your business, you may be limiting the use of borrowing as a means of financing the acquisition of *productive assets*, such as machinery and equipment. Unless your business is involved in buying and selling real estate, *I believe that using borrowed capital for brick and mortar is restrictive to your business operations*. This is true at least until your business is mature.

If your business is manufacturing, you are in the business of acquiring and using production equipment to produce a product that can be sold profitably. As such, you will understand the value of each piece of equipment, which warrants developing an equity in that equipment. If the lease is properly structured, it may be far more advantageous to lease the building or plant and borrow the money to purchase the needed production equipment. The same may be said of a service business: lease the building but own the equipment needed to provide your services.

A properly structured building lease should provide for optional renewals at appropriate time intervals, at prices determined in advance (such as using business indices for lease rate increases), with the option to purchase, if desired. The purchase option should be in accordance with a formula that is determined at the time the lease is structured and it should be set forth in the lease. Again, use your CPA and banker to help you in these determinations.

Incidentally, lease financing may also be desirable for various types of equipment that have a short useful life and little residual value. Computer equipment, office equipment, and smaller auxiliary equipment used in production are candidates.

Suppliers as a Resource

A good supplier can be a valuable financial resource for the small business. Too often, small businesses select a supplier because it offers its product at the lowest competitive price. This approach ignores the value of service, warranty, delivery, and payment terms.

Favorable payment terms offered by another supplier may more than offset a little higher price. The ability to deliver product on short notice, provide service after the sale, or stock product in your plant on consignment can

If you have borrowed extensively to construct a building to house your business, you may be limiting the use of borrowing as a means of financing the acquisition of productive assets, such as machinery and equipment.

be far more valuable to your operation than a small price break. In addition, many large suppliers are willing to provide payment terms to small businesses that are virtual borrowing arrangements. The value of an outstanding service policy (servicing the product supplied) or a favorable warranty policy may also outweigh the value of a minor price break. Make no mistake: I strongly advocate price comparisons so that you will be able to properly evaluate all of the factors. But a good supplier *offering more than a low price* can be a very valuable financial resource.

Chapter 13

Understanding Accounting–a Must!

Every transaction in business is ultimately translated into the language of finance—accounting. If you do not understand the language, you and your small business are at an extreme disadvantage.

Y OU MUST KNOW HOW THE BUSINESS DECISIONS YOU MAKE WILL affect your financial statements—*before* you make those decisions. You must understand how various business transactions are accounted for and how they will be recorded in your accounting system. If there is one common weakness among small business owners, it is their inability to understand and use the language of finance. Understanding accounting is a *must* if you are to be a successful small business owner or manager.

Why Do You Need to Know?

We know that many businessmen view accounting as a necessary evil and not as a valuable tool to help them succeed in managing their business. Too many turn the accounting task over to a bookkeeper and ignore the process until the financial statements don't turn out as expected. At that point, the bearer of bad tidings (the bookkeeper) is all but beheaded, for it must certainly be his or her fault that the statements don't appear as the owners thought they should. Wrong! Assuming that the bookkeeper is competent, it is the owner who is responsible for the appearance of the financial statements. The financials only report, in the language of accounting, the results of all of the decisions that were made by management. If this idea is unsettling to you, read on—it gets worse!

Let me give you some *reasons* why *you need to know* and understand accounting:

1. Without the knowledge of accounting, you will be unable to *develop a comprehensive business plan*, complete with *financial projections*, which directly affects your ability to attract a good banker and needed financial resources.
2. The lack of understanding of cost accounting may lead to decisions that *adversely affect the cost of products* acquired or produced and, therefore, the resulting profit margins.
3. If you do not understand inventory accounting, *adverse surprises*, such as inventory shortages, imbalances among inventory items, and inventory obsolescence may occur and surface when least expected.
4. Decisions to change the selling price of the company's products or services may not result in the *intended gross margins* unless you understand how gross profit is developed and accounted for.

Having spent several years in management consulting, I can tell you many horror stories that have occurred because someone in management (usually the top person) did not understand accounting. A few of these stories might be more easily understood than the reasons cited above. The stories that follow are *real* and *actually occurred*.

A company that secured a sizeable loan from its bank was required to have an audit as one of the positive loan covenants. The company had never been audited, even though its CPA firm had prepared its tax returns. The audit disclosed an inventory shortage of *several hundred thousand dollars, nearly 50 percent of the company's net worth!* Investigation revealed that production labor was being recorded in inventory at amounts *actually incurred*, but when inventory was relieved of the cost of product sold, it was relieved at a *standard cost*, a standard that did not include an allowance for labor inefficiencies.

This accounting process, *plus the company's failure to take frequent physical inventories*, allowed the cost of labor inefficiency to build up in the inventory account over the years. When the physical inventory was taken and priced at the standard cost (a cost that was appropriate for valuing the inventory), that value was far less than the value on the company's books.

A textile manufacturer was producing knitted goods, including T-shirts, in a variety of colors. The cost of the dyes used in coloring the T-shirts was *allocated equally* to all of the T-shirts, *regardless of color*. It was the company's policy to allow customers to select the colors they desired when ordering in lots of a hundred dozen or more. The company priced all T-shirts at the *same price per dozen, regardless of color*.

Investigation revealed that the cost of vivid color dyes (such as kelly green, navy blue, and dark red) could amount to 20 to 30 percent of the sell price, whereas the cost of lighter color dyes (such as white, pale yellow, and light blue) amounted to less than 5 percent of the sell price. The result was that *every time the company sold a navy, green, or red T-shirt, it incurred a loss!* Guess what the customers did? Right—they bought all vivid-colored T-shirts from this company and the lighter-colored shirts from their competitors. Unbelievable? No. Management simply did not understand their product costing!

Another company manufactured two types of product and used a job cost system to capture and report costs. However, the internal reporting segment of the accounting system did not develop *product line profitability reporting*. Product Line A accounted for 80 percent of the company's sales volume and was presumed to be quite profitable. Management emphasized Product Line A as the main thrust of the company's business. Product Line B had a smaller sales volume and was thought to have a relatively low margin of profit.

Well-conceived, accurate, and timely accounting and reporting systems are vital to a company's success.

Later, the entire cost reporting system was changed to permit product line profitability reporting. Guess what? They found that *Product Line A was generating a gross margin of 22 percent while Product Line B was generating a gross margin of more than 43 percent*. Subsequently, the company was split into two subsidiaries, one for Product Line A and the other for Product Line B. In less than three years, Product Line A company nearly went bankrupt and was sold for the residual value of its equipment. Product Line B Company is still alive and producing sizeable profits because its management increased the sales volume of its business by nearly 30 times!

I could provide additional illustrations but perhaps the point has been adequately stressed. Well-conceived, accurate, and timely accounting *and* reporting systems are vital to a company's success. We believe that owners of small businesses (or even managers of larger companies) must learn how accounting works and use it effectively to manage their business.

Cash or Accrual Accounting

The first accounting concept that you need to understand is the difference between the *cash* and *accrual* methods of recording transactions.

The *cash method* of accounting is much like the name implies. It reports income only when cash is received and records costs and expenses only when they are paid. This is pretty much the same as how you record your family income and expenses in your checkbook. You record income as you receive it and deposit it in the bank. You recognize expenses as you write checks to pay them.

Everything is great until you receive the credit card bill that is three times as big as you thought it would be and you don't have sufficient funds in the bank to pay it. So, either you borrow money from the bank to pay it or you borrow it from the credit card company (at very high interest rates) by paying only the minimum payment required.

Businesses that use the cash method run a considerable risk unless they keep track of how much they owe and how much others owe the business. These added records to capture transactions before cash is involved become much like the accrual method, discussed next. There can be tax advantages to using the cash method of accounting, and that method may be preferred for a personal service or professional business. However, the accrual method is much preferable as a useful (and necessary) tool in managing a business. Check with your CPA. He or she can advise you best.

The *accrual method* of accounting requires that *all transactions be recorded when they occur*, whether cash is increased or decreased at the time the transaction takes place. In the illustration above, every credit card transaction creates a liability that will ultimately require a cash payment. The accrual method requires that the liability be recorded *at the time it is created*. Income must be recorded *when earned (invoiced)*, even though the company may not get paid for 30 to 45 days.

When you ship product to a customer, title passes at the FOB point. (For example, when you put it on a truck going to the customer, the FOB point is your plant.) (More about FOB points later.) You record the sale based on the sales invoice rendered to the customer. When you receive products or services, you have incurred a liability and the accrual method requires that this liability be recorded at the time you receive the service or product (when title passes to you). You can begin to see how much more accurate and timely the accrual method reflects your business transactions.

The first accounting concept that you need to understand is the difference between the cash and accrual methods of recording transactions.

Because there are fewer businesses that use the cash method of accounting (and rightly so), we will confine our subsequent discussion of accounting to the *accrual* method. In most cases, that method is more beneficial and what businesses (probably including yours) should be using.

Understanding Debits and Credits (Double-Entry Bookkeeping)

There is no way around it: you really need to understand debits and credits, terms that are used in double-entry bookkeeping.

There is no way around it: *you really need to understand debits and credits,* terms that are used in *double-entry bookkeeping.* It does not matter whether your company's accounting records are kept manually or with the most sophisticated computerized accounting system, it still boils down to debits and credits. It is important that you understand these concepts. *They are most helpful in understanding the financial statements of your business.*

A good way to understand double-entry bookkeeping is to remember that *both a debit and a credit must be recorded for every transaction.* Hence, two parts to each entry or double-entry bookkeeping. *Debits and credits are terms that were applied to the two parts of each accounting entry,* probably about the time that Bob Cratchit began keeping books for Ebenezer Scrooge!

Business transactions are recorded in *accounts* that can later be summarized and displayed in financial statements. Think of an account as a box that has two compartments, a debit compartment and a credit compartment. The balance in the account is what is left after you subtract one compartment from the other. If the debit compartment value exceeds the credit compartment value, the account has a *debit balance.* If the credit compartment value exceeds the debit compartment value, the account has a *credit balance.*

The type of balance that an account typically has depends upon the nature of the account. *Asset accounts,* which represent things your company *owns*—including cash, accounts receivable, inventories, and plant and equipment—typically *have a debit balance. Liability and equity accounts,* which represent things your company *owes*—including accounts payable, accrued liabilities, notes payable, common stock and retained earnings—typically *have a credit balance.* If you add up all the debit balances in the asset accounts they should equal the total of all the credit balances in the liability and equity accounts. Hence, the equation:

assets (debits) = liabilities and equity (credits)

A better way to think of this equation, which will later help you under-

102

stand equity (or net worth), is set forth below:

assets − liabilities = equity

So if you were to start a company by putting $1,000 of your own money into the *company's bank account* in exchange for $1,000 worth of *common stock*, you would debit the company's bank account (or Cash) and credit the Common Stock account. This transaction is recorded in a *journal entry*, which derives its name from the good old days when a "bean counter," with pen and ink, recorded the entries diligently in a large book called the *general journal*. The entry would appear as:

Dr. Cash   **$1,000.00**

Cr. Common Stock   **$1,000.00**

We have used the abbreviations for debit (*Dr.*) and credit (*Cr.*) in this illustration and in others to follow. Fortunately, we no longer have to use pen and ink to make these entries. After all, it is hard to erase mistakes that are made in ink.

Today, the accountant would enter the journal entry into a programmed, computerized accounting system that would automatically put the amounts into the selected accounts. Even more interesting is the ability of the QuickBooks®, Peachtree Accounting®, and similar systems to make basic accounting entries in the background as the user creates various source documents, such as a sales invoice, a check, and so forth. As the user creates these documents, the program makes accounting entries to the appropriate accounts *automatically*. This great convenience, however, does not diminish your need to understand what accounting entries these systems are making and why.

We have discussed debits and credits as they impact the balance sheet accounts.

Lest we forget, a balance sheet is one of the main financial statements of a business: it reports the value of its assets, liabilities, and net worth at a given date.

By the way, the balance sheet accounts never get closed out, even at the end of the year. (Closing out an account is a process of calculating the balance of the account and then transferring it to another financial statement.)

The *income statement* (also called a *profit and loss statement*) is the *other primary financial statement* for a business: *it reports the revenue, costs and expenses, and (hopefully) profit for the year.* The accounts used in the income statement *do* get closed out at the end of the year, to a balance sheet account called Retained Earnings, so that the income statement accounts can start the next year with a zero balance. Income statement accounts that, during the year, typically show a *credit balance* include sales and other income. Income statement accounts that, during the year, typically have a *debit balance* include cost of sales, general and administrative expense accounts, sales expense accounts, and taxes on income. These accounts are closed and the net income (a credit total) is put into the Retained Earnings account.

The relationship of these accounts can be expressed by another equation:

Sales and Income Accounts (credits) − Cost and Expense Accounts (debits)

= Net Earnings (credit)

If the total of Cost and Expense amounts exceeds the total of Sales and Income amounts, the result is obviously a net loss (debit).

As you examine the following illustration that indicates typical account balances, remember that on the balance sheet *debit* balances represent the things your company *owns* and *credit* balances represent the things your company *owes*. The amount of net earnings for the year is ultimately added to the Retained Earnings account, part of the company's equity, and represents amounts owed to the shareholders. Hence, assets represent ownership, liabilities represent amounts due to others, and equity represents amounts due to the shareholders.

Debit Balance Accounts	Credit Balance Accounts
BALANCE SHEET ACCOUNTS	
Assets (cash, accounts receivable, inventory, plant and equipment, and expenses that have been prepaid) *Assets are things your company owns.*	*Liabilities and Equity* (accounts payable, taxes due, bank loans and capital stock plus retained earnings) *Liabilities and Equity are things your company owes.*
INCOME STATEMENT ACCOUNTS	
Cost of Sales (materials, labor, and overhead) *Expenses* (office expenses, travel, selling and advertising costs, and utilities)	*Sales* (all product sales or revenue from services rendered) *Other Income* (rental or interest income)

Figure 13-1. Typical account balances

If this seems confusing, everything is normal. But here is a way to reason it out. If there are earnings, they belong to the stockholders and, at the end of the year, the earnings (represented by the net of all income statement accounts) are closed to a stockholders' equity account, Retained Earnings, which carries a credit balance. The larger the credit balance, the greater the net worth of the company!

How can this be? The answer: the company *owes* the stockholders their investment (common stock) plus any earnings that are generated during the current and prior years.

Perhaps the following illustration will help you understand.

ASSETS *(things your company owns)*	
CURRENT ASSETS	
Cash	Debit Balance
Accounts receivable, less allowance for doubtful accounts (Credit Balance)	Debit Balance
Inventories	Debit Balance
Prepaid expenses	Debit Balance
Total current assets	Debit *Total*
PROPERTY, PLANT & EQUIPMENT, net	Debit Balance
OTHER ASSETS	Debit Balance
Total assets	Debit *Total*

LIABILITIES AND STOCKHOLDERS' EQUITY *(things your company owes)*	
CURRENT LIABILITIES	
Accounts payable	Credit Balance
Accrued expenses	Credit Balance
Income taxes payable	Credit Balance
Total current liabilities	Credit *Total*
STOCKHOLDERS' EQUITY	
Common stock, issued and outstanding	Credit Balance
Retained earnings	Credit Balance
Current year's earnings	Credit Balance
Total stockholders' equity	Credit *Total*
Total liabilities and stockholders' equity	Credit *Total*

Each of these line items on a balance sheet that is not a total is either an account or a collection of accounts, the balances of which are added together.

The income statement can be presented in much the same way, illustrating the terminology discussed earlier:

STATEMENT OF EARNINGS	
Sales	Credit Balance
Cost of sales:	
Materials	Debit Balance
Labor	Debit Balance
Overhead	Debit Balance
Total cost of sales	Debit *Total*
Gross profit	Credit *Total*
Operating expenses	Debit Balance
Operating income	Credit *Total*
Other income	Credit Balance
Earnings before taxes on income	Credit *Total*
Income tax expense	Debit Balance
Net earnings	Credit *Total*

Each line item on the Statement of Earnings that is *not* a total is either an account or a collection of accounts, whose balances are added together.

You can see that net earnings is represented by a credit total (assuming the company operated at a profit), which, when all income statement accounts are closed (at the end of the year) is added to the balance sheet account, Retained Earnings.

In this manner, all income statement accounts are zeroed out, ready for the next year's transactions. Refer back to the balance sheet illustration to observe the location of the Retained Earnings account. Note that *during the year* earnings are recorded in the Current Year's Earnings account.

How the Accounting System Works

Depending upon the nature of the business, accounting systems consist of most of the following elements.

Source documents are records of transactions, such as vendor invoices, sales invoices, time cards, check stubs (or copies), cash register tapes, expense reports, bank deposit slips, and credit card charge slips, to mention only the most common. These source documents display the origination (or source) of a transaction and should be retained, both for tax purposes and as evidence that the transaction occurred.

Journal entries are records of transactions, each being supported by one or more source documents and having debit and credit amounts that are equal.

Journals (or *transaction lists*) display and summarize a number of transactions, making possible a few large summary entries to the accounts rather than an entry for each transaction individually. For example, it is easier to summarize all the sales for a day or week into one entry than to make an entry into the accounts for each individual sale. This is especially true in a business that has a large number of sales daily.

Accounts can be one page in a book (called a *ledger*) or a "compartmentalized box" in a computerized system. In older manual systems, a *general ledger* had a page for each account to which handwritten entries were made. In computerized systems, the term "general ledger" is still used, but each account is a segment in a computer file rather than a page in a book. In computerized systems, the software normally checks entries automatically to determine that the debit amounts equal the credit amounts.

We have developed a typical chart of accounts such as might be used in a small service or manufacturing business, in Appendix K. A chart of accounts that might be used in a retail establishment is in Appendix L. Please note that account numbers are no longer required in automated systems like QuickBooks®; however, the use of account numbers often facilitates the understanding of the accounting system.

If you are not afraid of being overcome with accounting details, there are some simplified but typical accounting entries for a small business in Appendix M. Appendices K, L, and M are not intended to teach accounting but rather to further acquaint you with some of the elements of an accounting system. *If studying accounting details could ruin your day, don't even look at these appendices now!*

Trial balance is a term applied to a listing of all of the account balances in the general ledger to determine that the total of all accounts with credit balances equals the total of all accounts with debit balances. QuickBooks® and other automated systems automatically generate the journal, trial balance, general ledger, balance sheet, and income statements; they can be viewed and printed on command.

Subaccounts are created to keep track of details that support the balance in one account. For example, a subaccount may be created for each *customer's balance* owed to the company. All customer subaccounts, when added together, equal the balance in the general ledger account called *accounts receivable*. Similar subaccounts would likely be created to keep track of amounts owed to individual vendors, the total of which would equal the balance in the general ledger account, *accounts payable*.

A *balance sheet* is one of the most important financial statements required by a company. *This statement is a summary of all asset, liability, and equity accounts on a **specific date**.* A balance sheet should be prepared monthly and a copy should be kept in a safe, permanent file. Your banker and your accountant will likely want a copy of all financial statements to keep well informed of your company's activities.

The *income statement* (also called a *profit and loss statement* or a *statement of earnings*) is another very important financial statement necessary to display a company's operating activities. *This statement is a summary of all income, cost, and expense accounts for a given time period, usually a month or year.* It should be prepared no less frequently than monthly and a copy also kept in permanent safekeeping.

Statement of cash flow is the final financial statement that should be prepared. Although it is very useful, many companies do not prepare this statement more often than once a year. The decision to prepare it more frequently should be based on how valuable a tool it is to management in running the business. *This statement is a summarization of all cash transactions that occurred during the year.* I believe that this statement is very important to small businesses, especially start-up businesses, whose lifeblood is cash. Accordingly, it is recommended that small companies prepare a *statement of cash* flow monthly or, in some cases, weekly.

There are other statements or reports that provide management with information that can be helpful, if not essential, in managing the business. These should include a *product line profitability report*, which discloses the profitability of one product line or type of service relative to all others. *Job profitability reports* achieve the same objective for businesses that provide a service, such as contractors and personal service companies, who need to know the profitability of each job or project. A special *inventory report* can help advise management of the content (in summarized form) of the company's inventories so that out-of-balance or overstocked conditions can be avoided and inventory obsolescence can be kept to a minimum. *Production efficiency reports,* which compare estimated with actual materials and labor used in segments of production, help keep managers in manufacturing companies abreast of the effectiveness of their labor force.

*B*ased on source documents, journal entries are made and summarized in journals and, from the journals, summary entries are made to the accounts.

To summarize our comments: based on *source documents, journal entries* are made and *summarized in journals* and, from the journals, *summary entries* are made to the *accounts*. At the end of a period, usually a month, a *trial balance* is prepared to determine that the system is in balance (that debits and credits are equal) and *financial statements* are prepared.

Today, most of this activity is accomplished by a computerized system. There are many systems that are quite good, including QuickBooks®, Peachtree Accounting®, and many others. These systems automatically summarize journal entries into journals, post the entries to the accounts, and prepare a trial balance, financial statements, and other special reports, as requested.

Some companies have programming consultants customize computerized systems specifically for their special needs. Customization, although quite satisfying when completed, can be very costly and requires a considerable amount of time to develop (always longer than expected). This approach is often taken by larger companies that have networked systems developed by their own programming staffs.

Customization, although quite satisfying when completed, can be very costly and requires a considerable amount of time to develop (always longer than expected).

The entire accounting process can be summarized and illustrated in the following diagram. A review of Figure 13-2 illustrates the fact that the accounting process is relatively orderly and not very complicated.

It all starts with a transaction, which is supported or confirmed by a source document. Based on that transaction and a knowledge of the accounts that have been set up in the general ledger, a journal entry (using debits and credits) is prepared. From that point on, the process is largely one of summarization.

After accounting entries are made, a summarization process begins, to generate internal operating and statistical reports and financial statements.

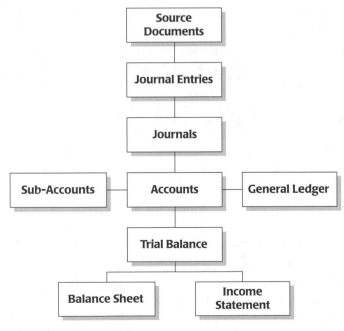

Figure 13-2. An accouning system

Computerized systems typically provide this result easily. For example, one of the programmed systems mentioned previously can produce these reports:

- journal entries
- trial balance
- general ledger
- balance sheet
- income statement
- cash flow statement
- job profitability report

Accounting for payroll is one of the most technically difficult and time-consuming of all accounting tasks.

Important note about payroll: Accounting for payroll is one of the most technically difficult and time-consuming of all accounting tasks. It is further complicated by the various tax rates that seem to be forever changing as our Congress and state legislatures see fit. In addition, there are many insurance and fringe benefit considerations, most of which are vital, even to a small business. Read the following and *give it serious consideration.*

> The author recommends that small business avail itself of payroll services that are provided by banks, accounting firms, and other institutions, which are well versed on payroll accounting, tax rates, and the required payroll tax reports. The cost is typically nominal and certainly worth the services that are provided.
>
> Those services would include preparing the payroll reports, related tax returns, and payroll checks for the employees and providing the entries needed to record the payroll transactions. All of these tasks are tedious.

Cost Accounting—a "Lost Art"

One of the most important pieces of information needed by a small business owner is the accurate cost of the products or services the company offers for sale. This information should typically come from the cost accounting segment of the company's accounting system. There are books devoted to this subject, including *Cost and Effect: Using Integrated Cost Systems to Drive Profitability and Performance*[1] and *Cost Accounting: An Introduction to Cost Management Systems*[2].

How many times have small contracting companies covered the cost of their materials and labor to perform jobs, only to find that they are not making money? The costs included in figuring the job did *not* include an *allocation of overhead* (payroll taxes, overtime premium, field supervision, and more) *or administrative costs* (office, general insurance, utilities, taxes, and so forth).

Because of the complexity of some cost accounting systems, I suggest that you read one or more of the books referenced here or others that are available in bookstores. As you read them, however, you should note that the majority of them were written for large companies and involve systems that small companies may not undertake.

Regardless of the system employed, I believe it should involve two types of costs: *standard* or *estimated* costs and *actual* costs. *Standard costs* is the term normally used in a manufacturing company and *estimated costs* is the term normally used in a service company (such as any type of contracting or personal services). *Actual costs*, also called *historical costs*, are those that are recorded in the company's accounting system. Both types of costs are important to the small business owner. Regardless of the nature of your business, the essential point here is to plan your costs (hence, estimated or standard costs) and then measure the actual costs against that plan.

Regardless of the system employed, I believe it should involve two types of costs: standard or estimated costs and actual costs.

For example, when a contractor of any type bids a job, he or she is actually developing an estimated cost of completing that job. If he fails to meet the plan, i.e. actual costs exceed planned costs, the job could result in a loss. The failure to meet planned performance should stimulate timely corrective action to prevent or at least reduce faulty estimating or poor execution on succeeding jobs.

If the jobs are large, they should be broken into job segments and the actual costs of each segment should be measured against an estimate for that segment. In many cases, poor performance on some segments (if known) may be offset by greater efficiency in other segments. Whatever your business, *the ability to compare actual performance against planned performance*, on a meaningful basis, *is an essential management tool.*

Most of the automated accounting systems, including QuickBooks® and Peachtree Accounting®, offer the ability to measure estimated against actual performance. Small business can effectively use a cost system that compares planned or estimated performance with actual performance and uses appropriate methods to allocate overhead costs. *Direct overhead costs* are for items that are used on jobs but cannot be specifically identified with one particular job, such as depreciation on equipment, maintenance costs, and the cost of job supervision. These costs can be accumulated in a segment of accounts and allocated to jobs on the basis of labor hours, material costs, or other similar statistics.

With good reporting and control systems, we believe that small business is adequately served with sufficient information to properly manage its activities. Temporary success may be attained without good systems, but in the long term business profitability results from well-informed decision-making. The following parable is intended to illustrate this principle!

Parable of the Tree

A turkey was chatting with a bull. "I would love to be able to get to the top of that tree," sighed the turkey, "but I haven't got the energy."

"Well, why don't you nibble on some of my droppings?" replied the bull. "They are packed with energizing nutrients."

The turkey pecked away, as instructed, and found that it gave him enough strength to reach the first branch of the tree.

The next day, following the bull's recommendation, the turkey reached the second branch. After the fourth day, the turkey was proudly perched atop the tree. Unfortunately, his silhouette was easily spotted by a farmer, who shot the turkey out of the tree.

Management Lesson: BS might get you to the top, but it won't keep you there.

Notes

1. Kaplan, Robert S., and Cooper, Robin. *Cost and Effect: Using Integrated Cost Systems to Drive Profitability and Performance*. Harvard Business School Press, 1997.

2. Jagolinzer, Philip. *Cost Accounting: An Introduction to Cost Management Systems*. South-Western College Publishing Co., 2000.

Chapter 14

Management and Control Systems

I N PREVIOUS CHAPTERS, WE HAVE REFERRED TO SYSTEMS, IN ADDITION TO
the accounting system, that are vital to the success of the small business. The ability to monitor operations with key internal reports, controlling jobs in a contracting business, ensuring quality in a manufacturing environment, or managing the investment in inventory in a retail operation, involves control systems that warrant further discussion.

Internal Reporting Systems

There are probably as many types of internal reporting systems as there are companies that use them. Internal reporting systems are defined here as the monthly financial reports that provide management with information beyond that provided in the annual balance sheet and profit and loss statement. Any system of internal reporting should include additional information about expenses, manufacturing overhead, and product or job profitability. I have seen companies that publish monthly statements that fill a two-inch-thick notebook and others that do not go beyond a bookkeeper's two-page trial balance. A happy medium is what I will refer to as *trend reports*.

It is always nice to be able to compare the current month results with results from prior months and with budget. Year-to-date results are more meaningful when compared with budgeted performance for the same period and with actual results for that period in the prior year. *To be able to see all of this data on a few pieces of paper is even better.* If last month's results can be discarded and new reports used in their place (without losing the prior month's information), internal reporting becomes simple and effective. A set of sample trend reports for a small business is presented in Appendix N. The use of trend reports is explained below and illustrated with a sample *Trend Income Statement* (Figure 14-1).

In this format, the plan for the *month* would be shown in the *Plan* column. This amount does not change from month to month, *unless* management has prepared a plan for *each month of the year*. Although the illustration appears small (to fit into this book format), it *is* possible to show all of the trend reports on a standard 8½-inch-by-11-inch page. The numbers are stated in *thousands of dollars*. If management wants to get into more detail, that information could be provided upon request.

For the month of April, for example, the *Plan* column will show the plan for that month and the actual results for the months of January, February, March, and April in their columns. The *year-to-date actual* is the aggregate of the four months' results and the *plan* and *last year's actual* are the aggregate amounts for the appropriate four-month periods.

When May's report is generated, the plan column may or may not stay the same (depending upon the planning approach), the month of May (actual) is added in its column, and the year-to-date columns are changed to reflect five months' activity. A new report is prepared and the April report is discarded.

Appendix N shows the following trend reports:

- ▶ Income Statement
- ▶ Variable Overhead Costs
- ▶ Balance Sheet
- ▶ Gross Margin Report

It is very important that these reports be completed and distributed to management *very shortly* after the end of the month. A good objective is five to seven working days—and five is better!

It is a definite advantage and convenience to be able to review the results of operations for your company for the past three years using just a few pieces of paper. I can attest that reports similar to these are currently being used in a number of small companies. They can be prepared on a word processor, using systems like Microsoft Excel® (such as the one illustrated),

TREND REPORT

NAME OF COMPANY
For the Year Ending December 31, 20XX

	Plan	Jan	Feb	Mar	Apr	May	Jun	Jul	Aug	Sep	Oct	Nov	Dec	YTD Actual	YTD Plan
Sales															
Cost of Sales															
Materials															
Labor															
Variable Overhead															
Total cost of sales															
Gross profit															
Gross profit %															
Expenses															
Salaries/wages															
Other payroll costs															
Office supplies															
Rent expense															
Auto/truck costs															
Utilities															
Advertising															
Bad debt expense															
Professional fees															
Travel expense															
Insurance															
Taxes															
Other expenses															
Total Expenses															
Operating Income															
Nonoperating Items															
Interest expense															
Other income/ expense															
Total other costs															
Pretax Income															

Figure 14-1. Sample trend income statement

or, in some cases, can be programmed into the system used for accounting purposes.

Credit Management

Today, all businesses, regardless of size, are expected to offer credit to their customers, either on open account or by accepting credit cards.

Many years ago everyone paid their bills with cash. Today, all businesses, regardless of size, are expected to offer credit to their customers, either on open account or by accepting credit cards. In fact, our entire economy is a credit economy. According to a recent Federal Reserve Statistical Release, total consumer credit outstanding (not including home mortgages) is approximately $2 trillion. If your small business offers credit terms to your customer (not credit cards), credit management (policy, extension, and collection) is critical. *It takes a lot of sales and related profit to make up for one bad debt!*

There are several credit bureau agencies that can offer assistance in the credit management area. The most notable is Dun & Bradstreet. The problem with D&B's ratings is that they are based on the information that is available to them. Quite often the customers of small businesses withhold key information from D&B, which lessens the agency's ability to provide meaningful credit data. For personal credit information, other agencies are available, including Equifax and TransUnion, that can provide data that is helpful to retailing establishments. Of course, if you accept credit cards, much of the work is done for you. However, all of these agencies charge a fee for their services.

Most small businesses can manage their own credit investigation when credit is to be granted on open account. Investigation that has proven reliable include the following important steps:

1. Credit application. Require the potential customer to complete a *credit application* form—*before you make the sale!* You can mail or fax this form to your pending customers and then use the information to evaluate their creditworthiness. There are many such forms available from forms companies; however, key information that should be on the form includes:

▶ *Information identifying the company or individual* (including federal tax I.D. or Social Security number).

▶ *Legal form of business* (corporation, partnership, LLC, or other), the state of incorporation (when applicable), and key officers of the company.

▶ *Names of persons authorized* to commit the customer organization to an order (sometimes orders are valid only with a written purchase order, which is much preferred).

116

▶ *Bank reference* information, including the name of the contact in the bank (preferably a bank officer).

▶ *Names* and *contacts* for at least *three trade references* with which the customer has established credit.

▶ *Current financial statements,* preferably the most recent year completed (preferably audited) and statements for the most recently completed month end.

You can design your own credit application form using your letterhead and return address or fax information. It is also helpful to indicate on the form, after the customer returns it, the *amount of the requested initial order.* Then the work begins.

You must assign someone in your organization (and it is best if this person is relatively assertive, but polite) to check out the referenced information. This person must call the bank and all trade references to find out the high credit extended, the current status (current or past due), and the length of time the credit relationship has been in force. The references may request that these inquiries be made in writing, which is quite acceptable but takes a little longer.

This information should be entered on the form. Then the form and the accompanying financial statements should be examined by whomever in your organization is authorized to extend credit—in a small business, often the owner. That person should indicate on the form whether credit is approved and the dollar value of the credit limit.

The customer should be advised when a credit decision has been reached; if credit is offered, the terms of such credit should be explained (such as net 30 days or two percent discount for payment in 10 days with net being paid in 30 days, etc.).

2. Credit follow-up. This is the next vital ingredient in the credit management system. If the account becomes *10 days past due (not 11 or 12!),* the *salesperson* who made the sale should call the customer to determine if the delay is because of a problem with the product or service purchased. If so, the problem should be resolved quickly and fairly. If the product or service is not the problem, the salesperson needs to ask when the company can expect payment. If the response is satisfactory, no further contact with the customer should be necessary. If the response is not satisfactory or the customer passes the promised date, the company must act promptly. *Time is of the essence.* A call to the customer's highest-ranking contact should be made to deter-

If credit is offered, the terms of such credit should be explained (such as net 30 days or two percent discount for payment in 10 days with net being paid in 30 days, etc.).

117

mine the nature of the payment problem. If this contact provides a reasonable answer and specific payment plans can be agreed upon, no further action should be necessary.

3. Collection efforts. If there is resistance to payment or an indication of a major financial problem, you have a choice: either work with the customer while they solve their financial problem or turn the account over to a collection agency. Collection agencies are hard-nosed outfits that make their money by collecting bad accounts. For this effort, they are compensated with a percentage of the amount collected. Find a good agency (ask your banker, attorney, or CPA for references) and rely on it. Remember, *50 percent of something is better than 100 percent of nothing.*

The real key to credit management is a sense of urgency. There must be no delay in following up and no delay in taking whatever action is appropriate.

The real key to credit management is a *sense of urgency*. There must be *no delay* in following up and *no delay* in taking whatever action is appropriate. *The older the past due account becomes, the less likely you are to collect it.* Make sure someone in your organization stays on top of your accounts receivable and studies the *aging report* diligently.

The aging report simply lists all customer balances and indicates whether each account is current or has become 30, 60, or 90 days past due. (See the example for the typical headings in an aging report.) *If the company has not taken definitive action by the time an account becomes 90 days past due, collection is quite unlikely!* When an account moves into the "30-60 days past due" column, the actions described in the previous paragraphs must begin.

Customer Name	Contact Name	Phone No.	Total Amount Due	Past Due Amounts		
				30-60 Days	61-90 Days	Over 90 Days

Sometimes there are legal issues involved when a customer fails to make payment. If that is the case, you should immediately contact your attorney and involve him or her to the extent that he or she believes is warranted. *Do not wait—take action!* You should also ask your attorney how the laws listed below and perhaps others may apply to your business:

▶ Truth in Lending Act

▶ Equal Credit Opportunity Act

▶ Fair Credit Billing Act

There are also some state laws that may apply to the extension of credit and the collection of credit amounts. He or she should also advise you on whether they apply to your business and, if so, how.

Order Entry and Billing

If your business is retail, the sales order and the billing are generated at the same time, typically by a point-of-sale device that records the sale, provides the customer a billing (sales receipt), and maintains a copy of the transaction documents for accounting purposes. On the other hand, if your business is in manufacturing or service, the order and the invoice are usually separated by time—the time it takes to fill the order or render the service. In these types of organizations, the sales order and the sales invoice may or may not be generated at the same time.

The order entry/billing function can be accomplished by hand (literally, using handwritten documents) or by automated computerized accounting systems. In the latter case, it is usually easier to capture the key information once and use that information for the sales quotation, the sales order, and the sales invoice.

Because there are so many types of order entry and billing systems available (also contained in the automated accounting systems referred to earlier, i.e., QuickBooks® and Peachtree®), our focus will be on the necessary data that should be generated and used rather than the designs of various systems.

In any business, large or small, it is vital to provide a *written quotation* to the customer so that there is *no misunderstanding about the nature of the product or service to be provided, the terms, pricing, warranty, and the time when the product or service can be expected to be shipped or provided.* The sales quotation should include:

▶ Date of the quotation and an identifying number

▶ Customer's name and I.D. number (if applicable)

▶ Billing address

▶ Ship-to address (if different)

▶ Customer's phone and fax numbers

▶ Indication of how long the quote will be honored

▶ FOB point (explained below)

▶ Payment terms

▶ Shipping method (as requested by the customer)

▶ Scheduled shipping or installation date

▶ Quantity of goods to be shipped (if applicable)

▶ Identifying product numbers (if applicable)

119

▶ Complete description of product or service

▶ Sales price per unit and extended total price

▶ Applicable tax amounts (with identification)

▶ Product limited warranty and warranty period

▶ Warranty remedies reserved to the seller

▶ Disclaimer of other or implied warranties

▶ Deposits or down payments required

An explanation of the *FOB point* is warranted. FOB means "free on board," an old term referring to being put on the ship, truck, or train. The FOB point is the *point at which title to the product is transferred from the seller to the buyer* and an indication of who will be responsible for shipping charges.

Typical FOB points include:

▶ **FOB plant or warehouse.** Buyer pays the freight from seller's plant or warehouse to the ship-to address.

▶ **FOB destination (customer ship-to address).** Seller pays the freight from seller's plant or warehouse to the ship-to address.

▶ **FAS (free alongside ship, seaport identified).** Seller pays the freight from seller's plant or warehouse to the seaport dock.

What is most vital about the sales quotation is that there be an absolute understanding between the buyer and the seller with regard to the nature of the product or service and what it is designed to do.

What is most vital about the sales quotation is that there be an *absolute understanding* between the buyer and the seller with regard to the nature of the product or service and what it is designed to do. Failure to achieve this understanding leads to disputes, unpaid bills, and sometimes the loss of customers.

Once all of the information is generated to prepare the *sales quotation*, it is reasonable to store that information so that it can be used again to generate the *sales order* and, later, to prepare the *sales invoice*. It is for this reason that many order entry and billing systems are integrated and performed by a computer. Even if the sales order is typed, proper design can eliminate the retyping of much of the same information to generate the sales invoice. Only additional information need be entered, such as customer purchase order number, ship date, and payment due date. You should investigate the automated accounting systems referred to earlier and/or consult your CPA to achieve the simplest and most appropriate system for your business.

Production Scheduling and Inventory Control

Several years ago, I visited with a small business owner (a manufacturer) who was complaining about having to build a 25,000-square-foot addition to his plant to accommodate the *ever-increasing amount of inventory*. Already in debt to the bank by nearly a million dollars, he did not look forward to increasing his obligation but believed there was no alternative.

I toured his plant and found an unbelievable amount of work-in-process inventory represented by *many skids of partially completed assemblies and subassemblies* of products being manufactured. A closer investigation of the paperwork supporting these items revealed that the work orders had all been issued within one to two weeks of each other about three to four months earlier. I asked when these items would be needed for the final assembly and learned that the *final assembly process was not scheduled for at least four to five weeks*!

Guess what? The small business owner didn't need to add to his plant and to his bank debt. *He needed a production scheduling system!* When the order for 120 of the finished product was issued to the floor, all work orders for all components, assemblies, and subassemblies were issued too. *Just the opposite of "just in time."*

The rest of the story is much better. After installing a simple but effective production scheduling system, the business owner had a great deal of *extra floor space* and about *$300,000 less in inventory*—and *within 18 months the bank debt was all repaid*. This real-life experience clearly illustrates the critical need for good production scheduling. You must remember that:

This book does not provide a detailed explanation of production scheduling and inventory control systems. There are many books that describe such systems thoroughly. However, I do want to emphasize their importance in providing *maximum customer service*, *minimum inventory investment*, and *efficient operations*.

> "Work expands to fill the time available for its completion."
> —C. Northcote Parkinson

> "Inventory expands to fill the plant or warehouse space available."
> —Unknown business owner

A common problem in achieving these three objectives is that they are often viewed as being in conflict with each other. Maximum customer service can always be achieved if inventories are maintained at high levels *and* if the plant is flexible in providing changes to production schedules to meet customer demand.

If you are the sales manager, this sounds great! If you are responsible for minimizing the investment in inventory or if you are the plant manager trying to develop efficient, low-cost manufacturing methods, this approach is no doubt frustrating. Production scheduling and inventory control is all about reconciling these objectives in the most profitable manner, consistent with maintaining a satisfied customer base.

Production scheduling and inventory control is obviously different for the job shop that manufactures to specific customer orders and for the company that continually manufactures to specified inventory levels. Regardless of the type of manufacturing, however, it is important to recognize that *production scheduling and inventory control are not separable functions.* Only where the product is purchased, placed in inventory, and then sold to the customer is inventory control a separate function. This would be the case in a retailing operation.

*R*egardless of the type of manufacturing, however, it is important to recognize that production scheduling and inventory control are not separable functions.

Production scheduling systems are clearly important for small businesses that manufacture a product, differing from plant to plant and industry to industry. As a result, the next few pages may be of interest only to small manufacturers. However, the *elements that are typically required* to make these systems work do have applicability to some contracting types of businesses. *(Those in retailing or pure service organizations, please bear with us or skip ahead.)*

1. Sales forecast. This is the same forecast, developed by the sales manager, that should have been used in preparing the current year's plan and determining the next two or three years' long-term business plan. This forecast must be in sufficient detail to enable the plant or production manager, with the aid of some production scheduling personnel, to develop a production plan.

2. Production plan. This plan "denotes what is to be produced monthly for each major product group. The plan sets the overall operating rate of the plant and determines the operating levels of major machines and the labor force requirements."[1] It should be noted that a sales forecast and production plan are needed even if the small business manufactures to customer order rather than to inventory. They are even needed in a nonmanufacturing business, such as a contracting business, whether or not it involves a product that is inventoried.

3. Master production schedule. This schedule is a detailed rendition of what the plant is expected to produce, in specific product types, colors, or finishes. It originates from a backlog of customer orders (in a typical custom manufacturing job shop) or a detailed sales forecast of individual product units or SKUs (stock-keeping units) in a production shop. The master production schedule must include the timing of the production of SKUs and, as such, when coordinated with bills of materials for the various products to be produced, it enables the preparation of a *material requirements plan* (MRP).

4. Bills of material. For each product or product component, there is a document, called a *bill of material*, that typically includes a part number, a description, a make-or-buy indicator, the quantity of various materials required per each unit (product or component), and a code that represents the level of the particular bill. For example, a level-one bill denotes a component at the lowest level of production, with no other components included within it. A level-two bill might represent an assembly that includes one or more level-one components plus some materials required to put them all together. The various levels continue to pyramid until the final level is the product itself. Depending upon the product and type of manufacturing, many other codes may be included on the bill, such as where-used information (the components on which this particular component is used), and a commodity code (indicating whether the component's materials are steel, hardware, chemicals, electrical, etc.).

5. Routing or operations sheet. This document lists all of the operations (sequential steps) necessary to manufacture the particular component, with a description of each operation. The routing sheet can include varying amounts of information, including time estimates (for setup and running), tooling requirements, machine assignments, machine feed and speed rates, and type of labor or operators required.

6. Production and backlog reports. These documents compare actual production performance with the plans and schedules. They must be generated on a timely basis and can be as simple as those discussed in the section on accounting or as complicated as those presented in various production and inventory control texts. The fundamental objective is still the same: to compare how well the company is performing relative to its plan and, if deviations occur, to provide information that will enable corrections to be made in an expedient manner.

7. Inventory management reports. Information relative to economic order points (EOP) and economic order quantities (EOQ), if required, may be integrated into the total system. It is important to know in advance, for planned production levels, how much raw material must be purchased, when, and at what price (preferably). It is also important to schedule the receipt of materials so as to avoid an excessive investment in inventory. This objective is partly what gave rise to just-in-time inventory management techniques.

As you can see, the subject of *production and inventory control* (PIC) can be very complicated. PIC involves assigning quantitative measures to a sound sales and production plan with controls that measure and report deviations from that plan with timely frequency. The good news is that there are computerized programs (software) available to help simplify the PIC function and professionals who are experienced in installing them. These systems, under various names and in varying forms, involve the basics of *computer-integrated manufacturing* (CIM). The CIM approach (or its equivalent) helps control and monitor the entire process, from product development and raw materials to the saleable goods that must be produced at the lowest possible cost and delivered to the customer in the shortest time.

If your business is involved in manufacturing, I believe that the PIC area is important and justifies the assistance of professional experts, either from your CPA firm (if they are qualified) or from consulting organizations.

If your business is involved in manufacturing, I believe that the PIC area is important and justifies the assistance of professional experts, either from your CPA firm (if they are qualified) or from consulting organizations. Sit down and discuss your operation with at least three reputable professional organizations and ask for their suggestions. That discussion will no doubt result in proposals from those firms to help you develop and install a PIC program. Give it some thought; if you engage a professional firm, it may be one of the best expenditures you could make. And remember: *nothing good is ever free!*

> **Warning!** Do not accept a plan that requires too much sophistication initially. Learn to walk before trying to run. Some professionals who are intimately familiar with PIC tend to oversimplify the problems, time, and cost involved in implementing a sound PIC system.
>
> My experience is that it requires twice as much time as planned to implement the system and, frequently, twice the estimated cost. Proceed cautiously!

Quality Control

In addition to having customers, one of the most important elements in business, large or small, is *the ability to provide a quality product or service*. The automobile manufacturers in the United States were taught this lesson so forcefully that they would probably like to forget it! Price is important, but without quality the sales incentive of low price is of a very short duration. It is easy to think about quality in familiar terms:

- ▶ Most of us avoid a repeat visit to a steak house where the steak is tough, even if the price is right.
- ▶ We probably don't rehire the services of a cheap plumber if he can't fix the leaks.
- ▶ Few of us would buy another car of the same make as the lemon we just got rid of.

A major company, Caterpillar, was featured in an article in *Fortune* magazine, which stated, "The company's operating principles seem to be an individual version of the Boy Scout law: the main principles are excellence of quality, reliability of performance, and loyalty in dealer relationships."[2] Maytag built its reputation on dependability and its ads still depict a repairman with nothing to do.

There have been at least three quality "gurus," according to Steven Silbiger, *The Ten-Day MBA*[3]: Joseph Juran, W. Edwards Deming, and Philip Crosby. Juran used the phrase "Consumers should be able to count on the product for what they need or want to do with it." Deming was the instigator of quality for the Japanese way back in the 1950s, who believed that quality could be achieved by identifying production problems early and monitoring production to prevent those errors as early as possible. Crosby proclaimed. "Quality is free," believing that if manufacturers improve quality, total production costs would be reduced. Whichever guru you favor, the indisputable fact is that *quality sells ... and at a higher price!*

Probably the best references on quality control come from the International Organization for Standardization (ISO). This organization was involved in the development of the original standards (American National Standards) for quality management and quality assurance, publishing documents for the selection and use of the standards, a definition of the elements, and guidelines for the standards and models for companies desiring to implement the standards. You have probably heard of the ISO 9000 program and its antecedents and the associated difficulties and benefits of implementing those standards. It is not necessary that small businesses comply with these standards, unless their major customers require it. However, the information contained in these documents, which have been adopted by the American National Standards Institute (ANSI), is excellent and forms a sound basis for quality management and control systems for any company. The documents referred to are available from the International Organization

125

for Standardization. You can view a listing of these publications and others on these web sites: www.iso.org, www.asq.com, and www.ansi.org.

Our emphasis in this section of the book is to help you better understand and evaluate the principles upon which standards of quality can be built for your small business. Stated below are the eight principles embodied in becoming certified within the parameters of ISO 9000:2000, from the document *Quality Management Principles*.[4] These principles are even more than a guide to quality; they are a guide to a sound business organization. If they seem basic, it is because *they are!*

Principle 1: Customer Focus
Organizations depend on their customers and therefore should understand current and future customer needs, should meet customer requirements, and strive to exceed customer expectations.

Principle 2: Leadership
Leaders establish unity of purpose and direction of the organization. They should create and maintain the internal environment in which people can become fully involved in achieving the organization's objectives.

Principle 3: Involvement of People
People at all levels are the essence of an organization and their full involvement enables their abilities to be used for the organization's benefit.

Principle 4: Process Approach
A desired result is achieved more efficiently when activities and related resources are managed as a process.

Principle 5: System Approach to Management
Identifying, understanding, and managing interrelated processes as a system contributes to the organization's effectiveness and efficiency in achieving its objectives.

Principle 6: Continual Improvement
Continual improvement of the organization's overall performance should be a permanent objective of the organization.

Principle 7: Factual Approach to Decision Making
Effective decisions are based on the analysis of data and information.

Principle 8: Mutually Beneficial Supplier Relationships
An organization and its suppliers are interdependent and a mutually beneficial relationship enhances the ability of both to create value.

These eight principles form the basis for companies seeking ISO 9000-type certification. But as you sit back and think about them, they really make good business sense and form a guideline for the quality control system in your company.

If you think about them *carefully*, they can apply to a pizza parlor, a lawnmower manufacturer, a general contractor, a corner drugstore, a dentist, a *Fortune* 500 company that is global in scope, ... and many others!

Notes

1. Greene, James H. *Production and Inventory Control Handbook*, 2nd edition. McGraw-Hill Book Co., 1987.

2. Peters, Thomas J., and Waterman, Jr., Robert H. *In Search of Excellence: Lessons from America's Best-Run Companies*. Warner Books, 1982.

3. Silbiger, Steven Alan. *The Ten-Day MBA: A Step-by-Step Guide to Mastering the Skills Taught in America's Top Business Schools*. Quill/William Morrow and Company, 1993.

4. International Organization for Standardization. *Quality Management Principles*. www.iso.org/iso/en/iso9000-14000/iso9000/qmp.html.

Chapter 15

Your CPA Firm

THE CHAPTER TITLE IMPLIES THAT WE BELIEVE YOUR BUSINESS SHOULD be served by a CPA firm. The implication is correct. There are many benefits to be derived from a relationship with a CPA firm, especially with someone in the firm at the partnership level. In this chapter, we will discuss the selection of a CPA firm, what the relationship should involve, and the benefits that we believe will accrue.

Selecting a CPA Firm

CPA firms come in all sizes with a variety of credentials. The selection process can be as interesting as it is rewarding. Unless you already know of a firm or a partner in a firm in whom you have confidence, one of the best ways to select a firm is to consult with your attorney or your banker. They will know about many of the firms and may also know some of the higher-ranking individuals in those firms. You should ask them for the names of *three firms* that they would recommend that have offices in the geographical area in which your business is headquartered. If they are unable to provide three names (unlikely), consult other businesspeople for their recommendations.

The size of the firm and its local office may be an important consideration. Although individual CPA practitioners often have as much skill and experience as partners in larger firms, their firms may not be able to offer all of the services needed for your company. Those services could include annual audits, tax return preparation, guidance in areas of computer technology, accounting systems design and implementation, assistance in the development of production scheduling, and inventory management and quality control systems. Larger firms, whether international in scope—such as Deloitte Touche Tohmatsu, Ernst & Young, PricewaterhouseCoopers, or KPMG—or medium-sized regional firms, will have professionals on their staffs who are experienced and specialize in many of these disciplines. Your goal is not to pick the largest or smallest, but rather to pick a firm that *offers the services you need* and promises a *relationship with a partner* in that firm who can serve as a sounding board for many of your business decisions.

After you receive references for three firms, invite their representatives individually to *visit your business* and discuss the services they can provide. These representatives should want a *tour* of your business facilities and evidence an interest in understanding the nature of your business. Determine how comfortable you are with the partner who would be assigned responsibility for your company as a client. The client partner will be the one you call when you have a question involving general business matters, taxation, audits, fees, and various services that may be needed. You must be very comfortable in dealing with this individual or the total relationship will not be successful.

After the initial meeting, each firm (at its own cost) should want to study your business further, including your accounting system and other control systems that are in place. Welcome them to learn as much as they require and meet with them as many times as necessary to enable your selection. The more informed they are, the better the relationship will be. Before you select the firm for your business, you should have a good idea of the services that your business will need. After you have determined which firms and representatives offer a relationship with which you will be comfortable, you should ask them to provide you with a firm quotation. The quotation is usually in the form of a proposal letter, which identifies the services they will provide for the ensuing year. The proposal letter should spell out clearly *what they will do, when they will do it,* and the *proposed fees* for such services.

The fees for any type of work provided by a CPA firm are based on the hourly billing rates of the personnel working on the engagement. Like your doctor or attorney, the partners' fees are in excess of $100 per hour and, in some locations, several hundred dollars per hour. The staff rates can vary

After you receive references for three firms, invite their representatives individually to visit your business and discuss the services they can provide.

129

from $50 per hour to more than $100 per hour. That is why most of the detail work is done by staff.

In all cases, however, the CPA firm should be willing to disclose its billing rates and give you a firm quotation for the work being done. Swallow hard and use them wisely! A *good* CPA is akin to a good doctor, but just in another line of work.

In the next few sections, we will discuss the services that we believe are appropriate for a small business and the reasons for such recommendations. The final selection of the firm will depend upon your comfort level with the professionals who propose to serve you, especially the client partner.

To Audit or Not to Audit: That Is the Question

Unless your company is small, under six people, and you do not anticipate it growing to more than ten employees, you likely do not need to have an annual audit.

Unless your company is small, under six people, and you do not anticipate it growing to more than ten employees, you likely do not need to have an annual audit. Quite often companies of this size consist of the owner, who runs the business; his wife or her husband, who keeps the accounting records; and other family members, all of whom are presumably competent and trustworthy.

If your firm has at least six members or your plans are for it to grow well beyond that level, you will need good accounting and control systems, maintained by persons who are trained in those areas. In this case, you need to have an annual audit, and here's why.

▶ An audit helps those responsible for the accounting and control systems to *keep current in their technical knowledge* of those systems.

▶ An annual examination of the financial statements *helps avoid unwanted surprises* of an accounting nature that can devastate a small business, such as discussed in previous chapters.

▶ Audited financial statements are essential in *helping obtain financing from banks or other financial institutions* and in obtaining credit from major suppliers. Small businesses that provide audited financial statements are *viewed as being well-managed and professional* in their approach to business.

▶ Audits help the client partner more fully understand the operations of your small business and *be better able to provide sound business advice* and counsel.

▶ As discussed later in this book, there will likely be an ultimate need for the major owner to attract other shareholders, take the business public, or retire and sell the business. Audited financials can be a major factor in being able to *successfully achieve* any of *these objectives*.

▶ An audit, although not intended to uncover fraudulent activities on the part of employees or associates, is certainly a deterrent and in many ways provides *peace of mind* to the small business owner.

There may be other compelling reasons for having an annual audit of the financial statements of the small business, but in our opinion these alone are sufficient. I began a company with just six employees and the benefits of having audited financial statements were immense. The respect received from the banker when seeking long-term financing, the ease with which the statements facilitated key leasing transactions, and the peace of mind among shareholders was more than enough reward for the time and fees involved. The fees for an audit are based on the CPA firm's estimate of the hours required and the personnel staffing on the job. Expect a few thousand dollars (more in most big-city locations) for an audit performed by a quality firm.

Tax Matters ... You Don't Have Time to Learn!

Whether the small businessperson decides to have an annual audit of his or her company's financial statements, he or she *must* use a competent CPA firm to advise on tax matters and to prepare the various tax returns demanded by all the governmental agencies. Keeping up with all of the tax laws is a full-time activity, even within CPA firms. Although the audit personnel are expected to maintain a working knowledge of income tax matters, it is the tax partner or manager who provides the in-depth tax advice and reviews all of the tax returns. Small business owners who themselves are CPAs (including this author) are the first to acknowledge that the task of keeping up with the tax laws is not only impractical but also detracts from the main thrust of their business.

The tax departments of CPA firms are well versed in all types of taxation, including income taxes at the federal and state level, payroll taxes, personal property taxes, and estate taxes. Their fee pales when compared with the savings that they can provide businesses by counseling and planning for the legal avoidance of taxes, in addition to the competent preparation of

Whether the small businessperson decides to have an annual audit of his or her company's financial statements, he or she must use a competent CPA firm to advise on tax matters and to prepare the various tax returns demanded by all the governmental agencies.

131

required tax returns. Whatever work they propose to do they should support with a proposal letter and a *fee quotation*. Sometimes fees can escalate when they are not agreed upon upfront.

Other Benefits of a CPA Relationship

In addition to the factors already discussed, there are a number of other ways in which a good CPA firm can be of benefit to a small business. In your selection process, you might inquire if the firms making proposals offer these types of services. The following listing could serve as a good checklist in making your final CPA firm selection. Your business may never need many of these types of assistance, but the CPA firm you select should be able to assist in most of these areas:

- ▶ Preparation of a business plan
- ▶ Personnel organization structures and planning
- ▶ Economic feasibility studies
- ▶ Mergers and acquisitions
- ▶ Compensation policies and planning
- ▶ Salary and wage administration programs
- ▶ Incentive compensation plans
- ▶ Deferred compensation plans
- ▶ Stock option plans (including phantom stock plans)
- ▶ Profit-sharing and retirement plans
- ▶ Policy manuals and employee handbooks
- ▶ Computer accounting system design and installation
- ▶ Computer equipment and software evaluation
- ▶ Production scheduling and inventory control systems
- ▶ Material handling systems
- ▶ Marketing planning and strategy
- ▶ Marketing compensation plans
- ▶ Pricing policies and practices
- ▶ Credit and collection policies and procedures
- ▶ Cash management systems
- ▶ Forms and records design

▶ Records retention programs

The list is rather imposing, but there are many good CPA firms that are able to assist in most of these areas. Many of the larger firms have split off their management consulting departments into a separate firm with a different name. The audit and tax firm may well recommend the consulting organization, but the split has been needed to avoid an apparent or real conflict of interest in serving their clients.

Working with Your CPA Firm

Assuming that you have decided to select a CPA firm and its fees have not scared you away, here are some suggestions on how to work with that firm.

1. Become well acquainted with your client partner. He is the one you will contact on most matters. He also has considerable background and experience. Yes, the hourly fee is eye-watering, but so it is with your doctor and your attorney. These professionals don't need a lot of time and research to provide assistance and counsel. Frankly, if they are good at what they do and care about your business, they are worth what they charge.

You should be able to discuss your company's business with your client partner without reservation. He can help in financing matters, direct you to his tax partner for competent tax advice, and provide counsel regarding other services that you may need in developing your small business.

2. Don't overuse the CPA firm's staff. These are less experienced personnel who often lack the background to provide answers without considerable research. They are well trained in conducting an audit, preparing tax returns, or assisting in the implementation of systems. They should not be used to *do* much of the implementation work, only to guide and direct.

3. Use a tax partner for estate planning. It is never too early to consider plans for business succession and estate matters. CPA firm tax partners are well suited to provide essential assistance in these areas. They will likely want to consult with your attorney on such matters as wills and trust documents.

Business succession is another issue that requires long-term planning. It is often more difficult to effectively remove yourself from your business than it was to get into the business. In the last chapter of this book, some ideas are presented relative to exiting the business without sacrificing either your net worth or your desires for the perpetuation of the business, if that is your choice.

4. Use your CPA firm to help with business contacts. The client and tax partners of your CPA firm typically have relationships with many businesses, both large and small. As a result, they can help you make contact with key personnel in these companies; such contacts are usually with higher-level executives. The ability to discuss various issues with other top-level businesspeople and other professionals can often benefit your company in several ways. Sometimes these contacts help develop a new customer relationship, an association with a new supplier, and, most often, a fruitful exchange of business information with other business owners.

In conclusion, your relationship with key partners in a well-rounded CPA firm can be most helpful in achieving your business objectives.

Your banker, your attorney, your insurance broker, and your CPA are all key resources that you must cultivate.

Chapter 16

Why You Need an Attorney

ONE OF THE INEQUITIES IN OWNING AND MANAGING A SMALL BUSIness (as compared with large corporations) is the lack of availability of an in-house legal staff to sift through the maze of laws and legal issues that confront business. Moreover, it seems with every passing year there are more and more laws and regulations that businesses of all sizes must consider. How does a small business deal with this issue? You need a solid relationship with a good corporate attorney.

There are many areas of business that are influenced by legal issues. These areas include:

▶ The *legal formation* of the business entity

▶ Legal issues involving all types of *business contracts*

▶ Laws governing the *hiring, treatment, and safety of employees* (see Chapter 4)

▶ State and federal laws governing *environmental issues* and the disposal of waste products

▶ *Tax laws*, other than income and payroll tax, including real estate and personal property laws

135

▶ State and federal laws affording protection to the *rights of consumers*, including credit issues

▶ Legal issues involving the *sale of company stock or other securities*

▶ *Estate and inheritance laws* relating to exiting business

▶ Laws governing *licenses and permits*

▶ Laws enabling the *protection of intellectual property*, including laws and regulations governing patents, trademarks, and copyrights.

In addition to dealing directly with the legal issues, your attorney can be of considerable assistance in the negotiation of important contracts, working in the background to provide you with prior experience he or she may have had in similar situations.

Formation and Maintenance of the Business Entity

Forming your business requires selecting the most appropriate form of legal entity for the business. Your attorney will help you select from several options, including the limited liability company (LLC), limited liability partnership (LLP), sole proprietorship, or the most commonly selected form, the corporation. He or she will explain the advantages and disadvantages of each.

If you have chosen the corporate form of legal entity, your attorney can help you prepare the *articles of incorporation* and *bylaws;* if you have selected an LLC, he can help formulate the *articles of organization;* or, if a partnership is selected, he will help write your *partnership agreement.* If your company is a corporation, the preparation and issuance of *stock certificates* and maintenance of a *stock ledger* are other matters in which you should involve your attorney. He can also provide guidance in developing the format for the *agendas for shareholder and directors meetings* and can advise you in preparing the *minutes* of these meetings and maintaining a *minute book.* Your attorney can also assist in obtaining federal and state (if applicable) *employer ID numbers.*

Incidentally, if you decide to form an LLC, in most states it is quite simple and the necessary forms can be downloaded from the Secretary of State or Corporation Commission web site. If you choose to do it yourself, I recommend that you have a SCORE® counselor or a representative of the local SBDC (Small Business Development Center) office review it. If they believe you need further legal assistance, they will so advise.

In addition to dealing directly with the legal issues, your attorney can be of considerable assistance in the negotiation of important contracts, working in the background to provide you with prior experience he or she may have had in similar situations.

136

Contractual Matters

There is a wide array of contracts in which your business will likely become involved. Contracts for *acquiring property*, *leasing equipment*, *borrowing money*, *selling products*, *buying materials*, *warranties for your products*, and the *employment* of key employees are but a few. All of these contracts must be *legally enforceable*. All but the employment contract need to be in compliance with the *Uniform Commercial Code* (UCC) and all should contain nothing that could later prove to be injurious to your company.

Earlier reference was made to the Robinson-Patman Act. This law, passed in 1936, is still in full force and effect and relates to discrimination in price, services, or facilities in the conduct of your business. Basically, it prevents the sale of large quantities of product to a buyer at a preferred price unless that price can be substantiated by proven cost savings relating to greater production runs or purchasing benefits. You should be aware of the provisions of this law and others affecting the conduct of your normal business transactions. Your attorney should assist you in this matter.

You should have your attorney review the contracts referred to above, as well as many of your business forms, before you execute the contracts and use the forms. Finally, he or she should be sufficiently knowledgeable of your business to help you avoid *product liability* issues that could result in sizeable lawsuits. You should discuss all of these issues with your attorney and follow his or her advice.

Your attorney be sufficiently knowledgeable of your business to help you avoid product liability *issues that could result in sizeable lawsuits.*

Employment Laws

As discussed in Chapter 4, the laws concerning the *hiring*, *firing*, and *treatment of employees* are many and complicated. Even the preparation of your company's *personnel manual* and related *forms* involves compliance with these laws. Your attorney needs to be involved in these issues, reviewing your company's forms and documents, when applicable, and available to consult with you on personnel matters having legal importance.

Environmental and Safety Issues

Federal and state governments have passed laws and regulations that are designed to protect the public in general and employees in the workplace from hazards to their *safety* and *health*. The Occupational Safety and Health

Administration (OSHA), under the jurisdiction of the U.S. Department of Labor, has issued standards involving a variety of issues, including *hazard communication*, *fire*, and *mechanical safety*. Additional federal legislation involves *emergency planning notification*, *community right-to-know* reporting, and *toxic chemical storage* and *release* reporting. These and other environmental issues may require the involvement of your attorney, if only in a counseling mode.

Tax Laws

Either your CPA or your attorney needs to be available to offer advice on matters relating to *sales* and *use tax*, *real estate*, *personal property,* and other forms of taxation, in addition to income and payroll taxes.

Consumer Laws

Federal and state governments have enacted many laws that afford protection to customers from *misleading advertising*, *bogus products* or *services*, *mail fraud*, and *product liability*. Some of these laws also contain requirements for what must be stated and what should not be stated in a consumer contract. Often the *product liability* matters involve the warranty of the product or service and can become very costly to any size of business. No one is apt to forget the Ford-Firestone tire recall issue involving millions of dollars of presumably faulty tires. There was a whole army of attorneys involved in that matter.

*U*nfortunately, we live in a society where many believe someone else is responsible for all of their misfortunes and hire lawyers to sue for large sums of money, regardless of where the fault lies.

Even on a smaller scale, problems can arise involving customers that require consultation with your attorney. Don't forget the McDonald's "hot coffee" incident followed by the "hot pickle" accident. In each case, McDonald's was sued for large amounts of money because the customer claimed severe physical and psychological damages from spilling hot coffee and eating a hot pickle. These matters were not inconsequential to McDonald's (the franchisor) or the McDonald's franchisee, a small business owner. Unfortunately, we live in a society where many believe someone else is responsible for all of their misfortunes and hire lawyers to sue for large sums of money, regardless of where the fault lies. You will have to protect your interest with your own attorney.

Licenses and Permits

Your attorney should make you aware of the licenses and permits that are required for your business. Although you can obtain information about these items from the state Office of Small Businesses (or similar title), chambers of commerce, or city government offices, it is good insurance to have your attorney review the requirements with you. Many types of professional firms, service organizations, and small businesses involved in the sale of certain products (firearms, liquor, food, gasoline, tobacco, and more) require certification, licenses, or permits. Make sure that you meet the requirements for your business.

Securities Laws

The issuance and sale of the common stock or securities of your company to a limited number of persons (in what is referred to as a "private placement") may allow an exemption from the more onerous provisions of federal and state securities laws. This is especially true if the investors are considered to be sufficiently sophisticated to understand the potential financial risks inherent in the investment.

You should always consult your attorney before considering issuing securities of your company.

However, you should *always* consult your attorney *before* considering issuing securities of your company, whether stock, warrants, notes, stock options, profit participation agreements, or other instruments representing a security interest in your company. He or she will tell you about the securities laws and if they apply to your proposed transaction.

Under no circumstance do you need to be the target of the Securities and Exchange Commission, the governmental body that monitors compliance with federal securities laws!

Protection of Intellectual Property

Intellectual property can include a wide variety of creative or unique works that are original with you or your company, such as an invention, a unique word or symbol, a literary work (such as an article or book), a dramatic and/or musical composition, or an artistic rendering. Under certain conditions, your right to the exclusive rewards from such works is protected by federal patent, trademark, and copyright laws.

Patents. A patent for an invention is the grant of a property right to the invention, issued by the U.S. Patent and Trademark Office, that is valid for 20 years from the date of the application filing. The patent excludes others from "making, using, offering for sale, or selling" the invention in the United States or "importing" the invention into the United States. You should note that a patent secured from the U.S. Patent Office *does not cover the use of your technology in foreign countries*. You will need to apply for patents in those countries as well.

If you have a patent pending, you should use the words "patent pending" on your potentially protected products; if you have a patent, the notification on each product should include the patent number on your protected items, such as *U.S. Patent No. 1,234,567*.

Trademark or Service Mark. A trademark is a word, name, symbol, or device that is used in trade with goods to indicate the source of the goods and to distinguish them from the goods of others. A service mark is exactly the same as a trademark except that it is for services, not goods. Examples of trademarks are brand names that identify a product, a logo, or other qualifying items and differentiate that item from any manufactured or sold by other businesses. Typically these items are so identified by a TM next to the name. An example might be CompactFlash™.

If the item being protected is a service and not a good, it is identified by a SM next to the name. Examples of service marks include **Rock of Gibraltar**SM (service mark of Prudential Insurance Co.) and **Greyhound**SM (service mark of Greyhound Bus Lines).

A trademark does not need to be registered with the U.S. Patent Office. However, federal registration has several advantages, including notice to the public of the registrant's claim of ownership of the mark, a legal presumption of ownership nationwide, and the exclusive right to use the mark on or in connection with the goods or services set forth in the registration.

If a trademark or service mark is registered, the designation to the public changes to the symbol ® next to the name. Examples of registered trademarks include Microsoft®, Adobe®, and Coca-Cola®. Note that, to remain valid, an affidavit of use must be filed both between the fifth and sixth years following registration and within the year before the end of every ten-year period after the date of registration. Check with your patent attorney for further details.

Copyright. A copyright is a form of protection for dramatic, musical, artistic, and certain other intellectual works. This protection is available to both published and unpublished works. The duration of the protection, if created on or after January 1, 1978, is from the moment of its creation and enduring the author's life plus an additional 70 years beyond his or her death. Similar to trademarks, copyrights do not need to be registered and the symbol © may be used to identify any creation eligible for copyright protection. However, registration provides significant additional protection to the author, including the right to sue for infringement (a right not accorded an unregistered copyright). Examples of copyrights include the following books: *Good to Great* © 2001 and *In Search of Excellence* © 1982. You will note that the symbol © and the date of the creation of the work must appear on the document and on this book as well.

However, registration provides significant additional protection to the author, including the right to sue for infringement (a right not accorded an unregistered copyright).

If you would like to learn more about patent and copyright law (and are not ready to pay a patent attorney to learn), go to the following web sites: www.uspto.gov (for patents and trademarks) and www.copyright.gov (for copyrights). The world of patent and copyright law is indeed unique and different and you will find that attorneys will specialize in this field to the exclusion of other fields of law. Your corporate attorney should be able to refer you to a patent attorney, should the need arise.

Litigation

Unfortunately, if a person is in business long enough, he or she is likely to do something or overlook doing something that will result in the business being sued or at least threatened with being summoned to court to answer a complaint. Court is a foreign environment to most businesspeople and evokes a fear of the unknown. At the very least, legal controversy distracts the business owner from the main thrust of his operations. It is not only helpful but also comforting, in this situation, to have available an attorney with whom you already have a good relationship and who is familiar with your business.

There may also be occasions in which you find that a supplier, a customer, a competitor, or even an employee has broken a contractual commitment to your company. In some cases, it may be sufficiently serious that you may want to know whether holding him accountable in court is an appropriate and available option. A good corporate attorney who is affiliated with other attorneys having proven litigation skills affords some security and protection for the small business.

Hopefully, these pages have convinced you that having a relationship with a good corporate attorney who is familiar with your business is crucial.

Unfortunately, many if not most small businesses do not have such a relationship and this has come back to haunt them. Good professionals are not inexpensive and attorneys are no exception. Their fees parallel those of the partner in a CPA firm or your doctor.

If you apply to your attorney the guidelines discussed for fee arrangements with your CPA, you should be comfortable. Do not waste his or her time and your money discussing the World Series or your last golf game. The clock will be running!

You must discuss fees upfront and a good attorney should understand the financial problems involved in developing a small business. In most cases, he or she will be reasonable in his or her fee schedule. Attorneys also know that small businesses grow up to be big businesses!

Legal Self-Help

There are some free sources of help regarding legal issues that are worthy of mention. Nolo Press has published books on legal matters but also has a very good web site: *www.nolo.com*. Here answers to many legal questions can be found.

Another source of legal information is located in the Small Business Administration's web site for legal and regulatory information: *www.business-law.gov*. This site is especially aimed at problems confronting small businesses.

I want to emphasize that sources such as these are not substitutes for a good attorney. They are, however, helpful in acquainting you with the background legal information that could prove helpful when you do contact your attorney.

Chapter 17

Involve an Insurance Broker

BECAUSE MY SMALL BUSINESS WAS FRIVOLOUSLY SUED BY A LARGER competitor for misleading advertising involving our respective products, my appreciation for good insurance brokers and insurers is significant. My insurance broker had placed the liability coverage with one of the best casualty insurance companies in the world and, after a countersuit by the law firm my insurer provided, the competitor dropped the case. The best part: my coverage included paying for my legal assistance from the first dollar of fees! My case rests!

So far we have determined that you need a good banker, an attorney (unless you are one), and a CPA (even if you are one!). The final professional needed is a good insurance broker. Because there are areas of specialization in the insurance field, we describe the need as an *independent insurance broker* who is familiar with all forms of insurance that may be required for a small business and can and should obtain competitive quotes from several insurance companies for those coverages.

In the past, and in some states still, brokers who performed this service may have been called *insurance agents*. Now, however, insurance agents typically represent one insurance company in a specialized field. When health insurance or other specialized types of insurance is needed, your insurance broker will likely refer you to an agent who deals primarily in that field of insurance coverage.

143

There are many forms of insurance that are essential for a small business and many are governed by laws, rules, and regulations, both at the federal and state levels. In addition, you will want to have competitive bids from various companies that offer these forms of insurance. A good insurance professional will know what you need and will also know where to find good companies that offer those coverages. The best part is that you don't have to pay this professional directly; he or she is paid by the companies providing the coverage. As you work with your broker, be sure to have him or her *explain fully (for each type of insurance) why you need the coverage and how you should determine the amount of coverage required.*

The *Small Business Kit for Dummies*[1] states that "estimates show that 80% of small businesses either do not have as much insurance as they should or they have the wrong kind of insurance." A good reason for having a *good* insurance broker!

The task of finding a good insurance broker is similar to that of finding a CPA firm or an attorney. Find the names of two or three brokers from business friend, your bank, or others. Interview each and ask for references from current clients and call them. Your "due diligence" will pay off!

Types of Insurance

Because of the many types of insurance that your small business may need, it is important to educate your broker about your business operation.

Because of the many types of insurance that your small business may need, it is important to educate your broker about your business operation. He or she will be in a better position to recommend the appropriate types of coverage for your company if he or she understands your business. It is no surprise that the coverage needed for a pizza parlor will differ substantially from that required for a dentist or a small manufacturing company.

Property Damage Insurance

This type of insurance is likely the most familiar to small businesspeople. It protects your business against loss from fire, accidents, theft, wind, and other catastrophes. The covered items include buildings, furniture and fixtures, machinery and equipment, and similar types of property.

You can cover the property for its *actual cash value*, which is the cost to replace the lost items less an allowance for depreciation, or for *replacement cost*, which does not include a deduction for depreciation. Obviously the replacement cost approach is more expensive, but it fully returns the value of the damaged property to the company.

Your broker may recommend that the cost of replacement coverage premiums be reduced by accepting a *higher deductible*, an amount that you will have to pay before the insurance coverage begins. At least the amount of the deductible is a known value and one that you can live with in case of loss.

Liability Insurance

In today's world, this may be the most important of the various types of insurance that a small business requires. There are many lawsuits filed against businesses of all sizes, with the potential for judgments that could bankrupt even a strong company. If someone slips on your front step, becomes disabled for life, and can prove even minor negligence on the part of your company, the resulting claim can be astronomical! Do not confuse this coverage with *product liability insurance*, which must be provided with a different type of policy.

Liability insurance is designed to protect your business from claims involving bodily injury to your employees, customers, and visitors. It also includes property damage that was caused by someone in your employ. Liability insurance also protects your business from claims resulting from misleading advertising or the infringement of patents or copyrights.

Liability insurance is designed to protect your business from claims involving bodily injury to your employees, customers, and visitors.

Business Interruption Insurance

This type of coverage complements the property damage insurance by covering the expenses (and profits lost) if your business is temporarily shut down (wholly or partially) by fire or other similar causes. This coverage is vital to the successful rebuilding of business operations and is a must for all small businesses that are exposed to the risks described.

Employment Practices Liability Insurance

This is another type of coverage that has evolved over the years from rarely needed to nearly mandatory. It seems that a day does not go by without an article in the newspaper about an employee who has filed a lawsuit against his or her employer for one or more of a variety of reasons, including being fired for inappropriate reasons or for being sexually harassed. This type of claim (or lawsuit), whether successful or not, is very damaging to a company (as discussed in Chapter 4) and the potential monetary damages can be very large.

Product Liability Insurance

Vital to businesses of all sizes, this type of policy protects the company against claims for injuries caused by its products. The past lawsuits against Ford Motor Company and Firestone Tire for liability involving deaths resulting from tire failure have resulted in claims in the billions of dollars. Your broker will be able to advise whether your products offer the types of risks that require this insurance. However, in our experience, some coverage of this type has proven to be much needed, regardless of the type of product being sold.

Other Insurance Types

Although those coverages listed above are perhaps the most commonly required types of insurance, in addition to health insurance, there are other types that may or may not be appropriate for your business. *Directors' and officers' liability insurance*, typically required for larger businesses, protects the directors and officers against losses incurred while functioning in those capacities for the company.

Professional organizations, such as doctors, dentists, accountants, and engineers, will need to consider *errors and omissions insurance,* which covers claims for malpractice or forms of negligence in providing their services. It is indeed unfortunate that litigation has forced the premiums for this type of insurance to unprecedented levels, resulting in medical care costs that are astronomical. The ultimate effect is that health care coverage for employees is nearly beyond the financial capabilities of small business.

We previously discussed *unemployment insurance*, required by federal and state laws, which covers employees who are terminated or laid off from their jobs. Everyone is familiar with the requirement for *automobile insurance* (also for trucks and other vehicles) that are used in connection with the business. Also mandated by law is *workers' compensation insurance,* which provides coverage for employees in the event of a work-related injury.

There is even *web site insurance,* which protects your company in the event someone claims some damage arising from your web site. More mature companies may wish to investigate the benefits of *key person insurance*, which is a form of life insurance covering the lives of key employees or owners of the business. Also available now is insurance that combines some of the coverages, such as casualty losses and liability, into one policy. Your broker will be familiar with these policies.

Selecting the Insurer

One of the most important services of the professional insurance broker is the selection of insurance companies to provide quotes for coverage. Some companies are quite strong in some types of insurance and weaker in other areas. Your broker will understand the market and select those that are appropriate for your needs. He should also be helpful in making sure that the companies are quoting "apples for apples," so that the resulting comparison of premiums is meaningful.

One of the most important services of the professional insurance broker is the selection of insurance companies to provide quotes for coverage.

Some insurance companies are much more stable in the administration of premiums than others. Your broker should protect you from having some insurer "buy" your business this year, only to significantly increase the premium for the same coverage next year. Jumping from insurer to insurer is not desirable and is also quite time-consuming. Your broker should know the reliable companies that have a record of stability, both in the prompt payment of claims and in their quotation of premiums. Premiums for insurance can be quite significant and your broker should help you shop for the right insurers.

Handling a Loss Claim

Although losses involving insurance claims will hopefully be few, when losses occur your broker is the first person to contact. He should be instrumental in helping you wade through the red tape that is typically a part of any insurance claim. He will have dealt with the insurers in filing claims and will know how and whom to contact to expedite your loss recovery. There are many steps to consider in perfecting a claim for an insured loss, including proving the right to your claim, assembling the supporting paperwork, and knowing when to contact your attorney to support your effort. Another good reason to have a good insurance broker!

Health Insurance

Because health insurance is specialized, your broker may wish to refer you to an insurance broker or agent who deals in this type of insurance. Health insurance is an ever-increasing cost of business, yet group health insurance for your employees is nearly an essential benefit. Many years ago, companies were able to absorb the entire cost of the premiums, but today the costs have risen to a point where small businesses (and many large ones) simply cannot afford to provide this coverage unless the employees share the cost. If you think about it, maybe that's the way it should be! When benefits cost people nothing, they can take them for granted. When they have to reach into their pockets, they are much more attentive to helping control the costs.

Health insurance and the other coverages (dental, life, and disability) that often go hand in hand are rather complicated and *require* the services of a good agent. There can be so many alternatives that significantly affect the premium, it is often difficult to know whether all of the appropriate coverage possibilities have been considered. Premiums can be affected by the size of the group covered, their ages, the number of dependents, loss history, deductible features, coinsurance features, and more. We will leave a detailed discussion of this subject to the broker or agent of your choice—but be sure to listen carefully.

Although this chapter is short, it is not because the subject is unimportant. Having assisted companies that were devastated by fire, explosion, and loss of life, I know from experience the importance of adequate insurance coverage. Adequate insurance coverage is critical to any size business and, having been blessed with a good insurance broker, it is easy for me to suggest that you also find a good one!

Note

1. Harroch, Richard D. *Small Business Kit for Dummies*. IDG Books, 1998.

Chapter 18

Be a Good Communicator

com-mu'ni-ca'tion *n.* a giving or exchanging of information, messages, etc.
—*Webster's New World Dictionary*

I BELIEVE WEBSTER'S DEFINITION MISSES THE MARK. THE GIVING OR EXCHANG-ing of information or messages does *not*, in my opinion, constitute communication *unless* the person receiving the information or messages *understands* the information given. Books can be written about various subjects, but there is no communication unless the reader comprehends what the author is saying. Perhaps this is why a student who is mentored by a good teacher learns more quickly than those who simply read the book.

I know that, on some occasion, you have told someone a joke, only to have him respond with a blank expression. Simply put, *he didn't get it!* You did not get your message across: there was *no communication*. If you are to be successful as a small business owner or manager, you must learn to communicate effectively ... with employees, customers, suppliers, and other people. We have all been a bit envious of the person who is able to communicate with anyone, regardless of their age, gender, educational level, or background. How does a person develop this ability? We believe the *key to good communication is listening*!

How frequently have you attempted to explain something to someone, who was mentally preparing a response, *even before you finished what you were saying?* Sometimes a person may even interrupt your explanation with a rebuttal. He did not listen to you and *no communication occurred.* When you are trying to communicate with another person, you need to listen carefully to his response to determine if he really "got it."

When you are trying to communicate with another person, you need to listen carefully to his response to determine if he really "got it."

Communicating with Employees

As a small business owner, you need the ability to communicate with your people. They are the ones who will accomplish the tasks necessary to make your business a success. In Chapters 4 and 5, we discussed the need to involve your employees in the business. This involvement will help in achieving a good line of communication; however, there are other ways for you to improve employee communication.

1. An "open door policy." Make yourself available to your employees as much as possible and be willing to answer their questions patiently. It has been said, "There are no stupid questions" and that is especially true in business. Also encourage (strongly) all of your managers and supervisors to adopt the same attitude, that of encouraging employee inquiry and comment.

2. Company-wide discussion sessions. In a company with fewer than 50 employees, it is useful to meet periodically to discuss specific issues and to encourage questions from employees. This should not require more than an hour each month and the benefits are significant. You as the owner and your key managers must be involved in these sessions and you *must be willing to deal with any question asked.* If you do not have the answer, write down the question, promise to find the answer, and deliver it at the next session. (In manufacturing operations, these sessions are often called "shop meetings.") The employees will be very impressed that the "big boss" is willing to talk with them and truly be interested in their comments.

As your company grows, you may need to break the employees into groups of a size that will enable a feeling of informality and encourage employee participation. When the sessions become more formal, the questions will cease and communication will not be achieved.

3. Training programs. Although such programs may be aimed at developing technical competence in your employees, they also serve to improve communication. Again, it is important that you become involved, if only for a brief period. This will let your employees know that you are interested in their technical improvement and in their growth as key people in your company. Be sure to allow a question-and-answer time when you are present.

4. Suggestion box. As simplistic as it may seem, recognizing and rewarding employees for providing suggestions for improving the company's operations goes a long ways toward improving real employee communication. If you don't intend to deal with the employees' suggestions, don't provide a suggestion box. Employees should feel free to make comments and suggestions—and to identify themselves or not with their suggestions. The bonus for the company is that some suggestions may improve profitability. Your employees are closer to the detailed day-to-day operations and so are often in a position to provide insights into solving problems that you might achieve no other way.

5. Informal outings. It is always helpful to be able to informally meet with employees and discuss whatever is of interest to them. You can involve the employees' families and gain even more from this activity. The activity might be a company picnic, a Christmas party (if your company isn't too large), or an in-house lunch or dinner. These can be relatively inexpensive if you ask each family to bring a vegetable, salad, or dessert dish and the company provides the main dishes (meat and vegetarian) and the drinks.

Speaking of drinks, my experience is that booze in any form is *not* a good idea at these gatherings. It is strange but true that people who do not drink alcohol regularly tend to overdo on such occasions—especially if it is free!—and react in ways that can be offensive to others or even cause major problems. Besides, avoiding booze helps avoid potential legal liabilities if some damage or violation of a law results from employees who overindulged. Please understand that this advice does not come from a teetotaler. I like martinis as much as anyone on this planet!

Other successful activities can be a golf league where the format is a scramble, with the teams being routinely changed but being sure to have some balance of skill among teams. Softball and volleyball games or bowling leagues can also be effective, if they don't become too competitive. Whatever the activity, be sure that it is designed to encourage communication among the employees and managers. The better the event is planned, the more effective it will be.

I debated whether these suggestions for developing improved communication with employees were worth including in this book. I included them because my personal experience in this area has been so positive. Your ability to communicate easily and directly with your employees will make them

As simplistic as it may seem, recognizing and rewarding employees for providing suggestions for improving the company's operations goes a long ways toward improving real employee communication.

151

significantly more loyal to the company and more willing to give extra effort to the company's objectives. You need this effort and they need your involvement with them!

Communicating with Customers

It is sad, but true, that customers, clients, or patients (whatever the definition) are no longer treated as personally and with as much concern as in years past. Perhaps the world is moving so fast or is so focused on money or other personal gratification that the extra service and attention to customers are overlooked.

The willingness to listen carefully to your customers' needs and attempt to fully satisfy that need, even if you must refer them to another source, is crucial to the success of your business!

Although this neglect may seem to be a negative, we believe it offers an *incredible opportunity* to those in business who *do communicate* with their customers and treat them as the valuable commodity that they are.

If your small business develops this capability, the benefits will be great. The key ingredient in developing this ability is ... *listening*. There are many ways to enhance your company's communication skills when dealing with customers.

Improve telephone sales skills. It should be the objective of your technical sales personnel to do whatever they can to understand and help satisfy customers' needs. Much of this is done over the telephone.

Your technical *sales personnel must be well informed* about your products or services. It is frustrating to call to find a product or service when the person who answers the phone is simply (and I hate to use the term) incompetent. Would you ever call that company again? Doubtful. If your salesperson does not know the answer to a customer's question, he or she should admit it, not guess, promise the customer to find out and call back promptly, ... and then do it!

The sales personnel must be taught to *listen* and to *listen carefully*. If they do not fully understood a customer's question, complaint, or request the first time, they should ask the customer to repeat it. There are too many occasions where the customer receives the wrong size, color, or model of product simply because the salesperson didn't listen carefully and write it down correctly.

Sales personnel should not tell the customer what he or she needs, even if it is obvious. Do not offend your customers by implying that you know their needs better than they do—even if you do! Your salesperson should explain whatever options are available, including the right answer, and then make the right answer the company's recommendation.

If your company cannot provide the product or service the customer needs, your personnel should be sufficiently knowledgeable to *suggest another source for the customer, even if it is a competitor*. You have competitors that are well managed and competent; it is vital to know who they are and what capabilities they have. It is better to make the referral to help your customer than to simply say you cannot provide what he or she needs. If you make a good referral, you will retain that customer even if he or she occasionally buys something from your most worthy competitor. This happened on more than one occasion in my company. We *never* lost a customer to the referral competitor!

Your sales personnel should *never make a claim for your product or service that cannot be achieved nor promise a delivery date that they suspect cannot be met*. They must never be guilty of saying what the customer wants to hear if it is not an honest response.

Follow up on successful sales by having your sales personnel contact customers to determine that the products or services are meeting your customers' needs. If all is well, customers will simply appreciate the follow-up call. If all is not well, your personnel need to take corrective action at the earliest possible time, staying on the problem until they either solve it or refer it to another source to provide a solution.

Regardless of the cost (and this is my personal opinion), *avoid telephone answering systems like the plague!* No one, repeat, no one wants to go through three or four menus, punching numbers on the phone, just to talk to a human being. There is absolutely no substitute for a pleasant voice answering the phone and inquiring how he or she may be of assistance.

If your business is so small that you answer the phone yourself when you are in, buy a cell phone and use a paging system so that you can reply to your customer's call promptly. Be sure to advise your customers of the paging number and the cell phone number.

If your business operations are geographically broad, *install a toll-free number* so that customers will not have to use their dime (Did I say dime? It used to be!) to call your company. It costs a little more, but it clearly encourages better communication with your customers. Also, it is helpful to have a *separate line for faxes or the internet* so that the phone is not tied up for those purposes.

It should go without saying that you should periodically check to determine that you have enough incoming lines to handle the customer traffic. The phone company will be delighted to help you! Just scrutinize their data carefully.

Your sales personnel should never make a claim for your product or service that cannot be achieved nor promise a delivery date that they suspect cannot be met.

153

Visit your customers personally. At a minimum, visit all of your key customers *at least once a year* and more often, if possible. If you cannot visit them personally, call and tell them that your schedule does not allow you to visit but your qualified representative will visit in your stead. You or your representative should take careful notes and *listen to your customer's comments* about his or her business and operating problems (especially if associated with the functioning of your product or service). You should inquire about his or her *recommendations for product changes or new product ideas* and the reasons. Your customer is your very best source for new product ideas and for product improvements—and *also your best source for new business.*

A visit by the top executive in the business (or his or her most trusted aide) is an excellent way to make a favorable impression on your customer and enhance your lines of communication with that customer. It is likely that you will be treated like royalty—unless your product or service has been faulty!

Use computerized communication methods. Your business should include adequate *e-mail* addresses so that your customers can send you information at their convenience if it is not essential to make a phone call. Also consider developing a *web site* as a means of improving communication. It should include the following:

▶ **Home page,** with a directory of the areas included in the web site and links to navigate to those pages and sections

▶ **Company page,** with some history about the company and its products and services

▶ **Product information pages,** listing the company's products and services, with appropriate technical information about each

▶ **Order page (shopping cart),** if appropriate for your business, to allow the customers to select and order products from the literature, complete with pricing data, except for shipping and handling charges

▶ **Communication page,** which enables customers to identify themselves and request information and literature, ask for an immediate return call, or critique the web site

Many internet service providers (ISPs) offer assistance for developing web sites, including identifying and selecting search engines that should be contacted to list your web site. There are also other aids that can be purchased or downloaded to help developing your site. Consider the need for a web site carefully. They are not free; however, they can be vital to business success when used appropriately. Contact a computer consulting firm. They should have personnel who can direct you in evaluating this option.

Develop an outstanding brochure. It does not matter if it is a one-page folded mailer. It should look professional (including quality paper and printing) and contain important information about your company that would invite further communication from prospective or present customers. (Refer back to Chapter 10.)

In some cases, it may be helpful to include a perforated postpaid reply card for requesting literature or a phone call. It should be updated from time to time so that the information does not become stale or obsolete. Seek the help of a good printer or ad agency if you don't know how to go about the design and printing.

Consider a "how are we doing?" questionnaire. Develop a questionnaire that you send periodically to your customers to ask them to assess your products, services, and responsiveness to their needs. It can be sent in conjunction with new product brochures, copies of press releases, or reprints of any articles about your products or services that have appeared in trade journals. Make the questionnaire very short and straightforward, requiring very little time for your customers to complete. Be sure that it is postpaid. Your local post office can help design a postage-paid card that is very cost-effective. Web sites have also proven effective in soliciting more honest answers from customers.

Develop a questionnaire that you send periodically to your customers to ask them to assess your products, services, and responsiveness to their needs.

Communicating with Suppliers

Your suppliers are also important to your small business. Their ability to supply you with needed materials, components, and supplies in an economical and timely fashion is critical to your company's success. Sometimes important advantages of suppliers are overlooked as businesses shop around for the cheapest prices so they can better compete with larger companies that have superior purchasing power. Invariably, the cheapest price is not the best price. *Quality, warranty, customer service, favorable credit terms,* and *delivery* can all be equally important to the buyer. A good working relationship with a supplier that offers these features, along with a reasonable price, results from good communication. Is it possible ... that I have said this before?

Seek out the best suppliers of key materials and/or components and invite them to visit your facility. Discuss the nature of your business and its needs with their key people. Visit their facilities to gain an appreciation of their ability to satisfy your requirements. Evaluate the suppliers and structure a working relationship with those you favor, including a willingness to enter into a purchase contract that would be beneficial to your business and the supplier. The suppliers selected should be willing to send a representative to your facility on a regular basis to better understand your operations and how they may better serve you.

Work out an understanding (or contractual relationship) with each of your key suppliers. Then, keep them informed of changes in your business and how effectively they have met your needs. Also, be sure to let them know if cash problems arise and how you will resolve a payment plan for them. They should want and deserve this information. Remember: little businesses that buy small quantities grow into larger businesses that buy large quantities. Your suppliers want just that type of customer.

> Your ability to communicate—with your employees, customers, suppliers, banker, CPA, insurance broker, attorney, and equity partners—will be a measure of your company's success!

Chapter 19

The Good Times ... and the Bad Times

THIS CHAPTER IS BASED ON THE PREMISE THAT SMALL BUSINESSES either do well or do poorly, but rarely stay the same. In a world where even a minimal growth rate is 3 to 4 percent annually, to stay the same is to do poorly.

The difficulty in managing a small business is that the "blood is so close to the surface of the skin" that a seemingly harmless mistake can blossom into a major problem. Moreover, when things are going right, it is easy for us to be lulled into a feeling of near euphoria, fostering the belief that we may actually be infallible. *Not!*

When All Is Well

Remember this: *when all is well ..., beware!* Never become complacent—*especially* when business is doing well. Always continue to look for new ways to improve your operations and creative ways to use marketing to open the door for growth opportunities and ... continue to innovate!

We are not saying that every successful period in the growth of a small business is followed by lean years. However, there are some precautions that the small business owner should take to ensure that a period of unusual growth does not precipitate decisions that could be harmful if the business climate reverses. Here is what you should consider doing during the good times.

Pursue product development projects. A period of good profitability and cash flow is an excellent time to develop new products, improve existing products, or broaden the scope of your line of products and services. Market test those products that you believe have real potential ... and don't forget to seek patent and copyright protection when applicable..

Prepay some of your long-term debt. Assuming there is no prepayment penalty, this is a good time to reduce future cash requirements and interest costs. Check with your banker and work out a new amortization schedule.

Delay lower-level personnel additions. Offer your direct labor or production people overtime opportunities, delaying hiring until it is absolutely essential. Nothing is worse than adding employees in the good times then having to lay them off if business takes a downturn. Steady employment is very attractive to present and prospective employees. If warranted, you can use part-time personnel or temps to shore up your personnel needs. I believe, that under these circumstances, overtime is cheap.

Avoid excessive pay increases. The fact that times are good does not warrant pay increases greater than normally granted. Pay increases become fixed in employees' minds and a relatively fixed cost for the company. If you want to reward employees, do so with discretionary cash bonuses. Do not tie the bonuses to a particular business statistic. Treat yourself and your key management personnel in the same manner, using bonuses rather than pay increases.

Add key equipment or productive facilities. Try to avoid heavy increases in debt to accomplish this. Use available excess cash or modest debt to buy or upgrade equipment that can help reduce future production costs. If you do not create excessive debt to accomplish this, the resulting future expense is depreciation, a noncash item.

Improve office or storefront facilities. These facilities can include new carpeting, furniture, equipment, painting, or even remodeling. These costs should not be significant and you should be able to fund them with the increase in cash flow from current operations.

Avoid major additions to your debt obligations. Even though you may be able to service the debt during the good times, any decision to add debt should be based on the company's ability to absorb those costs during periods of lower profitability. Added debt should result from good long-term planning, not from temporary business highs.

A period of good profitability and cash flow is an excellent time to develop new products, improve existing products, or broaden the scope of your line of products and services.

158

In summary, temporary periods of high profitability are good times to use the excess cash flow to help *reduce future cash costs*. Abnormal periods of growth are not good times to increase costs that are relatively fixed or increase the cash requirements of future periods.

Managing periods of abnormal growth, with the resulting increased investment in receivables and inventory, is one of the most difficult tasks confronting the small business owner. Do not allow your company to become "spread too thin."

If you need verification of the rationale of this opinion, simply look at the plagued operations of the dotcom businesses that grew too rapidly in the new millennium. Many increased their debt obligations when not advisable and others have been forced to lay off hundreds or thousands of employees, been acquired by more stable larger companies, or taken bankruptcy.

The road to small business success is *consistent growth within the scope of the business plan*. To do otherwise is like trying to time the stock market: it can be fun for a little while, but it is not the most effective investment philosophy in the longer term.

> *Turn down business from new customers if taking that business means reducing your ability to serve current customers properly.*

When All Is *Not* Well

You can count on having periods of time in your small business when sales volume drops, profitability declines or even disappears, and things look very bleak. Changing nothing because "good times are just around the corner" is a tactic reserved for ostriches. Panic action is not appropriate either. Instead, you must carefully manage your business, taking prompt but carefully considered action to offset the lost volume. Having helped many businesses through tough times, I believe there are some things that should be done and others to be avoided.

Prepare a new business plan (or plans). This plan to guide operations through the stormy period should be based on the reduced volume expected and outline the steps needed to compensate for the loss of profitability. You should review the plan with your banker, your CPA, and/or your SCORE management counselor. (Refer back to Chapter 11.) Some companies prepare more than one plan in anticipation of a significant change in volume, making it easier to deal with the change should it arise.

You need the banker's wholehearted support for the revised plan and your CPA can help attest to the plan's financial validity. Your SCORE management counselor may provide you with some "I have been there" advice—

and it is free! Some of the steps suggested for inclusion in the revised plan are discussed below.

Avoid sales price reductions. Even though your competitors may reduce their prices, try to avoid reducing the base prices of your products. Instead, offer discounts for ordering additional items or for preordering (for later shipment). Customers always forget price reductions but always remember price increases, *which may be needed later*. If prices must be reduced, select those products that are slow moving, are overstocked, or represent an out-of-balance condition in your inventory. Contact your key customers and discuss the situation with them. Reduce the sales prices of your main products only as a last resort, and preferably with a temporary discount arrangement.

A downtime is exactly the time when advertising is needed most, to keep the name of your company and its image in the marketplace.

Continue advertising or promotional efforts. A downtime is exactly the time when advertising is needed most, to keep the name of your company and its image in the marketplace. Retain a reasonable portion of your ad budget in your revised business plan. A slow period is also a good time for an inexpensive direct mail effort. Send out a new brochure or a special offer to your current customers. Too often, small companies stop all advertising and promotional efforts when times are tough, which can further hurt sales.

Consider outside services. In some companies, maintenance, repair, window cleaning, groundskeeping, and similar jobs are performed by employees. These employees represent a fixed cost (along with their benefits), especially if they are salaried. Investigate the cost of having this type of work performed by an outside contractor whose cost is known and incurred only when needed. We have known of situations where employees were terminated but rehired on a contractual basis to perform these services, allowing the company to reduce the cost and helping the former employees start a business.

Redouble efforts to collect receivables. If times are slow, sales personnel can be on the phone collecting accounts receivable that have become past due. Have them call the customers with whom they normally deal and, while asking for additional business, they should seek payment for past business. Get your past-due customers on some kind of regular payment plan if they are unable to pay their entire balance. Improving cash flow is vital.

Seek more favorable credit terms from suppliers. Your suppliers want your continued business and during slow times may consider granting your company longer credit terms, easing the demand on cash flow. Lower volume means slower-moving inventory. Try to slow down the payment cycle to match.

Ask your banker for help. If you have discussed your revised business plan with your banker, he or she may be willing to lengthen the term for repaying debt or even allow a moratorium on principal payments for a short, specified time. Ask for his or her help. You may be pleasantly surprised.

Reduce the cost of direct hourly workers. Try to reduce the cost through *lowering the normal business hours*. If your hourly personnel are working a normal 40-hour week, determine whether a 32-hour workweek will achieve the needed reduction. If so, you can avoid losing good, experienced personnel through layoffs. However, you must reduce the cost to match the volume of business, even if that means layoffs. Whichever approach, you should *avoid a second reduction if possible.*

When cuts are required, cut sufficiently to meet the planned volume so that the employees are not apprehensive about repeated reductions or layoffs. In other words, *"don't nibble at the bullet."*

Cut off overtime hours. Although there may be an imbalance in production if certain products lose volume while others remain normal, you should make a concerted effort to avoid paying overtime wages to any worker. Cross-train your employees, if you have not already done so. A slow time is a good time to work on your cross-training program, allowing good workers to expand their value to your business.

Communicate with your employees. After developing a new business plan with the aid of your key management personnel, discuss the situation with your employees. You need not divulge all the details of the plan, but advise them of the things that will affect them directly, such as reductions in hours, layoffs, and the curtailment of overtime. The absence of information breeds fear among employees that can affect performance and quality and may cause good employees to look for employment elsewhere.

An economic downturn and the resulting reductions in sales volume and profitability require a carefully devised plan for dealing with the problem. All of the steps that you believe you should take to mitigate the problem should be reflected in a revised business plan and your trend reports, discussed in previous chapters.

We believe your efforts in taking this approach will be rewarded. Moreover, I view difficult times as an opportunity to demonstrate the superiority of your company to deal with the problems.

When cuts are required, cut sufficiently to meet the planned volume so that the employees are not apprehensive about repeated reductions or layoffs. In other words, "don't nibble at the bullet."

Weak companies fail during bad times; well-managed companies survive and, quite often, become stronger from the experience!

Chapter 20

"The Rest of the Story"

I N 19 CHAPTERS, THE BOOK HAS COVERED WHAT I BELIEVE ARE THE ESSEN-tials for managing a small business successfully. These essentials are technical and it may be helpful for you to review them now. In short, *you need to know the following:*

1. The meaning and implications of leadership.
2. Your own personal strengths and weaknesses in managing a business.
3. What business you are in (what specific needs or wants your product or service will satisfy) and who your customers are.
4. Your product or service technically and how it is different from and better than that of your competition.
5. If your product or service can be protected by patent or copyright law, how to avail your business of that protection.
6. Your competition, the owners, management, products or services, how they price and sell their product, the ancillary services they provide, and, most of all, their strengths and weaknesses.
7. Whether you will make or buy your product and, if purchasing, from what sources.
8. How to price your product or service for a profit.

9. How your product or service will be sold—e.g., sales personnel, representatives, or others—and how the selling function will be compensated and evaluated.
10. What customer services your business needs to provide, both before and after the sale.
11. The sales, credit, warranty, and returns policies that your business requires.
12. The need for innovation and new product or service development and the procedures required.
13. If your business requires inventory, how the inventory of your product will be managed.
14. What packaging and labeling requirements must be met and what technical literature or user guides are needed.
15. How your business will be advertised and promoted and at what cost.
16. How to develop a business plan, complete with financial projections.
17. How to develop a relationship with a banker or lender and how to seek additional financing.
18. How to read and understand financial statements and how they are generated, including an understanding of the accounting system used in your business.
19. How to measure your operating results against the plan and develop internal reports that identify the steps needed to correct deviations.
20. How to select and work with a certified public accountant, a business attorney, and an insurance broker.
21. How to be a good communicator with customers, employees, suppliers, bankers, accountants, attorneys, and insurance brokers.
22. What to do when your business falters and you are no longer generating profits!

If this book were about becoming a successful golfer, these essentials might be thought of as grip, stance, swing plane, follow-through, and other vital but technical points. The fact is, most professional golfers and good amateurs know and practice all these essentials routinely. *Why then are they not all winners?* There must be other, more intangible factors that a few understand and the rest are trying to learn.

The Intangible Factors

So it is in business. Although this book has presented the essential skills involved in managing small businesses, there are other, more intangible factors that we must understand to fulfill our desire for business success. You may even see a parallel between business and golf relative to the factors we have chosen. With apologies to Paul Harvey (whose programs we have treasured and whom my younger readers may not even know), consider these *ten guidelines for successful small business management* as ... *"the rest of the story."*

1. Know and believe in yourself. Without confidence in your own abilities and a knowledge of your strengths and weaknesses, you will find it difficult to deal with the adversities that are part of building a small business. Building a successful small business is *not a "piece of cake."* It is an undertaking based on skill, passion, persistence, understanding, the ability to lead, and many other abilities.

Take heart, many have successfully gone before you and many will follow your lead!

2. Recognize that you cannot do it alone. You will need help to educate, guide, and assist you, especially in those areas of expertise where you have acknowledged weaknesses (your "flat sides"). You must rely on associates, professional advice, and/or a mentor who has knowledge of your business and the compassion to help you when help is needed. Moreover, you need the help of your people. They are essential to achieve your goals!

3. Be persistent in all things. Do not be discouraged by your failures. Use your failures as stepping-stones of learning. A person who has not had failures has not tried to achieve something that challenged his abilities. Failures are a blessing, for they provide a fertile learning ground applicable to the future.

My sociology professor in college once said, "Experience is no more than a recitation of our mistakes." After nearly 50 years in business, I believe him!

4. Strive constantly for innovation. Seek new ideas in products, methods, and marketing. An open and curious mind allows creativity, which leads to innovation. Without innovation, your business will stagnate and ultimately fail. Your business must either move forward, with new ways and new ideas, or it will move backward toward mediocrity and, ultimately, failure!

5. Listen to your customers! Your customers are your most reliable source of vital information. They are aware of their needs and wants and the needs and wants of the industry. They are your research department, your beta site, and your advisor when product or service innovation is the subject. Avoid satisfying your own ego or your desire to be recognized. Satisfy your customers: they are your lifeblood!

6. Make quality and service your hallmark. Providing your customers with quality products and responsive service will result in successful growth. Quality is rewarded by enabling reasonable pricing and profitability. Service is the mechanism that reinforces the quality. *Without quality and service, the success of your business is in jeopardy!*

7. Financially, you must know where you are ... and plan where you are going. Learn the financial management aspects of your business and use the information to guide your growth. I cannot tell you how many of my past and present clients have ultimately seen the benefit of "understanding the numbers." When others (your banker or your stockholders) read and critique your financial statements, you *must* know the answers. *It is not optional.*

Yes, learning accounting and financial management may be tedious and, at first, boring. Then, with so many people I have helped, the "light comes on" and they have affirmed, "I should have learned this before—it is a picture of my business."

8. Recognize your people as your greatest asset. Treat them fairly and involve them in your plans. You will be rewarded. Getting the "right people" in the "right places" in your business is essential to your business success. As Jim Collins so aptly stated in *Good to Great*[1], you have to "get the right people on the bus (and the wrong people off the bus)" and the right people must be "in the right seats."

9. Communicate clearly and effectively. You must create a meaningful line of communication with your people, your customers, your banker, and others. Remember that communication exists only when the "communicatee" understands what the communicator has said. Use your communication skills wisely. It is a very powerful tool!

10. Choose honesty and integrity as your guide. There is no substitute for the trust that will result when you follow these guidelines in all your business dealings. You must be first truthful to yourself, understand and assess your strengths and weaknesses, and find support for your weaknesses.

You must also be truthful with your people. They are the necessary ingredient that will take you to your objective. You must deal with them honestly and with integrity. In short, they must believe in you!

Your customers must believe that you and your company are honest in dealing with them. When things go wrong, they must believe that you will respond to the problem promptly and justly. Mistakes are made. *It is your ability to deal honestly and positively with those mistakes that will separate you from your competitors.*

The Ultimate Reward!

The ultimate reward is the satisfaction of knowing that your commitment and dedication to your ideals, your objectives, and your beliefs have resulted in a successful organization of people and ideas.

So if we have considered all of the tangible and intangible factors that affect success in the management of small businesses, what then is the ultimate reward?

If you own a small business that has weathered the storms of economic downturns and reveled in the glory of unprecedented growth to become a stable, consistently profitable entity, you already understand the ultimate reward. Quite honestly (as you know), the money you make in your small business is not the reward.

It is a continuing reward, fueled by constant challenges that are met and overcome. We have found that many small businesspeople become reluctant to either sell their business or turn over the reins to another. Why? They are enjoying the ultimate reward. It has become a part of their life. They have learned that *small is beautiful.*

Note

1. Collins, Jim. *Good to Great.* HarperCollins Publishers Inc., 2001.

Appendix A

Quiz for Small Business Success

Question	Points
1. What is the key to business success?	
a. Business knowledge	**5**
b. Market awareness	**4**
c. Hands on management	**3**
d. Sufficient capital	**2**
e. Hard work	**1**
2. Which is the largest potential trouble spot?	
a. Too much growth	**4**
b. Too little growth	**3**
c. Too fast growth	**5**
d. Too slow growth	**2**
e. Sporadic growth	**1**
3. My customers are:	
a. Always right	**3**
b. Too fussy	**2**
c. Demanding	**4**
d. Worth listening to	**5**
e. Dumb	**1**
4. Rank these in order of importance for small business *marketing* success:	
a. Word-of-mouth	**5**
b. Advertising	**2**
c. Signs	**3**
d. Location	**4**
e. Community events	**1**
5. Financially my firm:	
a. Has trouble with cash-flow	**2**
b. Has a good line of credit	**3**
c. Is financed totally by receipts—no credit	**1**
d. Is making better profits this year than last	**4**
e. Knows exactly where it is all the time	**5**

167

Question	Points
6. In hiring people:	
a. I take far too long	4
b. I look for the cheapest person	2
c. Personality is more important than experience	3
d. I look for the best person and am willing to pay	5
e. I only hire at the trainee level	1
7. The best competitive advantage is:	
a. Experience	5
b. Understanding what the market wants	4
c. Confidence	3
d. Conducting a business ethically	1
e. A detailed plan	2
8. I think business plans are:	
a. For the birds	1
b. Nice but not necessary	2
c. Something I can do with my accountant	3
d. Useful and informative	4
e. Essential—wouldn't do business without them	5
9. What makes a terrific entrepreneur?	
a. Creativity	4
b. Discipline	3
c. Consumer orientation	5
d. Technical proficiency	1
e. Flexibility	2
10. What is essential to marketing?	
a. "A sixth sense"	1
b. Market research	4
c. Customer awareness	5
d. Experience	2
e. Testing	3

Your point total is: _____

If Your Point Total Is	Your Business Success Quotient Is
38-50	You are a successful entrepreneur whose business operations reflect tried and true business practices.
25-37	Your business is probably headed for long-term success, but it will come sooner if you sharpen your awareness of solid management skills and marketing techniques.
13-24	While you may be enjoying customer loyalty and repeat business, never forget that savvy competition is always looking for ways to take the lead. Don't let comfort lull you into false security. Be creatively assertive!
0-12	You may well have the right product, but to sell it successfully, you need to increase your market awareness and improve your operating philosophy. Reach out for practical classes, seminars, and advice from people who have good business track records. And … keep persevering. It's the key ingredient to winning!

Appendix B

Employment Application

<table>
<tr>
<td colspan="2">Your Company Name

Application for Employment</td>
<td colspan="3">Date</td>
</tr>
<tr>
<td colspan="2" rowspan="2"></td>
<td colspan="3">Position</td>
</tr>
<tr>
<td colspan="3" align="center">PLEASE PRINT</td>
</tr>
<tr>
<td colspan="5">In accordance with state and Federal laws, applicants are considered for all positions without regard to race, color, religion, sex, national origin, age, sexual orientation, marital or veteran status, or the presence of non-job related disabilities, and the company is committed to maintaining an environment fre from sexual harassment and retaliation.</td>
</tr>
<tr>
<td>NAME</td>
<td>Last</td>
<td colspan="2">First</td>
<td>M.I.</td>
</tr>
<tr>
<td>ADDRESS</td>
<td>Street</td>
<td colspan="2">City</td>
<td>ST   Zip</td>
</tr>
<tr>
<td>TELEPHONE</td>
<td></td>
<td colspan="3">S.S. NO.</td>
</tr>
<tr>
<td rowspan="2">EMERGENCY CONTACT</td>
<td>Name</td>
<td colspan="3">Relationship</td>
</tr>
<tr>
<td>Address</td>
<td colspan="3">Phone</td>
</tr>
</table>

PLEASE ANSWER ALL QUESTIONS	YES	NO
Have you filed an application here before?		
Have you been employed here before?		
Do you understand that employment, if offered, is conditioned upon you providing satisfactory proof of identity and employment eligibility under U.S. immigration laws?		
Are you employed now?		
Are you on layoff and subject to recall?		
Can you travel, work overtime or weekends, if the job requires?		
Have you ever been convicted of (or plea bargained to) a felony conviction. If so, explain:		
Do you have relatives or friends employed by the Company?		
Do you have responsibilities or commitments that could prevent you from meeting work schedules or job-related meetings?		

EDUCATION	Name/Location of School	Diploma	Study Emphasis
High School			
College			
Graduate work			
Vocational or Special Studies:			

<table>
<tr>
<td rowspan="2">MILITARY SERVICE</td>
<td>Period</td>
<td>Branch</td>
<td>Attained Rank</td>
</tr>
<tr>
<td colspan="3">Work that could benefit job performance</td>
</tr>
</table>

SKILLS: Briefly describe the skills and/or abilities you have that qualify you for this position.

Employment Application

EMPLOYED	*Start with your present or last job. Exclude organization names which indicate race, color, religion, sex or national origin.*		
From	Employer	Beginning Pay Rate	Work Performed
To	Supervisor Phone	Ending Pay Rate	Reason for Leaving
From	Employer	Beginning Pay Rate	Work Performed
To	Supervisor Phone	Ending Pay Rate	Reason for Leaving
From	Employer	Beginning Pay Rate	Work Performed
To	Supervisor Phone	Ending Pay Rate	Reason for Leaving

JOB REQUIREMENTS *Due to the cross training techniques employed by the Company, there may be basic tasks that each employee is required to perform. Please check the appropriate column that indicates whether you can meet these job requirements.*

Yes	No	*Please answer honestly and completely*
		Do you have experience in answering a multiple line phone system? _____ If yes, the maximum number of lines with which you have experience handling is ___ lines
		Can you operate a computer (or computer terminal)? Describe your experience.
		Are you aware of the responsibilities of the job, for which you are a candidate? Yes:___ No: ___ If yes, do you have any physical limitations what would prevent you from fulfilling those responsibilities? Yes: ___ No: ___ If yes, explain:

APPLICANT'S UNDERSTANDING:

I certify that the information contained in this application is correct and complete to the best of my knowledge, and understand that falsification of this application in any detail is grounds for disqualification from further consideration or for dismissal from employment in accordance with Company policy. I understand that this is an application for employment and not a contract for employment. I understand that my employment and compensation can be terminated for any reason or for no reason at the option of either the Company or myself. I understand also that I am required to abide by all the rules and regulations of the Company.

Date _____   Signature of Applicant _____

Appendix C

Position Descriptions

As stated in Chapter 4, Position Descriptions constitute a written record of the duties and responsibilities for each position and serve as a factual basis for job evaluation decisions. They also provide the employee with a more clear understanding of what is expected from him in fulfilling the job assigned. Every employee should have a copy of the position description for the job he is filling. (*Note: For simplicity, we have used the masculine gender, such as his or he, for both male and female references in this Appendix*). A Position Description typically includes:

Title. References the type of work required by the position, the relative level or rank of the position and, where possible, the pay grade for the position.

Reporting Relationships. Lists the title of the position to whom this position is responsible and the titles of those positions immediately responsible to this position.

Position Summary. A general statement which best describes the responsibilities and authority of the position. The statement is limited to one or two sentences.

Principal Duties and Responsibilities. An enumerated listing of the major duties and responsibilities of the position. It is not an all inclusive list nor is it intended to be restrictive.

Qualifications. A statement of the minimum and desired qualifications for the position relative to each of the following areas (which should be defined and include a description of each of the relative qualification levels):

- ▶ Education
- ▶ Technical knowledge and skills
- ▶ Policy and planning responsibility
- ▶ Experience
- ▶ Unusual working conditions
- ▶ Decision making responsibility
- ▶ Supervision
- ▶ Outside contacts

There should be a position description maintained by the company for each position that they currently have and for those that are planned. All management personnel should have copies of the position description for their job and for all of the positions within the scope of their supervision.

A sample position description for an hourly and salaried position are illustrated.

ABC Company	**POSITION DESCRIPTION**
Policy Manual	**POSITION:** Office Manager

Reporting Relationships: Reports to: President Reporting to this position: Office Clerical Personnel	**Pay Grade: H2**

Position Summary:
Directs all office activities, including customer and vendor contact, communication with installers, estimators and supervisors. Responsible for accounting and internal management reporting systems, invoicing, collections, payables, payroll, taxes and insurance. Monitors cash flow and manages filing systems.

Principal Responsibilities:

1. Answers phone calls from customers and vendors and coordinates the flow of all information in the office. Assists in qualifying sales leads, communicating with estimators and sales personnel. Assists in the estimating function, preparing proposals, estimate spreadsheets, and tracks options and change orders to existing jobs.

2. Works with superintendents and installers to assign employees and trucks to jobs, reviews daily job summaries and maintains current employee personnel files.

3. Directs invoicing activities, working with superintendents to keep job files current reflecting any job changes and directs office staff to render accurate invoices to customers.

4. Assists in the scheduling and coordination of jobs, working with the Operations Manager to assure that work orders are prepared on a timely basis, with accurate maps to jobs, and contacts customers immediately prior to job starts.

5. Responsible for all accounting and internal management reporting, using QuickBooks and Excel to provide current and accurate financial and job information to management. Directs the activities of all accounting and clerical personnel. Prepares Job Profitability Reports and monthly financial statements reflecting accurately the operations of the Company. Follows up on accounts receivable collections and supervises the Company's payables and payroll systems.

6. Directs all other office activities, including the management of adequate insurance coverage, timely tax return preparation and payment, and maintenance of accurate and complete filing systems.

Qualifications:

Education:	Level 3	Policy & Planning Responsibility:	Level 4
Experience:	Level 4	Decision-Making Responsibility:	Level 3
Technical Knowledge & Skills:	Level 3	Supervision:	Level 3
Outside Contacts:	Level 2	Working Conditions:	Level 3

Approved:	**Date:**

173

ABC Company	POSITION DESCRIPTION
Policy Manual	**POSITION:** Senior Design Engineer

Reporting Relationships: Reports to: President Reporting to this position: Design Engineer	**Pay Grade:** S7

Position Summary:

Responsible for completing the engineering design of new products to be manufactured by the Company. Submits final designs to President for approval.

Principal Responsibilities:

1. Prepares and details engineering drawings of new products to be manufactured by the company.

2. Reviews engineering drawings and specifications with the President. Responsible for maintaining print files of all drawings of Company products.

3. May assist in trouble shooting to support President in solving design and processing problems involving the Company's products. Such assistance may include visiting customer plant locations.

4. Maintains close working relationship with customers relative to the Company's products and handles problem calls on the phone.

5. Assists in the development of new designs for new products and follows up on prototype testing and documents final results of all Research and Development Projects.

Qualifications:

Education: Level 1	Policy & planning responsibility: Level 3
Experience: Level 2	Decision-making responsibility: Level 2
Technical knowledge & skills: Level 1	Supervision: Level 3
Outside contacts: Level 2	Working conditions: Level 3

Approved:	**Date:**

Appendix D

Performance Appraisal System

Performance appraisal is the key element in the achievement of two of the most vital objectives of a Salary and Wage Administration Program:

1. Advising employees of their progress on the job so they may improve their effectiveness and growth potential.
2. Providing a basis for granting base salary or wage increases that are properly related to the employee's performance.

The Performance Appraisal should be prepared at least once a year, commonly on the anniversary of the employee's employment date, prior to granting any salary or wage increase. It may also be completed at any other time when:

▶ An interim salary or wage increase is granted for outstanding performance.

▶ Progress of an employee is below that which is normally expected.

▶ An employee is promoted from one pay grade to another, whether a pay adjustment is proposed or not.

A sample of a *Performance Appraisal Report for Non-Supervisory Personnel* is presented in the following pages.

ABC Corporation	PERFORMANCE APPRAISAL Non-Supervisory Personnel					
Name: **Position:** **Pay Grade:** **For period: from _____ to _____**	**Reason for Evaluation** ❏ **Annual appraisal** ❏ **Probationary period complete** ❏ **Other** _____					
TECHNICAL KNOWLEDGE: Understanding of job and related equipment through education and/or training.		OS	AN	NE	BN	UN	NA
	Self	❏	❏	❏	❏	❏	❏
	Supv	❏	❏	❏	❏	❏	❏
WORK PERFORMANCE: Accuracy, thoroughness and attention to details; completion of work on time with sense of urgency.	**Self**	❏	❏	❏	❏	❏	❏
	Supv	❏	❏	❏	❏	❏	❏
WORK ETHIC: Disciplined attention to business with minimal disruptions. Responsive to instructions. Dependability. On time. Low absenteeism.	**Self**	❏	❏	❏	❏	❏	❏
	Supv	❏	❏	❏	❏	❏	❏
ATTITUDE: Positive approach to job, company and co-workers. Reacts well to criticism. Desire to learn. Cooperative	**Self**	❏	❏	❏	❏	❏	❏
	Supv	❏	❏	❏	❏	❏	❏
SAFETY CONSIDERATIONS: Observes all safety rules. Keeps work area and equipment clean. Treats equipment carefully and helps keep in proper maintenance condition.	**Self**	❏	❏	❏	❏	❏	❏
	Supv	❏	❏	❏	❏	❏	❏
OVERALL: Summary of appraisal, giving proper weight to important factors. A composite evaluation of the employee.	**Self**	❏	❏	❏	❏	❏	❏
	Supv	❏	❏	❏	❏	❏	❏

COMMENTS OF EVALUATOR:

Employee's strong points

Employee's weak points

Signature of Evaluator:	Date:

COMMENTS OF EMPLOYEE:

1. Do you believe this evaluation is fair?   Yes ___   No ___
2. Do you have suggestions on how the Company could improve as a place to work?   Yes __   No __

Suggestions:

Signature of Employee:	Date:

COMMENTS BY EVALUATOR'S SUPERVISOR:

Do you and the evaluator recommend a pay increase? Yes _____ No _____

Recommended increase in pay rate. _____ per hour _____ per mo.

Change in pay grade? Yes ___ No _____   From_____ To _____

Signature of Evaluator's Supervisor:	Date:
Pay Increase Approval:	Date Effective:

Back of Form

Although the form illustrated is for Non-Supervisory Personnel (hourly and non-exempt), a similar form should be used for Salaried and Supervisory Personnel. An explanation of how to use the form follows:

Rating Degrees

Outstanding: Consistent, extraordinarily superior performance. The best that could be expected for this job.

Above Normal: Performance that is better than what is normally expected for the job. Some room for improvement.

Normally Expected: Performance meets the usual expectations for the job. Clearly satisfactory.

Below Normal: Performance that is not adequate to maintain the job over time. Improvement is necessary to rise to that which is normally expected of the job.

Unsatisfactory: Unacceptable performance. Except for unusual circumstances, is basis for dismissal.

Not applicable: Rater unable to evaluate.

Use of the Form

1. A self-evaluation is completed by the employee by rating his performance with an X in the appropriate column of one copy of the form. At the same time, the evaluator should complete the rating of the employee on the original of the form.
2. After the employee has completed his copy of the form, the form is returned to the evaluator. The evaluator reviews the self-evaluation and records the employee's ratings on the original of the form.
3. After attaching the employee's copy to the original, the evaluator should review the forms with his supervisor to reach agreement on salary (wage) or pay grade adjustments, if any. The back side of the original should be completed.
4. The annual performance evaluation interview is then held with the employee, showing the comparison of his ratings and those of the evaluator. The employee should then sign the form and add any comments that he believes appropriate.

The most important disclosure revealed by this process is when the evaluator and the employee are widely apart on the ratings. This indicates that they do not see the employee's performance in the same way. Such differences should be dealt with by discussion and further investigation. If the employee believes he is doing a great job and the evaluator believes the employee is giving a Below Normal performance, communication is critical and the issues must be resolved.

Appendix E

Personal Financial Statement

Name:

Personal Financial Statement		As of:	
What You Own (Assets)	**Current Value**	**What You Owe (Liabilities)**	**Current Value**
Checking Accounts	$	Unpaid Bills	$
Saving Accounts		Credit Card Balances Owed	
IRA Account		Installment Loans Owed	
Stocks and Mutual Funds		Student Loans Owed	
Cash Value of Life Insurance		Taxes Due and Unpaid	
Loans to Family or Friends		Amounts Owed Family/ Friends	
Home Value		Mortgage on Home	
Furniture Value		Home Improvement Loan	
Recreational Equipment Value		Personal Notes Owed	
Autos/Trucks Owned Value		Loans on Autos/Trucks	
Other Items Owned		Other Items Owed	
Total of What You Own		**Total of What You Owe**	

Personal Net Worth	
What You Own (Assets)	
Less What You Owe (Liabilities)	
Equals: Your Net Worth	

Appendix F

Schedule of Start-up Costs

Name of Small Business
Start-up Costs for Year 20XX

Type of Startup Cost	Month	Month	Month	Month	Month	Month	Total
Land Purchase (a)							
Building Purchase (b)							
Building/Office Rental (c)							
Equipment Purchases (d)							
Equipment Rentals (e)							
Utilities and Phone (f)							
Inventory (g)							
Property Taxes (h)							
Leasehold Improvements (j)							
Autos and Trucks (k)							
Advertising and Promotion (l)							
Licenses (m)							
Tax Deposits (n)							
Equipment Maintenance (o)							
Insurance (p)							
Professional Services (q)							
Payroll and Benefits (r)							
Office Supplies (s)							
Opening Promotional Costs (t)							
Loan Payments (u)							
Other Start-up Costs (v)							
Total Start-up Costs							
Cumulative Start-up Costs							

Explanation of Start Up Costs & Assumptions Used:
(Use this space to explain the source of data used, keying the description to the line above using a letter reference.)

Appendix G

Balance Sheet

Name of Small Business
As of December 31, 20XX
BALANCE SHEET

Assets				
	Year 1	Year 2	Year 3	Year 4
Current Assets				
Cash				
Accounts Receivable				
Inventory				
Prepaid Expenses				
Other Current Assets				
Total				
Property and Equipment				
Land and Buildings				
Leasehold Improvements				
Equipment and Furniture				
Sub-total				
Less: Accumulated Depreciation				
Total				
Other Assets				
Total Assets				
Liabilities and Equity				
Current Liabilities				
Short-term Bank Loans				
Accounts Payable				
Accrued Expenses				
Income Taxes Payable				
Other Current Liabilities				
Total				
Long-Term Debt				
Due Bank				
Due Others				
Total				
Owners' Equity				
Common Stock				
Retained Earnings				
Current Year's Earnings				
Total				
Total Liabilities and Equity				

Appendix H

Income Statement (P&L)

Name of Small Business
For the years ending, December 31, 20XX

INCOME STATEMENT				
	Year 1	Year 2	Year 3	Year 4
Sales				
Cost of Sales:				
Materials				
Labor				
Variable Overhead				
Total Cost of Sales				
Gross Profit				
GP %				
Expenses:				
Salaries/wages				
Other payroll costs				
Office supplies				
Rent expense				
Auto/truck costs				
Utilities				
Advertising				
Bad debt expense				
Professional fees				
Travel expense				
Insurance				
Taxes				
Other expenses				
Total expenses				
Operating income				
Non-operating items:				
Interest expense				
Other income/expense				
Total other costs				
Pre-tax income				
Income taxes				
Net income (loss)				

Appendix I

Cash Flow Statement

Name of Small Business
For the years ending, December 31, 20XX

CASH FLOW STATEMENT				
	Year 1	**Year 2**	**Year 3**	**Year 4**
Beginning Cash Balance				
Cash Received From:				
Owner Investment				
Loan Proceeds				
Cash Sales				
Receivables Collections				
Credit Card Payments				
Rental Payments				
Other Receipts				
Total Cash Receipts				
Cash Paid Out For:				
Payroll Costs				
Rent and Utilities				
Maintenance				
Office Supplies				
Taxes & Insurance				
Professional Fees				
Equipment Rental				
Selling and Advertising				
Loan Payments				
Other Disbursements				
Total Cash Disbursements				
Increase (Decrease in Cash)				
Ending Cash Balance				

Appendix J

Funds Flow Statement

Name of Small Business
For the years ending, December 31, 20XX

STATEMENT OF FUNDS FLOW				
	Year 1	Year 2	Year 3	Year 4
Beginning Cash Balance				
Funds Provided by:				
Net income				
Add: Non-cash charges				
Total from operations				
Owner Investment				
Loan Proceeds				
Increases (-decreases) in:				
Short-term bank loans				
Accounts payables				
Credit card payables				
Other payables				
Other Sources				
Total Funds Provided				
Funds Applied to:				
Increases (-decreases) in:				
Accounts receivable				
Inventory				
Prepaid items				
Other current assets				
Buildings				
Leasehold improvements				
Equipment				
Furniture & fixtures				
Long-term debt				
Owner withdrawals				
Other applications				
Total Funds Applied				
Increase (- Decrease) in Cash				
Ending Cash Balance				

Appendix K

Chart of Accounts
(Small Service Company or Manufacturer)

Chart of Accounts (for a small service company or manufacturer)	
Account Number	**Account Name**
100	Cash—National Bank (general account)
101	Cash—National Bank (payroll account)
109	Petty Cash
110	Marketable Securities
120	Accounts Receivable—Trade
121	Accounts Receivable—Employees
122	Accounts Receivable—Other
129	Allowance for Doubtful Accounts
130	Materials Inventory
131	Work In Process Inventory
132	Finished Goods Inventory
140	Prepaid Insurance
141	Prepaid Taxes
142	Other Prepaid Expenses
150	Other current assets
160	Land
161	Buildings
162	Machinery and Equipment
163	Office Furniture and Fixtures
164	Autos and Trucks
165	Leasehold Improvements
171	Accumulated Depreciation—Buildings
172	Accumulated Depreciation—Machinery & Equipment
173	Accumulated Depreciation—Office Furniture & Fixtures
174	Accumulated Depreciation—Autos & Trucks
175	Accumulated Amortization—Leasehold Improvements
180	Trademarks and Patents
181	Other Intangible Assets
182	Accumulated Amortization
190	Other Assets

Chart of Accounts (for a small service company or manufacturer)	
Account Number	**Account Name**
200	Notes Payable—National Bank
210	Accounts Payable—Trade
211	Accounts Payable—Officers & Employees
212	Accounts Payable—Other
220	Federal Withholding Taxes Payable
221	State Withholding Taxes Payable
222	FICA Taxes Withheld
223	Medicare Premiums Withheld
224	Health Insurance Premiums Withheld
230	Payroll Payable
231	Payroll Clearing Account
240	Accrued Salaries & Wages
241	Accrued Holiday Pay
242	Accrued Vacation Pay
243	Accrued FICA Taxes
244	Accrued Federal Unemployment Tax
245	Accrued State Unemployment Tax
246	Accrued Medicare Premiums
247	Accrued Health Insurance Premiums
250	Accrued Interest
251	Accrued Federal Income Tax
252	Accrued State Income Tax
253	Accrued Real Estate and Personal Property Taxes
254	Other Accrued Taxes
260	Long Term Notes Payable—National Bank
261	Other Long Term Notes Payable
270	Deferred Taxes on Income
271	Other Deferred Liabilities
280	Preferred Stock
281	Common Stock
290	Retained Earnings
291	Current Year's Earnings

Chart of Accounts (for a small service company or manufacturer)	
Account Number	**Account Name**
300	Sales—Service or Product A
310	Sales—Service or Product B
390	Sales Discounts and Allowances
391	Sales Returns
400	Cost of Sales—Service or Product A
401	Materials—Service or Product A
402	Labor—Service or Product A
403	Direct Overhead Costs—Service or Product A
410	Cost of Sales—Service or Product B
411	Materials—Service or Product B
412	Labor—Service or Product B
413	Direct Overhead Costs—Service or Product B
500	Supervisory Salaries
501	Indirect Labor
502	Maintenance Wages
510	Vacation and Holiday Pay (for 402 and 412)
520	Overtime Premium (for 402 and 412)
530	Payroll Tax Expense (for 402 and 412)
531	Health Insurance Expense (for 402 and 412)
539	Other Plant Payroll Costs (for 402 and 412)
540	Tools and Supplies
541	Maintenance Supplies
550	Power and Water
551	Insurance
552	Real Estate and Personal Property Taxes
559	Other Plant Facilities Costs
560	Depreciation Expense
561	Amortization Expense
580	Other Indirect Costs
599	Overhead Absorbed

Chart of Accounts (for a small service company or manufacturer)	
Account Number	**Account Name**
700	Administrative Salaries and Wages
701	Sales Salaries and Wages
710	Vacation and Holiday Pay
720	Overtime Premium
730	Payroll Tax Expense (for 700 and 701)
731	Health Insurance Expense (for 700 and 701)
739	Other Payroll Expenses (for 700 and 701)
740	Office Supplies
741	Sales Supplies
742	Maintenance Supplies
750	Heat and Light
751	Insurance
752	Real Estate and Personal Property Tax Expense
753	Telecommunication Expenses
760	Depreciation—Office Furniture, Fixtures & Equipment
762	Lease Costs—Office Equipment
770	Advertising Expense
780	Administrative Travel Expense
781	Administrative Auto Expense
782	Sales Travel Expense
783	Sales Auto Expense
790	Bad Debts Expense
791	Other Selling Expenses
792	Other Administrative Expenses
800	Other Non-Operating Income
801	Other Non-Operating Expense
900	Interest Expense
990	Provision for Federal Income Taxes
991	Provision for State Income Taxes

Appendix L

Chart of Accounts
(Small Retailer)

Chart of Accounts (for a small retail company)	
Account Number	**Account Name**
100	Cash—National Bank (general account)
101	Cash—National Bank (payroll account)
109	Petty Cash
110	Marketable Securities
120	Accounts Receivable—trade
121	Accounts Receivable—employees
122	Accounts Receivable—miscellaneous
129	Allowance for Doubtful Accounts
130	Inventory—Department A
131	Inventory—Department B
132	Inventory—Department C
140	Prepaid Insurance
141	Prepaid Taxes
142	Other Prepaid Expenses
150	Deferred Charges
160	Land
161	Buildings
162	Store Fixtures
163	Office Furniture and Fixtures
164	Autos and Trucks
165	Leasehold Improvements
171	Accumulated Depreciation—Buildings
172	Accumulated Depreciation—Store Fixtures
173	Accumulated Depreciation—Office Furniture and Fixtures
174	Accumulated Depreciation—Autos and Trucks
175	Accumulated Amortization—Leasehold Improvements
180	Trademarks
181	Other Intangible Assets
182	Accumulated Amortization
190	Other Assets

Chart of Accounts (for a small retail company)	
Account Number	**Account Name**
200	Notes Payable—National Bank
210	Accounts Payable—Trade
211	Accounts Payable—Officers and Employees
212	Credit Card Payables
220	Federal Withholding Taxes Payable
221	State Withholding Taxes Payable
222	FICA Taxes Withheld
223	Medicare Premiums Withheld
224	Health Insurance Premiums Withheld
230	Payroll Payable
231	Payroll Clearing Account
240	Accrued Salaries and Wages
241	Accrued Holiday Pay
242	Accrued Vacation Pay
243	Accrued FICA Taxes
244	Accrued Federal Unemployment Tax
245	Accrued State Unemployment Tax
246	Accrued Medicare Premiums
247	Accrued Health Insurance Premiums
250	Accrued Interest
251	Accrued Federal Income Tax
252	Accrued State Income Tax
253	Accrued Real Estate and Personal Property Taxes
254	Other Accrued Taxes
260	Long Term Notes Payable National Bank
261	Other Long Term Notes Payable
270	Deferred Taxes on Income
271	Other Deferred Liabilities
280	Preferred Stock
281	Common Stock
290	Retained Earnings
291	Current Year's Earnings

Chart of Accounts (for a small retail company)	
Account Number	**Account Name**
300	Sales—Department A
310	Sales—Department B
390	Sales Discounts and Allowances
395	Sales Returns
400	Cost of Sales—Department A
410	Cost of Sales—Department B
700	Admin Salaries and Wages
705	Sales Salaries and Wages
710	Vacation & Holiday Pay—Sales
720	Overtime Premium—Sales
730	FICA Tax Expense—Sales
731	Federal Unemployment Tax Expense—Sales
732	State Unemployment Tax Expense—Sales
733	Medicare Premium Expense—Sales
734	Health Insurance Expense—Sales
739	Other Sales Payroll Expenses
740	Sales & Office Supplies
741	Maintenance Supplies—Sales
750	Heat & Light Sales
751	Insurance Sales
752	Real Estate and Personal Property Tax Expense Sales
760	Depreciation—Store Fixtures, Furniture and Equipment
762	Lease Costs—Sales Office Equipment
770	Advertising Expense
780	Sales Travel Expense
781	Sales Automobile Expenses
790	Bad Debts Expense
791	Other Selling Expenses
900	Interest Expense
901	Other Non-Operating Income and Expense
990	Provision for Taxes on Income—Federal
991	Provision for Taxes on Income—State

Appendix M

Typical Accounting Entries

The accounting entries appearing in the following pages are common entries that are typical to most accounting systems. Refer to Appendix K to review a listing of the chart of accounts to help understand the entries that follow:

Accounting Entry	Debit	Credit
(1) Dr. Accounts Receivable – Doe Corp.	xxx	
Cr. Sales		xxx
To record the sale on credit of product to the Doe Corp., based on our sales invoice.		
(2) Dr. Inventory	yyy	
Cr. Accounts Payable – Jones Steel Co.		xxx
To record the purchase, on account, of materials from Jones Steel Co. based on our Purchase Order, Receiving Report and Jones Steel Co.'s invoice.		
(3) Dr. Cash	xxx	
Cr. Accounts Receivable – Doe Corp.		xxx
To record the receipt of payment on account from Doe Corp. based on check copy and our deposit slip.		
(4) Dr. Plant and Equipment – Machinery	xxx	
Cr. Accounts Payable – Smith Equip. Co.		xxx
To record the purchase of machinery from the Smith Equipment Co. based on our Purchase Order and their vendor invoice.		
(5) Dr. Cash	xxx	
Cr. Note Payable – National Bank		xxx
To record the borrowing of money from the National Bank based on our note payable to the bank, dated xx/xx/xx, with interest at x%.		

Accounting Entry	Debit	Credit
(6) Dr. Accounts Payable – James Steel Co.	xxx	
Cr. Cash		xxx
To record the borrowing of money from the National Bank based on our note payable to the bank, dated xx/xx/xx, with interest at x%.		
(7) Dr. Direct Labor	xxx	
Dr. Indirect Labor	xxx	
Cr. Federal Withholding Payable		xxx
Cr. State Withholding Payable		xxx
Cr. FICA Taxes Withheld		xxx
Cr. Accrued FICA Taxes		xxx
Cr. Accrued Federal Unemployment Tax		xxx
Cr. Accrued State Unemployment Tax		xxx
Cr. Medicare Premium Withheld		xxx
Cr. Accrued Medicare Premium		xxx
Cr. Health Insurance Premium Withheld		xxx
Cr. Payroll Payable		xxx
To record the direct labor payroll for the week of xx/xx/xx based on Job Time Cards (as summarized) and current tax rates. The accrued amounts are the employer's share of the taxes indicated. Indirect labor is an overhead expense for time spent in housekeeping activities.		
(8) Dr. Administrative Salaries and Wages	xxx	
Dr. Sales Salaries and Wages	xxx	
Dr. Payroll Tax Expense	xxx	
Cr. Federal Withholding Payable		xxx
Cr. State Withholding Payable		xxx
Cr. FICA Taxes Withheld		xxx
Cr. Accrued FICA Taxes		xxx
Cr. Accrued Federal Unemployment Tax		xxx
Cr. Accrued State Unemployment Tax		xxx

Accounting Entry	Debit	Credit
Cr. Medicare Premium Withheld		xxx
Cr. Accrued Medicare Premium		xxx
Cr. Health Insurance Premium Withheld		xxx
Cr. Payroll Payable		xxx

To record the administrative payroll for the month of xxx, based on existing payroll records and Time Slips for office personnel. Note: More about payroll in Chapter 8.

Accounting Entry	Debit	Credit
(9) Dr. Federal Withholding Tax Payable	xxx	
Dr. State Withholding Tax Payable	xxx	
Dr. Accrued FICA Taxes	xxx	
Dr. FICA Taxes Withheld	xxx	
Dr. Medicare Premium Withheld	xxx	
Dr. Accrued Medicare Premiums	xxx	
Cr. Cash		xxx

To pay the amounts due for Federal and state withholding tax, FICA taxes (employer & employee) and Medicare Premiums (withheld & accrued) to the Federal government based on tax returns filed.

Accounting Entry	Debit	Credit
(10) Dr. Accrued Federal Unemployment Tax	xxx	
Dr. Accrued State Unemployment Tax	xxx	
Cr. Cash		xxx

To pay the amounts due for Federal and state unemployment taxes.

Accounting Entry	Debit	Credit
(11) Dr. Payroll Payable	xxx	
Cr. Cash		xxx

To pay the payroll and issue checks to employees, based on payroll reports and time cards and slips, as previously used to record payroll distribution.

Accounting Entry	Debit	Credit
(12) Dr. Health Insurance Expense – Admin.	xxx	
Dr. Health Insurance Expense – Plant	xxx	
Dr. Health Insurance Premium Withheld	xxx	
Cr. Health Insurance Premium Payable		xxx

To record the liability for health insurance premiums as an expense, net of amounts withheld, based on the invoice received for the month of xxxx.

Accounting Entry	Debit	Credit
(13) Dr. Health Insurance Premium Payable	xxx	
Cr. Cash – National Bank		xxx
To pay the health insurance premium for the month of xx/xx/xx.		
(14) Dr. Prepaid Insurance	xxx	
Cr. Accounts Payable		xxx
To record the notice received from the insurance company of the premiums for casualty and liability insurance for the current year.		
(15) Dr. Insurance Expense – Administrative	xxx	
Dr. Insurance Expense – Direct	xxx	
Cr. Prepaid Insurance		xxx
To allocate one month's casualty and liability insurance premium to the office and to jobs based on an allocation factor, such as square footage.		
(16) Dr. Direct Overhead Costs	xxx	
Cr. Direct Overhead Absorbed		xxx
To allocate direct overhead expenses to jobs based on an overhead rate of x times direct labor dollars used on the jobs for the month. Note: *The rate selected should develop an amount that approximates total direct overhead expenses for a given month, thereby "absorbing" such costs into production for the month.*		
(17) Dr. Cost of Sales – Product A	xxx	
Dr. Cost of Sales – Product B	xxx	
Cr. Work in Process Inventory		xxx
To record the cost of jobs closed during the month (for which sales have been recorded) based on sales invoices and job reports.		
(18) Dr. Depreciation Expense – Administrative	xxx	
Dr. Depreciation Expense – Direct	xxx	
Cr. Allowance for Depr. – Plant and Equipment		xxx
To record depreciation for the month based on the cost and useful lives (developing depreciation rates) of the assets employed. The allocation between Administrative and Direct is based on the assets employed in each area.		

Accounting Entry	Debit	Credit
(19) Dr. Bad Debts Expense	xxx	
Cr. Allowance for Doubtful Accounts		xxx
To record as a reserve against accounts receivable an amount which, based on experience, will offset accounts that are likely to become uncollectible and must be written off.		
(20) Dr. Various Administrative Expenses	xxx	
such as Travel, Legal, Accounting, and Utilities		
Dr. Various Selling Expenses	xxx	
such as Travel, Commissions, and Advertising		
Cr. Accounts Payable		xxx
To record expenses associated with normal business operations.		
(21) Dr. Taxes on Income	xxx	
Cr. Accrued Federal Income Tax		xxx
Cr. Accrued State Income Tax		xxx
To accrue the liability for taxes on income for the current period.		

These entries are typical but not necessarily common to all companies. They are presented here to provide the reader with some understanding of how accounting entries, using debits and credits, are made to enter transactions into the accounts.

Appendix N

Trend Reports

The following charts can be used to track financial trends in different areas of operation and budgets for a small business. The charts include models for an income statement, variable overhead costs, a balance sheet, and a gross margin report.

Name of Company
For the Year Ending December 31, 20XX

	Plan	Jan	Feb	Mar	Apr	May	Jun	Jul	Aug	Sep	Oct	Nov	Dec	YTD Actual	YTD Plan
Sales															
Cost of Sales															
Materials															
Labor															
Variable Overhead															
Total Cost of Sales															
Gross Profit															
Gross Profit %															
Expenses															
Salaries/wages															
Other payroll costs															
Office supplies															
Rent expense															
Auto/truck costs															
Utilities															
Advertising															
Bad debt expense															
Professional fees															
Travel expense															
Insurance															
Taxes															
Other expenses															
Total Expenses															
Operating Income															
Nonoperating Items															
Interest expense															
Other income/ expense															
Total other costs															
Pretax Income															
Income Taxes															
Net Income (loss)															

Name of Company
For the Year Ending December 31, 20XX

Variable Overhead Expenses	Plan	Jan	Feb	Mar	Apr	May	Jun	Jul	Aug	Sep	Oct	Nov	Dec	YTD Actual	YTD Plan
Job Supv and Estimating															
Payroll Taxes – Direct															
Workers Compensation															
Supplies – Job-Related															
Freight in															
Dump Fees															
Small Tools															
Truck Fuel															
Truck maintenance															
Mileage reimbursement															
Insurance – Liability															
Commissions															
Inventory Adjustments															
Depr. – Job-Related															
Other Variable Costs															
Total Variable OH															

Name of Company Balance Sheet
For the Year Ending December 31, 20XX

Assets	Plan	Jan	Feb	Mar	Apr	May	Jun	Jul	Aug	Sep	Oct	Nov	Dec
Current Assets													
Cash													
Accounts Receivable													
Inventory													
Prepaid Expenses													
Other Current Assets													
Total													
Property and Equipment													
Land and Buildings													
Leasehold Improvements													
Equipment and Furniture													
Sub-total													
Less: Accumulated Depr.													
Total													
Other Assets													
Total Assets													

Liabilities and Equity	Plan	Jan	Feb	Mar	Apr	May	Jun	Jul	Aug	Sep	Oct	Nov	Dec
Current Liabilities													
Short-term Bank Loans													
Accounts Payable													
Accrued Expenses													
Income Taxes Payable													
Other current liabilities													
Total													
Long-Term Debt													
Due Bank													
Due Others													
Total													
Owners' Equity													
Common Stock													
Retained Earnings													
Current Year's Earnings													
Total													
Total Liabilities & Equity													

Name of Company
For the Year Ending December 31, 20XX

Gross Margin Report	Plan	Jan	Feb	Mar	Apr	May	Jun	Jul	Aug	Sep	Oct	Nov	Dec	YTD Actual	YTD Plan
Product Line A															
Sales															
Cost of Sales															
Gross Profit															
Gross Profit %															
Product Line B															
Sales															
Cost of Sales															
Gross Profit															
Gross Profit %															
Product Line C															
Sales															
Cost of Sales															
Gross Profit															
Gross Profit %															
Product Line D															
Sales															
Cost of Sales															
Gross Profit															
Gross Profit %															
Total All Lines															
Sales															
Cost of Sales															
Gross Profit															
Gross Profit %															

Appendix O

Sample Business Plan

You can use the sample business plan for ABC Services, LLC as a model for writing your own plan. It shows you what sections a business plan should include and the language you might use to write about your business. As you go through this plan, keep in mind that there are many ways to write a business plan and that there are many books available to help you in this process.

BUSINESS PLAN

For

ABC Services, LLC
Month, Year

<u>Confidential:</u>
This document is of a confidential nature and is not to be disseminated or reproduced without the express permission of the Company.

<u>Company Contact:</u>
Mr. John Doe
ABC Services, LLC
1234 Main Street
Oldtown, AZ 86301
doe@abcservices.com

Business Plan Illustration (Table of Contents)

TABLE OF CONTENTS

▶ **Mission Statement**

▶ **Executive Summary**

▶ **Marketing Plan**
    Products and Services
    Customer Base
    Competitive Position
    External Factors Affecting Marketing Efforts
    Pricing Strategy
    Sales Organization
    Sales Policies
    Advertising and Promotion

▶ **Operational Plan**
    Company Organization
    Personnel Policies
    Management Policies

▶ **Management Control Systems**
    Job Estimating and Pricing
    Job Profitability Reporting
    Nursery Products Inventory Management
    Credit and Collection Procedures

▶ **Financial Statements and Projections**
    Projected Financial Statements
    Commentary and Assumptions
    Projection Assumptions
    Schedule of Start-Up Costs
    Personal Financial Statement

▶ **Long-Range Strategic Plan**

The Mission Statement should be a brief paragraph that describes for the reader exactly the nature of your business. This reaffirmation of the business purpose, your target market, and the factors that separate your operation and value from your competitors is an essential part of your business strategy.

MISSION STATEMENT

ABC Services, LLC ("Company") is a start-up company founded by the principal owner, Mr. John Doe, to offer landscaping services, including landscape architectural design, in the tri-cities area. The Company also plans to offer a limited supply of trees, shrubs and plants for sale at retail from a small nursery. In the winter, ABC proposes to use its trucks for snow removal and the delivery of cut firewood. The Company's target market consists principally of homeowners, especially those whose homes are of recent construction. The owner, Mr. Doe, is an experienced graduate landscape architect whose background enables the Company to offer landscape design services provided only by a limited number of its competitors. Mr. Doe believes his knowledge and dedication to personalized customer service will create an image of professionalism differentiating ABC from its competitors and allow the Company to become a leading landscaping contractor in the tri-cities area.

EXECUTIVE SUMMARY

ABC Services, LLC was formed in January, 2003 by John and Jane Doe, the sole owners. The owners have invested $50,000 and have received an additional $25,000 loan from Mr. Doe's family. The loan bears interest at an annual rate of 8% to be repaid from the earnings of the Company, as available, with full payment not later than December 31, 2006. The Company began its operations as a landscaping contractor serving Oldtown and the tri-cities area. As indicated in the Mission Statement, John Doe is an experienced landscape designer and his role in the Company creates an image of professionalism combined with unique architectural landscaping services which he believes will set the Company apart from its competition.

Mrs. Jane Doe has an educational background in botany and directs the activities in the small nursery. She also oversees the work of the part-time accountant, Mrs. Numbers, who has several years experience in accounting with expertise in QuickBooks®. The Company's plans include the hiring of a man to supervise the activities of field personnel as soon as possible. The field workers are principally of Mexican descent.

The Company has done considerable demographics research and has carefully assessed its competition. The growth in the target market area is dynamic, both in population and in housing starts; which are key indicators for the future success of the Company. This information is discussed in the section on Marketing Plan. Although seasonality is a minor drawback to year 'round profitability, the Company believes its success during the landscaping and planting season will enable the retention of key personnel during the slow months.

The Company has leased a small building in Oldtown that can serve as its administrative office. The lease includes some adjoining land that will permit the development of a small nursery offering limited items at retail.

Although the owner's investment and family loan will cover the start-up costs other than fixed assets, the Company proposes to seek a term loan from the Oldtown Bank of $20,000 in January, 2003 (increasing to $50,000 in August, 2003 and $60,000 in December, 2003) to finance the start-up acquisition of assets. The Company also proposes to seek a seasonal revolving line of credit, with a maximum balance of $15,000 during 2003, to assist with the seasonal growth of inventory and receivables. The Company proposes to repay the term loan with cash flow from its operations beginning in 2005 and anticipates the loan to be fully repaid by December 31, 2006. The financing will be secured by the assets of the Company, including trucks, inventory, and accounts receivable and will be personally guaranteed by Mr. and Mrs. Doe.

A Schedule of Start-Up Costs, the Personal Financial Statement of the owners and Financial Projections of the Company's operations are included in this Business Plan in the section entitled Financial Statements and Projections.

The Company believes its future success lies in its ability to offer quality landscaping design services, the complete satisfaction of its customers' landscaping needs, and the adherence to sound financial and management principles.

MARKETING PLAN

The Marketing Plan discussing the Company's products and services is presented in the following pages. Included is information regarding the target customer base, the Company's competitive position, factors that afford the Company a unique position in the marketplace, external factors affecting the Company's marketing efforts, pricing strategy, sales organization and policies, advertising and promotional activities, and future marketing plans.

Products and Services. As residential development continues to grow at a rapid rate in the tri-cities area, the opportunities for providing landscaping services and related products has also increased. ABC Services is a start-up business as a landscaping contractor located in Oldtown, serving the tri-cities area of Old Valley, New Valley and Oldtown. In addition to the traditional landscaping services, the Company also proposes to develop a small nursery offering trees, shrubs, and plants for sale at retail. During the limited winter season from early December to late February, the Company plans to use its trucks for snow removal and the delivery of cut firewood. These additional services are targeted to the Company's proposed customer base.

Landscaping services to be offered by the Company include landscaping design, utilizing the educational and technical background of the owner, Mr. Doe. The Company plans to focus on quality residential builders to help target new business in connection with related construction opportunities. Landscaping services will include rock and gravel coverage in addition to the sale of nursery items, planting, garden design and construction, fountain installation, residential site clean-up, and other related services. The Company is negotiating a contract with a local rock and gravel supplier to enable the purchase and delivery of quality rock and gravel products to the contract site. Contacts developed by Mr. Doe for the purchase of trees, shrubs, and various plants from specialized large nursery locations should allow the Company to offer its customer a wide variety of options for their landscaping needs.

Customer Base. The customer base for the Company consists of current and prospective residential homeowners in a market area with a population over 100,000. Demographic research provided by the State Department of Commerce, disclosed that the population growth in the combined tri-cities area during the period 1900 to 2002 increased 75.5%. Although no information for population growth for the entire tri-cities area is available, the Oldtown Economic Development Department projects a 16.2% growth for that community over the next eight years.

New building permits for the tri-cities area during the period 1900 to 2002 increased 59.4%; taxable sales for the area increased 379.6% during the 1900-2002 period. It is clear that continued growth in the tri-cities area is expected. The tri-cities community is located in Yahoo County, a primarily rural and agricultural area, it does account for about two-thirds of the county's population. Population growth projections for the county, prepared by the State Department of Economic Security, show an increase of 8.5% by 2005 and 23.3% by 2010. It is the Company's belief that these indicators clearly represent an opportunity for the growth of its targeted customer base.

Competitive Position. The Company's principal competition currently comes from three nurseries that provide landscape design and contracting in addition to their sale of trees, plants, shrubs, and flowers. Rivers Nursery, one of the leading nurseries in Oldtown, offers a good selection of plantings and provides landscape design, but does not sell rock nor install sprinkler and drip systems. New Valley nursery operates in much the same manner. The third nursery, Lestimer Nursery, does offer plantings, design, and also has a modest offering of rock and gravel.

There are forty-two landscape contractors in the tri-cities area. However, many of them are small two-three person operations. Only one of the landscape firms has a degreed landscape architect, such as Mr. Doe. Because of Mr. Doe's educational background and experience, ABC has a distinct advantage over the majority of the competition. In addition, the proposed contract with the rock and gravel supplier plus the attractively designed new nursery gives the Company a full-service approach that only a few of the competition can offer.

Finally, during the winter months, the Company offers cut firewood for sale and uses its trucks for snow removal. Although this activity should develop only limited revenue, it does help defray the costs of a seasonally slow two to three months.

External Factors Affecting Marketing Efforts. The only external factors that impact the Company's projected operations, in addition to weather conditions, are building covenants in the various residential developments where potential customers are either building or residing. Because of the trend to specify more (rather than less) landscaping and area beautification, these covenants serve to enhance the Company's opportunity to serve its customer base.

Pricing Strategy. Because of the Company's position relative to the competition (as discussed above), Mr. Doe believes ABC's pricing should be among those in the top 33%. Hence, the Company intends to price their services higher than two-thirds of their competition. The quality of the work and the design capability offered by the Company should enable them to price a bit above most of the competition. However, the Company has developed a pricing technique that involves a careful estimate of materials and labor costs, and considers the cost of its variable and fixed overhead. This technique, developed using an Excel spreadsheet, enables the Company to select a price for a landscaping job that can range between a net profit (before tax) of its targeted 10% to a breakeven price. The latter would be selected when business is slow and work is needed to keep the employees actively engaged.

Prices for nursery products are set more competitively with the objective of being at or near the prices charged by it quality competitors. The Company's vendor contracts should help in assuring a reasonable return for these items. In the winter, the pricing strategy is to make a small profit but, more importantly, keep valued employees at work.

Sales Organization. Mr. Doe will be primarily involved with landscape design and sales. His wife, Jane, will serve as an inside salesperson for nursery products and customer service. She has two years of college with a major in botany and is well suited for landscape and nursery sales. Nearly all of the Company's sales will likely result from the efforts of John and Jane, and part-time college students hired during the summer season for inside sales.

John has made preliminary contacts with eight residential builders who build homes in the upper price class ($350,000 to $2,500,000) and has secured their agreement to refer clients to ABC for landscaping design and services. Each of these builders constructs 5 to 8 homes per year and the landscaping contracts for these residences will vary from $6,000 to more than $15,000, with an average estimated at $9,000. Although there is no guarantee that ABC will secure contracts with the builders' customers, John believes he can sell 4 to 5 contracts per month through the busy season from April through October. If an average of 4 per month for 7 months can be secured, the revenue from this source alone would be approach $250,000. In addition, John believes he can perform additional landscape design services for existing home owners who are trying to upgrade the appearance of their homes.

Sales Policies. The Company's sales policies are simple and straightforward. The Company proposes to provide a high quality product and service at a reasonable price. Mr. Doe's willingness to assist customers in preliminary landscape design, without charge, should help to attract business. The final design and landscaping service is priced to enable this helpful approach to satisfy customers' needs. The Company plans to warrant their nursery products for one growing season, provided that Company personnel are engaged to do the planting of the products.

Advertising and Promotion. Although the Company occasionally will place ads in the local newspapers to highlight special sales, most of the ad budget is dedicated to establishing a recognition of the Company, its products and the quality of services. A simple two-fold color brochure with a reply card that explains the Company's services and can also be used as a mailer will be the promotional vehicle used at the start. Initial sales promotion costs are included in the budget and start-up costs.

OPERATIONAL PLAN

This section of the Business Plan describes the management and personnel organization, a brief description of the procedures for hiring, training, and communicating with personnel and a discussion of management and operational policies.

Company Organization

The Company will have four full-time employees and two to three part-time employees during the summer season, depending upon sales demand. The part-time employees are used both in the nursery and in landscaping jobs, as required.

Mr. John Doe is President of the Company and will work full time. John and his wife, Jane, are the sole owners of the Company. John's primary activities will involve landscape design, consultation, sales, and the direction of the other key employees. John is 34 years of age and attended State University receiving a Bachelor of Science degree in Landscape Architecture. He worked ten years in landscape design for a large landscaping firm in Big City. Some of his designs were featured in the Homes Section of Big City Times.

Mrs. Jane Doe is a Vice-President of the Company and will be primarily responsible for the operation of the nursery and inside sales. She met John at State University where she completed two years of college, majoring in Botany. She directs the activities of the seasonal part-time employees used at the nursery and will also monitor the work of the Company's part-time accountant, including the payment of bills, preparation of financial statements, and payroll.

Other Employees include two full-time landscape workers who will work for John in the field on landscaping jobs. When they are not in the field, they help around the nursery or do other odd jobs, as required. Although their educational background is limited, they are both hard workers. Both are of Mexican descent.

During the summer season, Jane will likely hire one or two part-time local college students to help around the nursery. They will assist customers and care for the plants and shrubs, under Jane's direction. John will hire two to three part-time field workers as jobs require.

Key outside contacts. The Company also has key professional contacts that are used in their area of expertise. The Company uses J.M. Smith & Co., CPA's, for tax return preparation and general management and financial consultation; John Henry is the Company's insurance broker and the Company consults with L.L. Jones & Co., Attorneys at Law in all legal matters. These professional contacts are an important factor in the ongoing success of the Company.

Personnel Policies

The Company's personnel policies are being developed for inclusion in a planned *Company Handbook*. The handbook will present policies regarding the hiring process, the definition of salaried and hourly personnel, working hours, pay for funerals and jury duty, performance evaluations, basis for disciplinary action, raises, vacations and holidays, and other data relating to employment at ABC. The handbook will also contain Position Descriptions for the jobs in the Company.

Management Policies

In addition to personnel policies, the *Company Handbook* will contain the Company's management policies regarding warranties, delivery, and planting of products from the nursery, granting of credit to customers, product and service pricing, merchandise returns, and other matters relating to Company operations. These policies, already documented informally, will serve as a reminder for all personnel of the position taken by the Company with regard to important operational issues.

The Management Control Systems used by the Company to monitor its operations are discussed in this section of the Business Plan.

MANAGEMENT CONTROL SYSTEMS

The systems the Company plans to use to control and monitor its operations are part of the QuickBooks® capabilities coupled with the use of Microsoft Excel® spreadsheets. The systems include: Job Estimating and Pricing, Job Profitability Reporting, Nursery Products Inventory Management, and Credit and Collections Procedures.

Job Estimating and Pricing. This technique was discussed in the Pricing Strategy section of the Marketing Plan. Landscape jobs are estimated and bid using a fairly complex Excel® spreadsheet. Based on an approved landscape design, this document enables the Company (usually completed by Mr. Doe) to develop a listing of the cost of materials, labor required, and the application of variable and fixed overhead, to generate a base price aimed at the Company's target profit percentage. The bid is then accomplished by quoting a price between the base price and a higher price (considering the competition, the customer, and location of the work). During the off-season and based again on competition, the Company may deviate below its target profit percentage to gain work allowing the full-time employees to be productively utilized.

Job Profitability Reporting. The Company will utilize QuickBooks Pro® accounting software to generate profitability reporting by job. The actual results of each landscaping job will be compared to the bid estimate and deviations will be investigated. The Company plans to maintain a spreadsheet that summarizes the totals of its jobs, the estimate and actual amounts of materials, labor, and other costs. This information should be helpful in revising or updating the job estimating system, as required by higher prices or increased labor costs.

Nursery Products Inventory Management. The accounting software will also enable the management of inventory of nursery products (trees, shrubs, and other types of landscaping accessories). Order points and quantities will be developed for the various products, and revisions will be made depending upon the stage of the sales season. Jane Doe will monitor this system to minimize the investment in inventory on hand, but providing sufficient stock for walk in trade. As the season grows to an end, she plans to be especially careful to monitor additional ordering of stock to minimize the inevitable losses due to natural causes. Despite the greatest care, there is a normal loss factor for nursery stock that must be considered in the overall pricing strategy.

Credit and Collections Procedures. The Company plans to use a simple credit application form that will require trade and financial references which will be verified. After receiving the completed application forms, Jane Doe will call all references to help determine the creditworthiness of the applying customer. Once approved by John Doe, based on the reference information, the accounting software should allow the monitoring of amounts due by reference to aging reports.

FINANCIAL STATEMENTS AND PROJECTIONS

This section of the Business Plan presents the following financial projections, including assumptions to facilitate the understanding of management's financial objectives:

Projected Financial Statements

- ▶ Balance Sheets, by month for 2003, and annually as of December 31, 2004 and 2005

- ▶ Income Statements (with Variable Overhead Costs), by month for 2003, and annually for the years ending December 31, 2004 and 2005

- ▶ Funds Flow Statements, by month for 2003, and annually for the years ending December 31, 2004 and 2005

Commentary and Assumptions

The Company plans to begin operations, effective January 1, 2005, with $50,000 of invested capital and borrowings from family members of $25,000. The Company proposes to seek a term loan from Oldtown Bank to assist in financing the acquisition of fixed assets and inventory. The value of the Company's beginning assets is several times the amount of the loan proposed ($20,000) and should satisfy the collateral requirements of the bank. The owners (Mr. and Mrs. John Doe) recognize the need to provide their personal guarantee of the indebtedness. It is also proposed that the term loan of $20,000 (to be increased to $50,000 in August, 2005 enabling the purchase of an additional truck, and to $60,000 as the Company works down their credit card payables) provide for a moratorium on principal payments for a 24-month period, with interest being paid currently at the annual rate of 8%. Principal payments of $5,000 per month projected to begin in January or February,

2007 and continue monthly to the end of that year. The complete repayment of the term loan is anticipated in the spring of 2008.

The Company further proposes the use of a revolving line of credit with the bank, not to exceed $15,000, to supplement the other sources of financing during the high seasonal months. During the spring and summer months, increases in inventory and accounts receivable necessarily precede the cash flow resulting from sales during those months.

The Company's projected growth to nearly $300,000 in sales during the year 2003 is based on the Marketing Plan included in this Business Plan, coupled with the unique capabilities and experience of the owners. In addition, the remarkable growth in the areas of the Company's targeted customer base further supports the financial projections.

Projection Assumptions

Sales. The growth to $45,000 in sales during the peak months of June and July will require a limited number of new residential landscaping contracts supplemented by smaller landscape upgrade jobs and nursery sales. A high quality residential landscaping contract can average $9,000 and above. Mr. Doe's relationship with quality home builders who build in the higher value residential market (as discussed in the Marketing Plan), is expected to be a strong basis for this growth. Mr. Doe believes his experience in landscape design, which is critical to the higher value residential home owner, will set the Company apart from most of its competitors.

Cost of Sales. The first year (2005) reflects the expected higher materials costs due to purchasing contracts less favorable than in following years. Materials costs as a percentage of sales (11.7%) are conservative and do not reflect expected future economies resulting from better purchasing contracts. However, the projections conservatively do not project these anticipated savings during 2006 and 2007. Direct labor costs have been projected at an approximate 20% of sales volume. This relationship is consistent with Mr. Doe's past experience with Big City Landscaping and has been calculated, based on the number of employees needed and their wage rates. Variable overhead costs in 2003 are projected at 25% of sales. With the projected increase in sales volume, the percentage relationship of Variable OH to sales is expected to drop slightly in 2006 – 2007. Some semi-variable costs, such as supervision, will not increase in direct relationship with sales.

Expenses. The largest costs are salaries and wages which are based on calculated amounts to be paid to planned personnel. The other large expense is rent, which is based on a tentative lease agreement as offered by the proposed landlord. Interest is calculated at 8% per annum on all outstanding borrowings.

Receivables. The growth in receivables is based on the seasonal nature of the business. Thirty to forty days of sales is an anticipated range for receivables. The Company has targeted the better builders who have a record of paying within a reasonable time period.

Inventory. This asset will grow as a result of the seasonally increasing sales volume and the improved offerings at the nursery. As the nursery matures and sales volume further increases in 2006 and 2007, the Company has projected related increases in inventory investment.

Payables. As the Company's cash flow increases and cash balances are easier to maintain, Accounts Payable and Credit Card Payables are expected to moderate. However, during the first two years of the Company's existence, it is expected that vendors and credit card payables will be used to level the peaks and valleys in cash flow needs.

Other Factors. Although the Company is an LLC, the election to be taxed as a Sub-Chapter S corporation has been deferred until 2006. The owners will make no withdrawals in 2005 or 2006. Some withdrawal may be considered for 2007 to allow for the payment of income taxes that flow through to them. By electing the Sub-S Corporation, self-employment taxes for the owners are minimized.

Schedule of Start-Up Costs

A Schedule of Start-Up Costs has been prepared and is included in this section. It presents the initial costs required and how those costs are expected to be paid. All numbers in this schedule are consistent with the monthly Statement of Funds Flow.

Personal Financial Statement

The Personal Financial Statement of John and Jane Doe, as of December 31, 2004, is also included in this section. The statement reflects a net worth of more than $150,000 and indicates a life insurance policy on the life of John Doe of $500,000 face value.

ABC SERVICES LLC
Project Start-up Costs for 2005

Type of Start-up Cost	Jan	Feb	Mar	April
Inventory	15,000	1,830	660	17,490
Accounts Receivable		7,500	11,000	18,500
Leasehold improvements	20,000			20,000
Office Furniture and Fixtures	8,000			8,000
Vehicles and Equipment	50,000			50,000
Utility and Tax Deposits	750			750
Insurance	5,000			5,000
Negative cash flow from operations (see Funds Flow Stmt)	7,930	4,237	−2,435	9,732
Add back: non-cash charges	−535	−535	−535	−1,605
Total Start-up Costs	106,145	13,032	8,690	127,867
Cumulative Start-up Costs	106,145	119,177	127,867	132,877

Source of Funds for Start-up Costs			
Owner investment	50,000		
Family loan	25,000		
Vendor payables	13,500	1,647	5,594
Other payables	2,850	1,359	−1,135
Credit card payables	1,500	11,000	1,000
Total of Funds Sources	92,850	14,006	5,459
Cumulative Funds Available	92,850	106,856	112,315

Cumulative Start-up Funds Needed	13,295	12,321	15,552
Proposed Bank Loan Outstanding	20,000	20,000	20,000

Projected Cash Balance	6,705	7,679	4,448

ABC SERVICES, LC
Projected Balance Sheet
As of December 31, 2005, 2006, and 2007

Assets	Jan	Feb	Mar	Apr	May	Jun	Jul	Aug	Sep	Oct	Nov	2005 Dec	2006 Dec	2007 Dec
Current Assets														
Cash	6,705	7,679	4,448	3,573	3,663	2,105	3,964	5,553	2,641	5,025	4,804	4,433	12,656	4,426
Accounts Receivable	0	7,500	18,500	28,500	43,500	46,500	43,500	41,500	40,000	36,500	29,500	28,500	38,500	39,400
Inventory	15,000	16,830	17,490	25,980	29,715	35,450	39,770	38,750	38,000	37,500	35,000	35,000	44,650	47,500
Prepaid Expenses	4,465	3,930	3,395	2,860	2,325	1,790	5,255	4,720	4,185	3,650	3,115	2,580	7,150	9,100
Other Current Assets	250	250	250	250	250	250	250	250	250	250	250	250	350	400
Total	26,420	36,189	44,083	61,163	79,453	86,095	92,739	90,773	85,076	82,925	72,669	70,763	103,306	100,826
Property and Equipment														
Land and Buildings	20,000	20,000	20,000	21,500	21,500	21,500	21,500	21,500	21,500	21,500	21,500	21,500	21,500	21,500
Vehicles and Equipment	50,000	50,000	50,000	50,000	50,000	70,000	70,000	100,000	100,000	100,000	100,000	100,000	120,000	120,000
Furniture and Fixtures	8,000	8,000	8,000	8,000	8,000	8,000	8,000	8,000	8,000	8,000	8,000	8,000	8,000	10,000
Sub-total	78,000	78,000	78,000	79,500	79,500	99,500	99,500	129,500	129,500	129,500	129,500	129,500	149,500	151,500
Less: Accumulated Depr.	895	2,100	3,305	4,510	5,715	7,100	8,915	10,740	12,565	14,390	16,215	18,040	39,040	60,440
Total	77,105	75,900	74,695	74,990	73,785	92,400	90,585	118,760	116,935	115,110	113,285	111,460	110,460	91,060
Other Assets	500	500	500	500	500	750	750	750	750	750	750	750	2,500	3,500
Total Assets	104,025	112,589	119,278	136,653	153,738	179,245	184,074	210,283	202,761	198,785	186,704	182,973	216,266	195,386

Liabilities and Equity	Jan	Feb	Mar	Apr	May	Jun	Jul	Aug	Sep	Oct	Nov	2005 Dec	2006 Dec	2007 Dec
Current Liabilities														
Bank Revolving Credit Line	0	0	0	10,000	10,000	15,000	15,000	0	0	0	0	0	0	0
Accounts Payable	13,500	15,147	20,741	20,741	29,830	31,905	35,793	34,875	34,200	33,750	31,500	30,055	40,185	43,540
Credit Card Payables	1,500	12,500	13,500	13,500	8,500	13,500	7,500	14,500	10,000	10,000	5,000	2,500	2,500	5,000
Accrued Liabilities	1,500	2,695	1,500	1,500	4,170	4,170	1,500	3,727	1,500	1,500	3,195	3,077	6,000	9,000
Other current liabilities	1,350	1,514	1,574	1,574	1,774	1,930	1,959	1,823	1,792	1,717	1,593	1,575	2,835	3,600
Total	17,850	31,856	37,315	37,315	54,274	66,505	61,752	54,925	47,492	46,967	41,288	37,207	51,250	61,140
Long-Term Debt														
Due Bank	20,000	20,000	20,000	20,000	20,000	20,000	20,000	50,000	50,000	50,000	50,000	50,000	60,000	10,000
Due Others	25,000	25,000	25,000	25,000	25,000	25,000	25,000	25,000	25,000	25,000	25,000	25,000	25,000	15,000
Total	45,000	45,000	45,000	45,000	45,000	45,000	45,000	75,000	75,000	75,000	75,000	85,000	85,000	20,000
Owners' Equity														
Common Stock	50,000	50,000	50,000	50,000	50,000	50,000	50,000	50,000	50,000	50,000	50,000	50,000	50,000	50,000
Retained Earnings	0	0	0	0	0	0	0	0	0	0	0	0	10,766	29,746
Current Year's Earnings	-8,825	-14,267	-13,037	-9,074	4,464	17,740	27,322	30,358	30,269	26,818	20,416	10,766	18,980	34,500
Total	41,175	35,733	36,963	40,926	54,464	67,740	77,322	80,358	80,269	76,818	70,416	60,766	79,746	114,246
Total Liabilities & Equity	104,025	112,589	119,278	136,653	153,738	179,245	184,074	210,283	202,761	198,785	186,704	182,793	216,266	195,386

ABC Services, LLC
Projected Statements of Income
For the Years Ending December 31, 2005, 2006, and 2007

	Jan	Feb	Mar	Apr	May	Jun	Jul	Aug	Sep	Oct	Nov	Dec	Total 2003	Total 2004	Total 2005
Sales	10,000	20,000	30,000	45,000	45,000	45,000	40,000	30,000	25,000	20,000	15,000	10,000	290,000	365,000	410,000
Cost of Sales															
Materials	0	1,170	2,340	3,510	5,265	5,265	4,680	3,510	2,925	2,340	1,755	1,170	33,930	42,705	47,970
Labor	0	1,970	3,940	5,910	8,865	8,865	7,880	5,910	4,925	3,940	2,955	1,970	57,130	71,905	80,770
Variable OH	500	1,312	1,875	5,932	6,647	6,674	6,438	6,014	5,739	5,576	5,077	4,875	56,659	73,690	82,445
Depreciation	760	1,070	1,070	1,070	1,070	1,250	1,680	1,690	1,690	1,690	1,690	1,690	16,420	19,000	19,000
Total Cost of Sales	1,260	5,522	9,225	16,422	21,847	22,054	20,678	17,124	15,279	13,546	11,477	9,705	164,139	207,300	230,185
Gross Profit	−1,260	4,478	10,775	13,578	23,153	22,946	19,322	12,876	9,721	6,454	3,523	295	125,861	157,700	179,815
GP Percent	0.0%	44.8%	53.9%	45.3%	51.5%	51.0%	48.3%	42.9%	38.9%	32.3%	23.5%	3.0%	43.4%	43.2%	43.9%
Expenses															
Salaries/wages	3,000	6,000	6,000	6,000	6,000	6,000	6,000	6,000	6,000	6,000	6,000	6,000	69,000	72,000	75,000
Other payroll costs	600	1,200	1,200	1,200	1,200	1,200	1,200	1,200	1,200	1,200	1,200	1,200	13,800	14,400	15,000
Office supplies	1,500	25	25	25	25	50	50	50	50	50	50	50	1,950	2,340	2,800
Rent expense	1,200	1,200	1,200	1,200	1,200	1,200	1,200	1,200	1,200	1,200	1,200	1,200	14,400	32,400	35,850
Utilities	100	100	100	100	100	100	170	170	170	240	240	230	1,820	2,150	2,240
Advertising	0	500	125	125	125	125	125	125	125	125	125	125	1,750	1,400	1,500
Professional fees	200	80	80	80	80	80	80	80	80	80	80	80	1,080	1,020	1,100
Travel expense	35	35	35	35	35	35	35	35	35	35	35	35	420	560	650
Insurance	60	60	60	60	60	60	60	60	60	130	130	130	930	1,600	1,850
Taxes	50	50	50	50	50	50	50	50	50	75	95	125	745	850	975
Depreciation	135	135	135	135	135	135	135	135	135	135	135	135	1,620	2,000	2,400
Other expenses	185	35	35	35	35	35	35	35	35	35	35	35	570	500	750
Total Expenses	7,065	9,420	9,045	9,045	9,045	9,070	9,140	9,140	9,140	9,305	9,325	9,345	108,085	131,220	140,115
Operating Income	−8,325	−4,942	1,730	4,533	14,108	13,876	10,182	3,736	581	−2,851	−5,802	−9,050	17,776	26,480	39,700
Interest expense	500	500	500	570	570	600	600	700	670	600	600	600	7,010	7,500	5,200
Net Income (loss)	−8,325	−5,442	1,230	3,963	13,538	13,276	9,582	3,038	−89	−3,451	−6,402	−9,650	10,766	18,980	34,500

ABC Services, LLC
Projected Variable Overhead Costs
For the Years Ending December 31, 2005, 2006, and 2007

	Jan	Feb	Mar	Apr	May	Jun	Jul	Aug	Sep	Oct	Nov	Dec	Total 2003	2004	2005
Job Supervision	0	0	0	2,940	2,940	2,940	2,940	2,940	2,940	2,940	2,940	2,940	26,460	35,280	38,890
Payroll taxes - direct	0	394	788	1,770	2,361	2,361	2,164	1,770	1,573	1,376	1,060	903	16,520	21,437	23,932
Workers compensation	0	59	118	177	266	266	236	177	118	118	71	47	1,653	2068	2304
Supplies – Job related	0	38	43	58	59	57	53	47	43	42	41	40	521	600	750
Freight in	0	111	121	157	181	185	180	140	130	120	50	30	1,405	1,600	1,700
Dump fees	0	0	20	20	30	30	30	30	25	25	25	20	255	400	450
Small tools	0	35	35	35	35	35	35	35	35	35	35	35	385	500	600
Truck fuel	20	175	250	250	250	250	250	300	300	200	150	150	2,545	3,800	5,000
Truck maintenance	0	0	0	25	25	50	50	75	75	45	30	35	410	780	975
Insurance - liability	475	475	475	475	475	475	475	475	475	650	650	650	6,225	6,725	7,345
Other variable costs	5	25	25	25	25	25	25	25	25	25	25	25	280	500	500
Total Variable OH	500	1,312	1,875	5,392	6,647	6,674	6,438	6,014	5,739	5,576	5,077	4,875	56,659	73,690	82,446
Depreciation – job related	760	1,070	1,070	1,070	1,070	1,250	1,680	1,690	1,690	1,690	1,690	1,690	16,420	19,000	19,000
Total payroll															
Administrative	3,000	6,000	6,000	6,000	6,000	6,000	6,000	6,000	6,000	6,000	6,000	6,000	69,000	72,000	75,000
Workers	0	1,970	3,940	5,910	8,865	8,865	7,380	5,910	4,925	3,940	2,955	1,970	57,130	71,905	80,770
Supervision	0	0	0	2,940	2,940	2,940	2,940	2,940	2,940	2,940	2,940	2,940	26,460	35,280	38,890
Total	3,000	7,970	9,940	14,850	17,805	17,805	16,820	14,850	13,865	12,880	11,895	10,910	152,590	179,185	194,660
Total payroll costs (at 20% of Payroll)															
Administrative	600	1,200	1,200	1,200	1,200	1,200	1,200	1,200	1,200	1,200	1,200	1,200	13,800	14,400	15,000
Workers & Supervision	0	394	788	1,770	2,361	2,361	2,164	1,770	1,573	1,376	1,179	982	16,718	21,437	23,932
Total	600	1,594	1,988	2,970	3,561	3,561	3,364	2,970	2,773	2,576	2,379	2,182	30,518	35,837	38,932

ABC Services, LLC
Projected Statements of Funds Flow
For the Years Ending December 31, 2005, 2006, and 2007

	Jan	Feb	Mar	Apr	May	Jun	Jul	Aug	Sep	Oct	Nov	Dec	Total 2003	2004	2005
Beginning Cash	0	6,705	7,679	4,448	3,573	3,663	2,105	3,364	5,553	2,641	5,025	4,804	0	4,433	12,656
Funds Provided by:															
Net income	-8,825	-5,442	1,230	3,963	13,538	13,276	9,582	3,036	-89	-3,451	-6,402	-9,650	10,766	18,980	34,500
Add: Non-cash charges	895	1,205	1,205	1,205	1,205	1,385	1,815	1,825	1,825	1,825	1,825	1,825	18,040	21,000	21,400
Total from operations	-7,930	-4,237	2,435	5,168	14,743	14,661	11,397	4,861	1,736	-1,626	-4,577	-7,825	28,806	39,980	55,900
Funds Applied to:															
Increases (-decreases):															
Accounts receivable	0	7,500	11,000	10,000	15,000	3,000	-3,000	-2,000	-1,500	-3,500	-7,000	-1,000	28,500	10,000	900
Inventory	15,000	1,830	660	8,490	3,735	5,735	4,320	-1,020	-750	-500	-2,500	0	35,000	9,650	2,850
Prepaid insurance	4,465	-535	-535	-535	-535	-535	3,465	-535	-535	-535	-535	-535	2,580	4,570	1,950
Other current assets	250	0	0	0	0	0	0	0	0	0	0	0	250	100	50
Other assets	500	0	0	0	0	250	0	0	0	0	0	0	750	1,750	1,000
Leasehold improvements	20,000	0	0	1,500	0	0	0	0	0	0	0	0	21,500	0	0
Vehicles & equipment	50,000	0	0	0	0	20,000	0	30,000	0	0	0	0	100,000	20,000	0
Furniture & fixtures	8,000	0	0	0	0	0	0	0	0	0	0	0	8,000	0	2,000
Total Funds Applied	98,215	8,795	11,125	19,455	18,200	28,450	4,785	24,445	-2,875	-4,535	-10,035	-1,535	196,580	46,070	8,750
Incr (- Decr) in Cash	6,705	974	-3,231	-875	90	-1,558	1,859	1,589	-2,912	2,384	-221	-371	4,433	8,223	-8,230
Ending Cash	6,705	7,679	4,448	3,573	3,663	2,105	3,364	5,553	2,641	5,025	4,804	0	4,433	12,656	4,426

LONG RANGE STRATEGIC PLAN

The Company's objective is to become the leading landscaping contractor in the tri-cities area. To that end, the Company's long range plans include the expansion into the New Valley area with a business location and small nursery in that city. Mr. Doe believes his education and experience in landscape architecture and design gives the Company an advantage over the majority of their competition. He plans to use that advantage to develop relationships with the quality builders in the Oldtown area, offering outstanding landscape design service to these custom homebuilders.

Because the Company is in a start-up mode, Mr. and Mrs. Doe understand that the Company's initial disadvantage in the marketplace is the lack of unlimited financial resources. Accordingly, they plan to grow the Company slowly and within the resources available, not overextending in search of rapid growth.

Although two to three years in the future, John plans to start soliciting landscape design services in the New Valley and Old Valley communities, again concentrating on custom homebuilders who are perceived to be the leaders in their field. A physical move into the New Valley area would require additional equipment and a new location. This move, if consummated, would likely occur in 2006 or beyond.

The development of a stable and profitable Company is the primary objective for the long range future of the Company. With that growth will come the ability to invest in additional locations to serve other areas.

JOHN AND JANE DOE
Personal Financial Statement
As of December 31, 2004

Assets	
Checking Account (Oldtown Bank)	2,450
Savings Account	4,500
IRA Retirement Account	2,500
Mutual Funds	56,500
Cash Value of Life Insurance ($500,000 face)	4,325
Residence (1238 Oldtown Road)	197,500
Furniture & Household Items	24,600
Automobiles Owned (1999 Buick & 2001 Honda CRV)	36,600
Total Assets Owned	**328,975**

Liabilities	
Unpaid Bills	1,250
Credit Card Balances Owed	1,475
Taxes Due & Unpaid (Federal & State Income Tax)	3,100
Real Estate Mortgage - Residence (25 year)	134,300
Auto Loan (2001 Honda CRV)	12,500
Total Liabilities Owed	**152,625**

Net Worth	**176,350**

Total Liabilities and Net Worth	**328,975**

Notes:
(a) $50,000 of the Mutual Funds are set aside for investment in ABC Services, LLC.
(b) Neither John nor Jane are endorsers or co-makers of a loan, nor are contingently liable for any amounts.
(c) John Doe earned $55,000 in salary and bonus in 2002 from Big Town Landscape Designs, Big Town, ST.

Index

A

Accountants
  audits, 130–131
  benefits of services, 132–133
  review of leasing agreements by, 95–96
  selecting, 128–130
  tax preparation by, 131–132
  tips for working with, 133–134
Accounting
  cash vs. accrual, 101–102
  for costs, 99–100, 110–112
  double-entry bookkeeping, 102–106
  importance of understanding, 98–100, 165
  systems of, 106–110
Account numbers, 107
Accounts, defined, 102, 107
Accounts payable, 107
Accounts receivable, 107
Accrual accounting, 101–102
ACS Technologies, 14
Actual cash value coverage, 144
Actual costs, 111
Administrative costs, 111
Advertising
  during bad business periods, 160
  in marketing strategies, 40–41
  variety of methods, 72–74
  for workers, 20–21
Affiliated research companies, 42
Aging reports, 118
Alcohol at company outings, 151
American Management Association, 43
American Marketing Association, 43
American National Standards Institute
  (ANSI), 126

American Society of Appraisers, 94
Annual business plans, 78
Annual performance reviews, 30, 33
Answering systems, avoiding, 153
Antilock braking systems, 49
Antitrust laws, 65
Application forms, 23
Appraisals, 90–91, 94
Assembly instructions, 67
Asset accounts, 102, 104
Association of Machinery and Equipment
  Appraisers, 94
Attorneys
  involvement in collections, 118–119
  need for, 135–142
  patent, 51–52
Audits, annual, 130–131
Automobile insurance, 146

B

Backlog reports, 123–124
Bad business periods, 159–161
Balance sheets
  purpose, 103, 108
  typical line items, 104, 105
Bankers
  conferring with, 93, 161
  selecting, 91–92
Bank loans
  creditworthiness for, 83–84
  importance of business plans for, 76–77
  renegotiating during down times, 161
  requirements for, 86
  steps in securing, 93–95
Belonging, sense of, 30

Benefits plans
    cafeteria plans, 36
    presenting to new employees, 25, 33
    retirement plan features, 35–36
Beta sites, 51
Big Bertha driver, 15
Bills of material, 123
Bonuses, 158
Borrowing. *See* Loans
Borrowing power, focusing, 96
Bridge construction and repair business, 14
Brochures, 73–74, 155
Building leases, 96
Business cards, 73
Business contacts, from CPA firms, 134
Business hours, reducing, 161
Business interruption insurance, 145
Business operations
    defining, 13–14
    explaining to new employees, 26
    forming legal entity, 136
Business partners, 87–88
Business plans
    for bad business periods, 159–160
    elements of, 77–82
    importance of accounting knowledge for, 99
    need for, 76–77, 93
Business schools, training from, 27
Business succession planning, 133
Buy/sell agreements, 91

C

Cafeteria plans, 36
Callaway, Ely, 15
Callaway Golf Company, 15
Campbell, Hal, 14
Canon, 49
Capital leases, 86
Cash accounting, 101–102
Cash flow statements, 108
Caterpillar, 125
Certified public accountants. *See*
    Accountants
Charts of accounts, 107

Chevrolet trucks, 16
Church management software, 14
CIM (computer-integrated manufacturing), 124
Claims (insurance), 147
Claims, unrealistic, 153
Client partners (accounting), 129, 133
Codes on bills of material, 123
Collateral, 94
Collection agencies, 118
Collection efforts, 117–119, 160
Colleges and universities, 27, 43
Colors, company identification with, 72, 73
Combination plans, 68–69
Comments and suggestions from employees, 150, 151
Commerce Department market data, 43
Commission plans, 68, 69
Commitment, 11
Commodity codes, 123
Communication
    with customers, 152–155, 165
    with employees, 150–152, 161
    importance of skills, 149–150, 165
    importance to motivation, 30
    with suppliers, 155–156
Company-wide discussion sessions, 150
Compensating New Sales Roles, 69
Compensation
    administration programs, 31–33
    during good and bad times, 158, 161
    importance in hiring, 24
    policies, 33–34, 68–69
Competencies of partners, 88
Competitors
    comparing products and services with, 55
    described in marketing plans, 80
    getting information about, 42, 44–45
    importance of understanding, 40
    learning prices of, 55
    market data from, 44
    product ideas from, 49
    referring customers to, 153
Complacency, avoiding, 157–159
Compromises in hiring, 19

Computer Dimensions, Inc., 14
Computer-integrated manufacturing (CIM), 124
Computerized accounting systems, 103, 109–110
Computerized communications, 154–155
Conference Board, 43
Confidential information, withholding from business plans, 79
Consigning inventory, 87
Consumer laws, 138
Consumer reporting agencies, 83–84
Contact information, in business plans, 79
Contacts, from CPA firms, 134
Continual improvement principles, 126
Contracts, 137
Control systems
  credit management, 116–119
  described in business plans, 81
  internal reporting, 113–116
  order entry and billing, 119–121
  production scheduling and inventory control, 121–124
  product/service quality, 125–127
Copying machines, 51
Copyrights
  assessing product potential for, 51–52
  defending, 140–141
  described in marketing plans, 80
  importance of knowing about, 49
Corporations, forming, 136
Cost Accounting, 110
Cost and Effect, 110
Costs
  accounting for, 99–100, 110–112
  reducing during down times, 160, 161
  relation to selling prices, 53, 56–58
Covenants in loan agreements, 86, 94–95
Cover pages of business plans, 79
CPA firms. *See* Accountants
Credit applications, 116–117
Credit management systems, 116–119
Credit reports, 83–84, 116
Credits and debits, 102–106

Credit scoring, 84
Credit terms, renegotiating, 160
Creditworthiness, 83–84
Crosby, Philip, 125
Cross-training, 161
Current assets, 105
Current liabilities, 105
Current ratios, 94
Customer base
  defining, 40, 41–44
  described in marketing plans, 80
Customer focus, 126
Customers
  asking about competition, 42, 55
  asking about service, 70
  as beta sites, 51
  communicating with, 152–155, 165
  hiring employees away from, 19
  identifying, 38–39
  market data from, 44
  product ideas from, 48–49, 154
Customized accounting systems, 109

D
Data sources, 41–44
Deaths, partnership/stockholder agreement provisions for, 89
Debits and credits, 102–106
Debts. *See* Financial resources; Loans
Debt-to-equity ratios, 94
Deductibles, insurance, 145
Default events, in loan agreements, 94
Dell, 73
Deming, W. Edwards, 125
Design patents, 52
Direct costs, 57
Direct mail advertising, 74
Directors' and officers' liability insurance, 146
Direct overhead costs, 111
Disabilities, partnership/stockholder agreement provisions for, 89
Discounts, 64–65, 160
Discriminatory pricing, 65, 137
Display advertising, 72, 73

Distribution
  by competitors, 45
  described in marketing plans, 80
  elements of, 66
  in marketing strategies, 40
Divorces, partnership/stockholder agreement
  provisions for, 90
Documentation
  determining needs, 67–68
  financial, 85, 86 (*see also* Financial state-
    ments)
  loan agreements, 93–95
  partnership/stockholder agreements, 88–91
  sales quotations, 119–120
Donkey, parable of, 11–12
Double-entry bookkeeping, 102–106
Down times, 159–161
Draws, 68–69
Drinking at company outings, 151
Drucker, Peter, 48
Dun & Bradstreet reports, 43–44, 116

E
Earnings statements, 106
Effectiveness of sales, monitoring, 70
E-mail addresses, 74
Employee bulletin boards, 21
Employees
  attracting, 23–25
  communicating with, 150–152, 161
  finding, 19–21, 165
  indoctrinating, 25–26
  interviewing for, 21–23
  motivating, 27–30, 150–152
  reducing costs of, 161
  training, 26–27, 150–151
Employment agencies, 20
Employment application forms, 23
Employment contracts, 24–25
Employment laws, 21–23, 137
Employment practices liability insurance, 145
Employment preferences lists, 23
Enjoyment of work, 29–30
Entrepreneur self-assessment, 1–7
Environmental factors, in marketing plans, 80

Environmental protection measures, 137–138
Equal employment opportunity laws, 21–23
Equifax, 84, 116
Equipment and facilities leasing, 86–87
Equipment upgrades, 158
Equity accounts, 102, 104
Equity investments, 85
Errors and omissions insurance, 146
Estate planning, 133
Estimated costs, 111
Events of default, 94
Excess cash flow, how to manage, 158–159
Excessive pay increases, avoiding, 158
Executive summaries, 80
Experian, 84
Express warranties, 65

F
Facilities upgrades, 158
Failures, learning from, 164
Fair Credit Reporting Act, 84
Family members, financing from, 85–86
Federal government market data, 43
Fees
  attorneys, 142
  CPA firm, 129–130, 131, 132
Financial resources. *See also* Accounting
  ability to gather, 10
  annual audits, 130–131
  bankers as, 91–92
  business partners, 87–88
  creditworthiness and, 83–84
  leasing benefits, 95–96
  overview of options, 84–87
  suppliers as, 96–97
  taking out loans, 93–95
Financial statements
  auditing, 130
  bankers' interest in, 92
  in business plans, 81
  creating from accounting systems, 102–110
  with credit applications, 86, 117, 130
Financing. *See* Financial resources; Loans
Fire safety programs, 26
Five P's of Selling, 69

Fixed costs, 57–58
Floor plan financing, 87
FOB point policies, 65, 120
Follow-up on sales, 153–155
Ford-Firestone tire recall, 138, 146
401(k) plans, 35–36
Friends
    candidate referrals from, 19–20
    financing from, 85–86
Fuji, 73

G
Gates, Bill, 15
General journal, 103
General ledgers, 107
Getting-acquainted phase of hiring, 25–26
Golf club maker, 15
Greyhound Bus Lines, 140
Gross profit percentage, 61–62
Growth periods, 157–159
Guarantees, 67

H
Harvard Entrepreneurs Club Guide to Starting Your Own Business, 78
Hasselblad, 54
Health insurance, 147–148
Hiring
    application forms, 23
    delaying, 158
    finding good workers, 19–21, 165
    getting-acquainted phase, 25–26
    legal requirements, 21–23
    reference checking, 23–24
    selling points, 24–25
Historical costs, 111
Honesty, 88, 165–166
Hourly workers, reducing costs of, 161
"How are we doing?" questionnaires, 155
Human resources. *See* Employees

I
IBM, 73
Image, 16–17
Image Stabilization lenses, 49
Imaging software, 67
Implied warranties, 66

Income statements, 103–104, 108
Indoctrination phase for new employees, 25–26
Industry research, 49
Industry schools, 27
Industry trade magazines. *See* Trade magazines
Informal outings with employees, 151–152
In-house training, 27
Innovation, 48, 157, 164
Installation instructions, 67
Instructions with products, 67
Insurance brokers, 143–148
Intangible factors in success, 164–166
Integrity, 88, 165–166
Intellectual property protections, 139–141. *See also* Copyrights; Patents; Trademarks
Intermediaries, market data from, 44
Internal reporting systems, 113–116
International Organization for Standardization (ISO), 125–127
Internet advertising, 74
Interviews, 21
Introductory pricing, 60, 61
Inventories
    consigning, 87
    importance of accounting knowledge for, 99–100
    production scheduling impacts on, 121–124
    status reports, 108
Invoices, 120–121
Involvement, employee motivation and, 30, 150–152
ISO 9000, 125–127

J
Job costs, 111
Job evaluation systems, 32
Job postings, 21
Job profitability reports, 108
Journal entries, 103, 106, 107
Juran, Joseph, 125

K
Kennedy, John F., 9, 14–15
Key person insurance, 146

Knowledge self-assessment, 1–7
Kodak, 73

L

Labeling requirements, 67
Labor inefficiency costs, 99–100
Lanford Brothers Company, 14
Laws
  antitrust, 65
  equal employment opportunity, 21–23
  potential impact on small businesses,
    135–142
Lawsuits
  consumer protection, 138
  liability insurance for, 143, 145
  working with attorneys on, 141–142
Layoffs, 161
Leadership, 8–11, 126
Leasing, 86–87, 95–96
Legal business entities, forming, 136
Legal self-help, 142
Letterheads, 72, 73
Level 5 leadership, 8
Lexus, 16, 54
Liability accounts, 102, 104
Liability insurance, 145, 146
Libraries, 43
Licenses, 139
Limited liability companies (LLCs), forming,
  136
Limited warranties, 66
Listening, 149–150
Loan agreements, 86, 93–95
Loan guarantees, 83, 86
Loans
  creditworthiness for, 83–84
  importance of business plans for, 76–77
  potential sources, 85–86
  renegotiating during down times, 161
  steps in securing, 93–95
Logos, 72–73
Long-range strategic plans, 81–82
Loss claims, insurance, 147

M

Machinery Dealers National Association, 94
Make-or-buy decisions, 47

Management
  communication in, 30, 149–156
  credit, 116–119
  described in business plans, 81
  internal reporting systems for, 113–116
  partnership/stockholder agreement provi-
    sions for, 90
  of production schedules and inventories,
    121–124
  quality control, 125–127
Management consultants, 133
Management control systems. *See* Control
  systems
Manufacturers' representative organizations,
  42
Marginal contribution pricing, 60–61
Marketing. *See also* Advertising
  advertising and promotions, 71–75
  during bad business periods, 160
  customer identification, 38–39
  sales and service policies, 64–66
  strategy development, 39–41
Marketing plans, 80–81
Market research, 41–44
Markets
  defined, 39
  obtaining information about, 41–44
  price sensitivity, 54
Markup, 61–62
Master production schedules, 123
Matching contributions in 401(k) plans, 36
Material requirements plans, 123
Maytag, 125
McDonald's "hot coffee" incident, 138
Microsoft, 16, 48
Missing loan payments, 95
Mission statements, 79–80
Monitoring sales effectiveness, 70
Motivating employees, 27–30, 150–152
Mutually beneficial supplier relationships, 126

N

Negative covenants, 94–95
Net earnings equation, 104
Net worth equation, 103

Net worth requirements, 94
New products. *See* Product development
Newspaper advertising, 72, 73
News releases, 71–72
Niche markets, 38–39
Nikon, 49
Nolo Press, 142
Northwestern Mutual Life Insurance
    Company, 16

O

Objectives
    in business plans, 78
    defining, 13–14
    image and, 16–17
    leadership toward, 9–11
Occupational Safety and Health
    Administration (OSHA), 25–26, 137–138
Offer letters, 24–25
Open-door policies, 150
Operating expenses, 57
Operational plans, 81
Operations sheets, 123
Order entry and billing systems, 119–121,
    154
Outdoor advertising, 74
Outside services, 160
Overhead costs, 110, 111
Overtime, 158, 161
Owners, personal guarantees from, 95
Owner's manuals, 67

P

Packaging requirements, 67
Parable of the donkey, 11–12
Parable of the tree, 112
Parties, 151
Partner selection, 87–91
Partnership formation, 136
Partnership/stockholder agreements, 88–91
Parts manuals, 68
Past-due accounts, 117–119, 160
Patents
    assessing product potential for, 51–52
    defending, 139–140
    described in marketing plans, 80
    held by competitors, 45
    importance of knowing about, 49
    pending, 50, 52, 140
Pay grades, 32–33
Pay increases, 32, 158. *See also*
    Compensation
Payment problems, 117–119
Payroll accounting services, 110
Peachtree Accounting, 103, 109, 111
Penetration pricing, 54
Performance appraisals, 30, 33
Permits, 139
Persistence, 164
Personal credit reports, 84
Personal knowledge of candidates, 19–20
Personal loan guarantees, 95
Personal resources, 85
Personal strengths, assessing, 1–7
Personal visits to customers, 154
Personnel handbooks, 25, 33, 34–35
Planning, 10, 76–82. *See also* Business plans
Popularity, 11
Position descriptions, 32
Positive cash flow guarantees, 94
Positive covenants, 94–95
Positive net earnings guarantees, 94
Postpaid reply cards, 155
Premium increases, 147
Prepaying debt, 94, 158
Price cycles, 54
Price reductions, avoiding, 160
Pricing
    for bad business periods, 160
    described in marketing plans, 80
    discriminatory, 65, 137
    gross margin vs. markup, 61–62
    in marketing strategies, 40
    overview, 53–54
    in product development process, 51
    profit maximization approach, 55–61
Primary market research, 41, 44
Private placements, 139
Process management, 126
Product definitions, 50
Product descriptions in marketing plans, 80

Product development
   emphasis during good times, 158
   finding new product ideas, 47–50, 154
   in marketing strategies, 40
   steps in process, 50–52
Production and backlog reports, 123–124
Production efficiency reports, 108
Production planning, 122–123
Production scheduling, 121–124
Product liability insurance, 145, 146
Product liability issues, 137, 138
Product line profitability reporting, 100, 108
Product planning, 46–47
Product prices. *See* Pricing
Profitability
   calculating, 51, 57–58
   determining needs, 56
   managing fluctuations, 157–161
   pricing and, 53
   of product lines, 100, 108
Profit allocations, 90
Profit maximization approach, 55–61
Profit participation notes, 85
Promotional activities, 74–75, 80, 160. *See also* Advertising
Promotional materials from competitors, 45
Property damage insurance, 144–145
Proposal letters, 129, 132
Prudential Insurance Co., 140
Publicity, 71–72
Purchase options in building leases, 96
Purchase orders, 117

Q
Quality control, 125–127, 165
Quality Management Principles, 126
Questionnaires, 155
QuickBooks, 103, 107, 109, 111
Quiz for Small Business Success, 5–7
Quotations from CPA firms, 129
Quotations, sales, 119–120

R
Radio stations, contacting, 71–72
Realism in business plans, 79
Receivables, collecting, 117–119, 160

Recognition, importance to motivation, 28–29
Reference checking, 23–24, 117
Registered trade or service marks, 140
Registering copyrights, 141
Repayment provisions in loan agreements, 94
Replacement cost coverage, 144–145
Reply cards, 155
Research foundations, 43
Research organizations, 49
Resource gathering, 10
Retail method of inventory valuation, 62
Retained Earnings account, 103, 104, 105
Retirement plans, 35–36
Return on assets, interest on loans vs., 93
Rewards of small business, 166
Robinson-Patman Act, 65, 137
Routing sheets, 123

S
Safety programs, 25–26, 137–138
Salaries. *See* Compensation
The Sales Compensation Handbook, 69
Sales effectiveness, monitoring, 70
Sales forecasting, 122
Sales organizations
   compensation policies, 68–69
   of competitors, 45
   described in marketing plans, 80
   improving, 152–155
   policy management, 64–66
   technical literature, 67–68
   training programs, 69–70
   variables determining, 63, 64
Sales projections, 50
Sales quotations, 119–120
Schumpeter, Joseph A., 48
SCORE counselors
   help revising business plans, 159–160
   help seeking loans, 86
   help with business formation, 136
   seminars with, 27
Screening new product ideas, 50
Search firms, 20
Secondary market research, 41, 44

Section 125 cafeteria plans, 36
Securities laws, 139
Segmenting jobs, 111
Self-assessment, 1–7, 9
Self-confidence, 164
Selling points in hiring, 24–25
Selling prices. *See* Pricing
Seminars, 27, 71
Service after sale, 66
Service manuals, 68
Service marks, 52, 140
Service personnel, product ideas from, 49
Service quality, 165
Sherman Anti-Trust Act, 65
Shipping charges, 120
Shop meetings, 150
Signs, 74
Silbiger, Steven, 125
Skills, 1–7, 88
Small Business Administration, 83, 86, 142
Small Business Advisor, 78
Small Business Development Centers, 27, 136
Small Business Kit for Dummies, 78, 144
Small Business Magazine, 5–7
Software
    accounting, 103, 107, 109, 111
    business plan, 82
    computer-integrated manufacturing, 124
Source documents, 106
Special discount pricing, 60
Sports leagues, 151
Standard costs, 111
Standards of quality, 125–127
Statements of cash flow, 108
Statements of earnings, 106, 108
Statistical Abstract of the United States, 43
Stockholders' equity, 105
Straight commission plans, 68, 69
Straight salary plans, 68
Strategic alliances, 87
Strategies in business plans, 81–82
Strengths and weaknesses, assessing, 1–7
Subaccounts, 107
Success, reinforcing, 28

Success factors, 164–166
Succession planning, 133
Suggestions, soliciting, 30, 150, 151
Suppliers
    communicating with, 155–156
    as financial resources, 96–97
    mutually beneficial relationships with, 126
    renegotiating credit during down times, 160
    soliciting quotes from, 47
Support information, 67
System approach to management, 126

T
Tables of contents, of business plans, 79
Tax partners, 131, 133
Tax preparation, 131–132, 138
Technical articles, 71
Technical competence of partners, 88
Technical sales literature, 67–68
Technical schools, 43
Technical service personnel, product ideas from, 49
Telephone answering systems, 153
Telephone sales, 152–153
Temporary employees, 20
The Ten-Day MBA, 125
Terminations, partnership/stockholder agreement provisions for, 90
Terms in loan agreements, 94
Testing new products, 51
Toll-free numbers, 153
Towers Perrin, 69
Trade magazines
    market data from, 43
    market research by, 41–42
    writing articles for, 71
Trademarks, 52, 80, 140
Training programs
    communication benefits of, 150–151
    cross-training, 161
    for new employees, 26–27
    for sales representatives, 69–70
Tree, parable of, 112
TransUnion, 84, 116
Trend income statement, 115

Trend reports, 113–114
Trial approach, 61
Trial balances, 107
Troubleshooting information, 67
T-shirt company, 100
Tuition reimbursement, 27
TV stations, contacting, 71–72

U
Undercapitalization, 88
Unemployment insurance, 146
Uniform Commercial Code, 137
Unique objectives, 9–11
Universities, 27, 43
User's guides, 67
U.S. Industry & Trade Outlook, 43
Utility patents, 52

V
Valuation methods, 90–91
Values of leadership, 8–11
Variable costs, 57–58
Vendor financing, 87
Venture capital firms, 87
Vibration Reduction lenses, 49
Vision, 9–10, 14–16
Visiting customers, 154
Vocational technical schools, 27, 43

W
Wages. *See* Compensation
Warranties
   liability issues, 138

types, 65–66
writing, 67
Weaknesses, self-assessment, 1–7
Web site insurance, 146
Web sites
   as advertising venue, 74
   appraisal organizations, 94
   business plan resources, 82
   consumer reporting agencies, 84
   customer contact via, 154–155
   employment laws, 21
   government data sources, 43
   legal and regulatory information, 142
   Nolo Press, 142
   partnership/stockholder agreements, 89
   patent and copyright law, 141
   quality standards, 126
   research foundations, 43
   SBA loan guarantees, 86
Windows operating system, 48
Withdrawals, partnership/stockholder agreement provisions for, 89
Workers. *See* Employees
Workers' compensation insurance, 146
Work-in-process inventory, 121
Written sales quotations, 119–120

X
Xerox copying machines, 51

Y
Yellow Pages advertising, 73